"A noted business leader joins America's preeminent business strategist to diagnose what ails our political system and prescribe a cure. Timely indeed."

"Gehl and Porter's powerful book is a deep and persuasive analysis of our current political dysfunction and practical steps for change. Let us hope the public and our leaders take heed."

"This book is an actual manual for how Americans can reclaim our democracy and make it work for the people rather than for the political-industrial complex. Gehl and Porter's writing is clear and lively; their analysis of the two-party duopoly is devastatingly accurate; their timing is perfect. Read it and act!"

"*The Politics Industry* outlines a unique framework that challenges the traditions of our political system. Whether you are the candidate on the ballot or the citizen casting the vote, we can all learn from Gehl and Porter's blueprint to improve our democracy."

"This crucial book dissects America's electoral and legislative machinery to provide a revealing perspective on why our $16 billion political industry is failing its most important customers: the American people. The authors' assessment is eye opening, and their proposed solutions reflect the heart of the American ethos—innovation, determination, courage, and the will to reinvent the status quo."

"Katherine Gehl and Michael Porter deliver a stunning indictment of American politics and government and the way economic competitiveness and broader national welfare have been diminished by its failings. But Gehl and Porter provide us with much more than analysis and diagnosis. They offer practical reforms to end this destructive political gridlock and dysfunction. This is an impassioned and timely book that deserves wide readership."

—**DREW GILPIN FAUST,** former President, Harvard University

"Gehl and Porter are true experts. They provide not just analysis or endless commentary but a plan for real change—all for the better. This is a fresh look at American politics."

—**BUD SELIG,** Commissioner Emeritus, Major League Baseball

"This is the best book I've read about our divided politics. Gehl and Porter provide a clear and compelling solution."

—**BILL WALKER,** former Governor of Alaska (Independent)

"Americans everywhere are frustrated by the state of politics, but doing something to actually fix it can feel like an overwhelming or impossible task—until you read this book!"

—**KATIE FAHEY,** Executive Director, The People

"Katherine Gehl and Michael Porter's timely and imaginative new book, *The Politics Industry,* examines today's political dysfunction from an original perspective, and in that context proposes political innovation to break partisan deadlock and foster a fuller and more productive range of political expression."

—**ROBERT ZIMMER,** President, University of Chicago

"Too many Americans feel unrepresented by our two political parties or their representatives in government, and Gehl and Porter give a clear explanation why. They eschew the tired finger pointing about 'breaking the system' that both parties engage in. In this book, Gehl and Porter put forward a number of serious, innovative, and nonpartisan reforms. If more people in America thought about democracy the way Gehl and Porter do, our country would be in a lot better shape."

—**SARAH LONGWELL,** Publisher, The Bulwark

"I've been deeply dismayed about Washington, D.C.'s performance for years. Gehl and Porter turned the light on for me and returned my hope—as they will for you. Their analysis is brilliant, but more importantly, their solution will transform our political system. There is no more important book in 2020."

—**AUSTIN RAMIREZ,** CEO, Husco International

The
POLITICS
INDUSTRY

The POLITICS INDUSTRY

How **Political Innovation** Can Break Partisan Gridlock and Save Our Democracy

KATHERINE M. GEHL
MICHAEL E. PORTER

HARVARD BUSINESS REVIEW PRESS

BOSTON, MASSACHUSETTS

Library of Congress Cataloging-in-Publication Data

Names: Gehl, Katherine M., 1966- author. | Porter, Michael E., 1947-
    author.
Title: The politics industry : how political innovation can break partisan
    gridlock and save our democracy / Katherine M. Gehl and Michael E.
    Porter.
Description: Boston, MA : Harvard Business Review Press, [2020] | Includes
    index.
Identifiers: LCCN 2019057395 (print) | LCCN 2019057396 (ebook) | ISBN
    9781633699236 (hardcover) | ISBN 9781633699243 (ebook)
Subjects: LCSH: Politics, Practical--Economic aspects--United States. |
    Political culture--United States. | Political corruption--United States.
    | Gerrymandering--United States. | United States--Politics and
    government--2009-2017. | United States--Politics and government--2017-
Classification: LCC JK1726 .G45 2020 (print) | LCC JK1726 (ebook) | DDC
    324.0973—dc23
LC record available at https://lccn.loc.gov/2019057395
LC ebook record available at https://lccn.loc.gov/2019057396
ISBN: 978-1-63369-923-6
eISBN: 978-1-63369-924-3

To my mom. I still miss you.

—Katherine

To my granddaughter, Elliot Teal. For your future.

—Papa Michael

Contents

Foreword

—Republican Congressman Mike Gallagher
(WI, elected 2016)

—Democratic Congresswoman Chrissy Houlahan
(PA, elected 2018)

Before serving the United States as members of Congress, we each served as members of the armed forces. Chrissy earned a systems engineering degree from Stanford University on an ROTC scholarship and served in the Air Force, helping design defense systems for ballistic missile attack. Mike joined the Marines the day he graduated from Princeton University and served in intelligence across the world. Both of us felt we owed this service to our extraordinary country.

During our time in the military, we served under and led men and women of great diversity—each with their own family backgrounds, stories, and belief systems. We came together united by our common goal to protect this country we treasure. Military duty was a great honor and formed the foundation for our continued service today— service to our districts, our states, and our country.

While we are immeasurably honored and privileged to now be serving again in Congress and to be working on behalf of our constituents and our country, we are both dismayed by the current state of play in Washington, D.C. Like many of our colleagues, we are deeply frustrated. We know you are too.

As veterans, we know what it means to fight on the same team for the America we love so much. That love hasn't changed. That desire to fight for America hasn't changed. So why aren't we now on the same for-America team? Why is our status as members of different political parties seemingly more potent than our shared love for America, our many areas of agreement, and our shared responsibility to solve problems and get results? Why are we more often opponents than colleagues? Why are we collectively allergic to the compromise and teamwork required to do what Americans want and expect of their Congress? Why can't we get big things done for the American people?

Because the system is built to tear us apart. In American politics, winning isn't winning unless the other side is losing, and losing badly.

This shouldn't be.

And it doesn't have to be. This book proves it.

Katherine and Michael argue that "it's the system." Most importantly, they propose specifics on how we can fix it together. Their prescription is powerful. It is nonpartisan. What's more, it's doable.

The next generation of elected leaders is not required to carry on the dysfunctional legacy of gridlock and bad blood that has defined our recent politics. We must match our love of country with a system that's designed to serve the people, not the "political-industrial complex." We want to look back on our careers in public service and see that we were able to make American lives better, coast to coast.

We know you want the same. We're excited about the possibilities.

This book arrives not a moment too soon. Please engage—we owe it to our extraordinary country to do so.

Authors' Note

Pandemic 2020

As publishing deadlines pass for *The Politics Industry*, the world is racing to beat back a nationless, faceless, dangerous adversary: the coronavirus (COVID-19) pandemic.

Currently, one in four Americans have been ordered to "shelter in place."[1] Metropolitan hospitals are becoming overwhelmed, medical supplies are running short, and getting infected appears to be easier than getting tested. Many predict a trailing economic depression, with impacts that could be more painful for our country than those of the virus itself.[2]

It is surreal.

There will be a time to review in detail how our public officials responded throughout this crisis. That time is not now. As we fight to "flatten the curve" of infection, there are only three observations we are comfortable sharing.

First, we are yet again dismayed by the hyper-partisanship, the self-interest, and the opportunism the political-industrial complex exhibits—but we are not surprised. We seem paralyzed, no matter the gravity of the situation, by a poisoned politics. There are bright spots within the chaos—certain elected and unelected government officials stepping forward, heroic service by health-care professionals, selfless volunteerism around the country—glimmers of what could be. *If only* our system weren't so screwed up at the core.

Second, the obvious system failures that have put millions of Americans at risk over the last weeks and months make it even more apparent that the solutions we prescribe in this book are of critical importance. The threat of the next binary election continues to outweigh at times the pressing concerns of the day when it comes to proactive lawmaking in Congress.

Finally, as with the Cold War, 9/11, and the Great Recession, there will be American children who remember where they were when the news of the coronavirus pandemic first broke and what happened to their families during the nation's response to it. The pandemic and its aftermath will define generations. But it could also *redefine* our politics.

When a new normal comes, there will be a moment; a window for big, sweeping change. For the good of all Americans, and to honor those we will have lost and the sacrifices made by so many, we pray that enough of us will put country over party and invest in the political innovation that can revivify our politics with healthy competition—and make sure we don't get caught unprepared again.

There is a path forward. Let's take it, together.

—Katherine & Michael
March 23, 2020

Preface

My name is Michael E. Porter, and I am an economist, a scholar, an author, an adviser, and a teacher. My Five Forces framework for understanding the competitive forces in an industry, which I introduced in a *Harvard Business Review* article in 1979, started a revolution in the strategy field and continues today to shape business practices and academic thinking worldwide.

Over my career, I have written nineteen books on various topics, including economic theory and policy, competition and competitive advantage, national and state competitiveness and economic development, health-care delivery, and business strategy. American politics was literally the last topic I ever thought I'd tackle. That all changed because of Katherine Gehl.

For most of my life, I paid little attention to politics—I was too busy with policy and strategy and was working to actualize them in practice with leaders of companies and nations around the world. For me, the "game" of politics was more like noise. I assumed that developing optimal public policies was the biggest challenge. And if we could do that, good policy would be implemented based on merit. Like many of you, my primary involvement in politics was voting in elections and holding out hope for that presidential or gubernatorial candidate who could get us on the right track again. Looking back,

I see now that I accepted as normal the toxic gridlock and learned helplessness our political system teaches.[1]

This started to change when I again turned my attention to American economic policy. In 2010, I began cochairing, with Professor Jan W. Rivkin, the U.S. Competitiveness Project, a multiyear endeavor by Harvard Business School to understand the root cause of the country's disturbing economic performance, which began well before the Great Recession. While the United States retains great strengths, its competitiveness has been steadily declining. We face an alarming array of weaknesses that are likely familiar to you, challenges such as education, worker skills, complex regulation, and crumbling infrastructure.

The economic agenda, however, is only half of the job for government. The other half is social. In 2013 I led, with Scott Stern and other partners, the development of the Social Progress Index, a new framework and methodology for objectively measuring and comparing key social, environmental, and quality-of-life indicators in countries across the world. We discovered something most Americans don't recognize: in the same way that our economic competitiveness has been declining, we are falling behind in many aspects of social performance, including some in areas we cherish and often pioneered. This decline in social performance has contributed to our economic challenges, too—especially inequality.

As we advanced the U.S. Competitiveness Project from diagnosis to action, my Harvard Business School colleagues and I put forward what we called the "eight-point plan," which consisted of the most pressing policy priorities needed to revitalize our economic competitiveness. I traveled to Washington, D.C., multiple times to meet with members of Congress, and they unanimously agreed on what needed to be done.

But nothing got done. No results. How could our pathfinding policy prescriptions for reversing decades of fundamental economic decline—which was leading to cascading impacts on citizens' opportunity and standard of living—not produce reforms? How could our plan gain bipartisan support behind closed doors but generate absolutely no legislative action in public?

I was mystified.

Katherine wasn't. She was a veteran of high-level politics and political-change efforts. Having already gone through what she calls "the five stages of political grief," she was the ideal pastor for my political enlightenment. Katherine already left partisan politics behind and was deeply engaged in political innovation. But our collaboration in politics started with a business challenge.

In 2013, Katherine asked me to consult on her company's strategy. She was the president and CEO of Gehl Foods, a $250 million high-tech food manufacturing company in Wisconsin. With more than a century of innovation under its belt, the company found itself faced with precipitously declining fortunes. Katherine had been leading a turnaround effort at the company and was wrestling with how to best protect her father's legacy and keep the company competitive for another hundred years. Little did I know that while we were using the Five Forces and other tools of competitive analysis to analyze and develop a strategy for Gehl Foods, Katherine was conducting a parallel analysis of what she came to call the politics industry.

Her epiphany is the basis of this book: the competitive-forces framework and other tools used for understanding competition in any industry could also be used to reveal the nuances of American politics. Katherine subsequently convinced me that politics was not some untouchable insider game immune to rigorous analysis. And she had the audacious idea that by demystifying politics, by looking at it as any industry, we could fix it.

Soon after Katherine sold her company in 2015—in part to dedicate more time to political innovation—she asked me to join her work as a coauthor. I was way out of my league here but was willing to give it a shot. In 2017, our report "Why Competition in the Politics Industry Is Failing America" was published by Harvard Business School and became the precursor to this book. The work was powerful and inspiring. I was hooked.

Ours is a partnership I never would have predicted. But kismet aside, origin stories have a funny way of rewriting themselves once ideas become papers, and papers become books, and books become—we hope—the basis for big change.

People often assume that I am the parent of these ideas. I am not. Katherine is the originator of both Politics Industry Theory and the strategy for political innovation we prescribe in this book. She is also the driving force in spreading and implementing these ideas around the country. I am proud to be involved.

One last thing: *The Politics Industry* is my twentieth book. I don't plan for it to be my last, but after decades building a career around the strategic thinking and insights that make or break companies and nations—and influencing generations of students and helping leaders in business and government—this book might just be my most important. Why? Because it's a book about solutions, taking action, and achieving results at a time in America when the stakes couldn't be much higher. This book is a road map for breaking partisan gridlock and saving our democracy. As you will read, Americans have done it before.

Katherine and I will show you how we can do it again.

—Michael Porter

Introduction

In 2005, celebrated author David Foster Wallace delivered a commencement address at Kenyon College. He started with a fish story: "There are these two young fish swimming along, and they happen to meet an older fish swimming the other way, who nods at them and says, 'Morning, boys. How's the water?' The two young fish swim on for a bit, and then eventually one of them looks over at the other and goes, 'What the hell is water?'"[1]

After Wallace assured the new graduates that he wasn't positioning himself as an embodiment of the wise old fish, he got to the point of the story: "The most obvious, ubiquitous, important realities are the ones that are hardest to see and talk about."

For most Americans, the political system surrounds us in much the same way water surrounds fish. It's just what we know. It's normal. And while we complain about its performance, we don't question its nature because we don't believe it can change. We accept dysfunction, gridlock, and government inaction—even in the face of national adversity—as normal. And when we return to our polling places on Election Day and yet again see only two choices on our ballots—neither of which we really like—we accept that as normal, too. Here's what else has become normal for far too many Americans over the last fifty years: a quality-of-life downturn so significant that, when compared with the thirty-six other peer democratic countries with advanced economies, we Americans are near the bottom across numerous dimensions we once pioneered. We are thirty-third in access to quality education, thirty-third in child mortality, twenty-sixth in discrimination and violence against minorities, and thirty-first in clean drinking water—just to name a few.[2]

The *actual* water in America is getting bad now.

Couple this distressing societal collapse with a major slide in our global economic competitiveness, historically high levels of gridlock, and historically low trust in government, and it is not an overstatement to say the great American experiment is at risk of unraveling.

Yet political normalcy has enveloped us. Apathy and abdication blunt our personal agency—our ability to bring about change—and tamp down momentary flashes of outrage. Those who haven't succumbed to learned helplessness try to do something about it, often by doubling down on their political party, certain that the other side is the problem. Others pin their hopes on that mythical change candidate who will finally fix things, whether through "hope and change" or by "draining the swamp." Some dedicate themselves to major policy concerns, like the national debt or immigration. But this is about much more than people or parties or policies. The root cause of our political dysfunction is deeper, where nobody cares to look, and is centered around one unifying theme—the forces of competition—in a system that doesn't work like you probably think it does.

Most people think of our American political system as a public institution that follows a set of high-minded principles and impartial structures and practices derived from the Constitution. But that's hardly the whole story. Much of today's system is a self-serving, self-perpetuating private industry composed of gain-seeking actors who write their own rules. They compete to grow and accumulate resources for themselves—not necessarily to serve the public interest—and create artificial barriers to prevent new competition from threatening their hold on the industry. What should be a problem-solving, outcomes-driven cycle of elections and legislative leadership is instead an industrial-strength perversion that fosters unhealthy competition and blocks the innovation and progress for which American democracy is known. Politics has become the preeminent barrier to addressing the very problems it exists to solve.

The engines of this regression are the unheralded but all-powerful rules, structures, norms, and practices (what we call the *machinery of politics*) that quietly determine everything from how candidates get on a ballot and how we vote to how a bill becomes a law. And both sides of the ideological divide are to blame. Waves of unchecked engineering of these rules and practices—orchestrated jointly by Democrats and Republicans—have optimized the elections and lawmaking machinery to protect and perpetuate the politics industry itself and grow its power, not to produce results. The power of new competition to rein in the runaway system has been intentionally and systematically neutralized, augmenting a state of play now bound to its own dysfunction and inaction.

Washington, D.C., is broken, right?

We say it all the time, throwing our hands in the air, ceaselessly condemning the nerve center of our politics. And the claim must be true, because seemingly every candidate for office, regardless of political party, repeats it as a rallying cry. But as former congressman Mickey Edwards (R-OK) brilliantly explained, this hackneyed phrase represents a fundamental misunderstanding of—or worse, a slippery misdirection from—what's really going on. In fact, Washington is working *exactly* how it is designed to work and delivering exactly the results it is designed to deliver, because it wasn't designed to work for us—for the citizens, the voters, the public interest.[3] What appears broken to us is humming right along for the industry itself, and it will not self-correct. To force a correction, we must revive the American tradition of political innovation. To change the results our system delivers, we must change the rules of the game. That's the singular power and sole purpose of this book, and the only legacy we care about.

Power and purpose flow from clarity; we must first—like those two young fish—see the water we're swimming in. In the politics industry, it all boils down to the corrupted cycle of elections and legislation—and they don't work as you think they do. They don't work for us at all.

How Elections and Legislation Really Work Today

Imagine you are a member of the US House of Representatives. You are deliberating over a bill that addresses a critical national challenge that should be handled on a bipartisan basis. As an elected representative, you should consider several seemingly obvious questions: *Is this a good idea? Is this the right policy for the country? Is this what the majority of my constituents want?* But as a participant in our current political system, you have only one question to answer: *Will I make it back through my party's next primary election if I vote for this?* If the answer to that question is no, and it virtually always is for the tough problems, then the other questions are irrelevant because the rational incentive to get reelected—to keep your job—compels you to vote against this bill.

But perhaps this time you decide to put country over party. You take the risk and publicly endorse the bill's artful compromise solution. You ignore the pleas of your party leadership. You weather threats and temptations from special interests. And you vote in favor of the bill.

You are in trouble.

For the purposes of your upcoming reelection, it doesn't matter if the bill passes or not. It doesn't matter if you are lauded by pundits, good-government reformers, or local constituents for your bipartisan leadership. It doesn't really matter if the bill is likely to produce good outcomes. What does matter, assuming you want to keep your job, is how your side of the partisan system you just bucked is going to respond.[4]

Here's where one of the most powerful verbs in American politics comes into play: you're about to get *primaried*.[5] In the next *party primary election* (or *partisan primary*), a contest for the party's nomination dominated by special interests and sharply ideological voters, you can expect an überleft challenger if you're a Democrat and a hard-right opponent if you're a Republican.[6]

You'll probably lose, because rampant unhealthy competition in politics means that for an elected official there is virtually no intersection between acting in the public interest and the likelihood of getting reelected. In our current system of running for office and legislating, if you *do* your job the way we need you to, you're likely to *lose* your job. Party primaries create an eye of the needle through which no problem-solving politician can pass. This is absurd.

Look at it from another perspective.

Suppose you're *not* an elected official. Instead, you're a person who has made a successful career in business, and like the vast majority of citizens across America, you are deeply dissatisfied with Congress. Your success in business comes from your ability to identify opportunities in the marketplace, and when you look at politics, the demand for better options couldn't be more obvious—particularly in your district, where another lesser-of-two-evils election is just around the corner. So, ever the entrepreneur, you throw your hat in the ring, perhaps as an independent, or maybe, quite boldly, you launch a startup: a new political party.

In the beginning, the race is promising. Your policy platform and solutions-oriented messaging strikes a chord. Despite your newcomer status, you gain ground quickly. Voters are paying attention to your candidacy, and, at the least, they want to see you on the debate stage. Most of your would-be constituents favor compromise over gridlock, so you pledge to work across the aisle on Capitol Hill. Perhaps most audaciously, you commit to a *positive* campaign, eschewing the demonization of your opponents in favor of talking about the issues.

Your poll numbers rise. You're beginning to seem competitive.

But there's a hitch. With your momentum building, local opinion makers, political insiders, and even close friends reach out and implore you: Drop out. Winning is a long shot, they say, and every vote you earn is a vote stolen from a major-party candidate—the candidate you would be resigned to support if you weren't in the race yourself. If you don't drop out now, you might *spoil the election* by stealing the votes that this major-party candidate needs to win. This argument strikes you as deeply unfair. How could fewer choices—fewer new ideas—be better for voters who are craving other options? The reality of American elections becomes clear: staying in the race might well mean handing a victory to the *greater* of two evils—the very candidate you were working so hard to defeat in the first place.

You ran for office because you spotted an opportunity to act in the public interest—to deliver solutions ignored by the current players. Your startup campaign was poised to fill a gap in the marketplace. But in American elections, *plurality voting*—the dominant, first-past-the-post, winner-take-all voting system—creates the spoiler phenomenon and dissuades would-be elected officials like you from running altogether.

Frustrated and amazed by this truly un-American abuse of the free market, you do what any good, civic-minded citizen would do: you pursue legal action, believing you have a promising antitrust case. But you are quickly flummoxed yet again. Ever so conveniently, and unlike in most industries, antitrust regulation doesn't apply to politics—and no independent regulator is coming to the rescue.[7]

Welcome to the politics industry, where party primaries and plurality voting combine to punish the public interest. There are few incentives to solve problems. There is little accountability for results. And there are no countervailing forces to restore healthy competition . . . yet.

Fundamentals of Politics Industry Theory

At the center of the politics industry are two rivals that can only be described as a textbook duopoly: the Democratic Party and the Republican Party. Around this duopoly has arisen a massive arrangement of actors and organizations, including special interest groups, lobbyists, big-money donors, super PACs, think tanks, pollsters, consultants, and the media that bridges Washington, D.C., to the rest of the country. By nearly every measure, the duopoly and the supporting bodies around it—what we call the *political-industrial complex*—is thriving. A recent result will hammer the point home: spending in federal elections during the 2016 cycle was more than $16 billion, which is greater than the annual budgets of at least a dozen states.

How can an industry so successful fail its customers—the American public—so mightily? In any other industry this large and thriving, with this much customer dissatisfaction, some entrepreneur would see this as a phenomenal opportunity and create a new competitor responding to what customers want. But that doesn't happen in politics. Why not? The answer to these questions lies in understanding the nature of competition in elections and legislating.

The key methodology we apply is the Five Forces framework, which was originally developed four decades ago to understand industry structure and its effects on the nature of competition in for-profit industries.[8] The framework has been the gold standard ever since. The approach recognizes that an industry is a complex system, involving numerous actors who compete but also collaborate.

As we will see, the politics industry is driven by the same five forces that shape competition in any industry: rivals, buyers, suppliers, the threat of new entrants, and the threat of substitutes. By exploring each of these competitive forces and how they relate to one another, we will illuminate the grave implications of unhealthy competition—the perverse incentive structure, the poor results and lack of accountability, and the absence of countervailing forces to inject competition—and reveal how to address other essential questions:

- Why is the United States innovative in so many areas, but not in politics?

- Why is it normal to have limited—and often disappointing—choices at the ballot box?

- Why doesn't Washington, D.C., get anything done?

- Why does an independent candidate rarely stand a chance of getting elected?

- What outcomes *should* we expect from an optimally functioning political system?

- And, most importantly, what can we do to start achieving those great outcomes?

Looking at politics through this new lens, we can see why our political challenges have not been solved by substituting one party with the other, or one elected official with another. Nor have new policies or any number of well-meaning political reform efforts solved these problems. This lens also empowers us to fulfill the promise of this book: the political innovation needed to break partisan gridlock and save our democracy. By understanding how the system works, we can more objectively determine how our innovation energy is best spent.

Currently, most efforts to change the politics industry revolve around a laundry list of reforms spanning myriad ideas, such as ending gerrymandering, reducing money in politics, instituting term limits, or establishing Election Day as a national holiday. While we endorse elements of the popular reform agenda, many of its propositions fail to address the root causes of system failure, or aren't viable from the start. Or both. What is doable *and* worth doing? What is powerful and achievable? *Political innovation.* (See figure I-1.)

Let's distinguish these two elements of political innovation. *Powerful* innovations address the root causes of dysfunction (not just the symptoms) and are designed to help the political system deliver results in the public interest. *Achievable* innovations are uncompromisingly nonpartisan (no Trojan horses for partisan gain), and success is theoretically possible in years, not decades (constitutional amendments, for example, do not pass this bar).

FIGURE I-1

Political Innovation Is a Nonpartisan Framework for Targeting Root Causes of System Failure in Order to Deliver Measurable Results

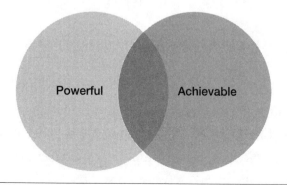

Politics Industry Theory is the key to unlocking this framework. By demystifying the nature of politics and mapping the complex forces at work, the prescription for innovation becomes clear: change the machinery of politics—the rules that govern elections and legislating. As is always the case in life, the rules of the game affect how the game is played and the outcomes of that game. The net result of the rules of the game in the politics industry is unhealthy competition. And the result of unhealthy competition, in any industry, is that customers are not well served. So, let's change the rules. Here's what we propose.

For elections machinery, we propose "Final-Five Voting," a package that (1) replaces closed, party primaries with nonpartisan open primaries that send the top five finishers to the general election, and (2) replaces plurality voting in the subsequent general elections with ranked-choice voting. (Don't worry, this will all be clear—how it works, and its transformative power—when you get to chapter 5.)

For legislative machinery, we propose replacing the bloated and outdated rules, practices, and norms of lawmaking with a model, modern approach designed from the ground up to foster cross-partisan problem solving.

Collectively, these innovations will change the very nature of competition in American politics—and get results.

Our Purpose, Process (and Politics)

Our core endeavor is unlocking the forces of healthy competition in American politics to restore a system that fixes real problems in real people's lives—more choice, more voice, better results.[9] This endeavor revolves around a handful of key distinctions that clarify our research and inform our conclusions.

First, from the beginning our purpose has been action, not merely analysis. Analysis, no matter how insightful, is not enough. We work hard to understand the politics industry only to figure out how to fix it. So much of political analysis dwells on commentary, lamentations, or explanations. But it is often short on prescribing real, substantive solutions. As we've said, that's the legacy we care about.

Second, do not confuse our use of this competition lens drawn from business with the idea that government should be run like a business. We don't believe this. Government has mandates and structures that are profoundly different from those of business. We are concerned here with the political system—not the government itself (the agencies, the departments, the civil service, etc.). The tools used to understand competition in business help illuminate the challenges of, and solutions for, our political system.

Third, our focus is on the *results* that government delivers to its citizens. It is not centered on theoretically better or more fair democracy, or representation as an end in itself. We are committed to democracy and the freedom and equality it promises. For us, no other system compares. But we are practical as well. Freedom, equality, and representation are not enough to support American democracy on their own. The innovations we propose support democratic values, representation, and democracy writ large. But critically, they will increase the likelihood that *government delivers results* in the public interest. When government does not deliver, people become angry. As history shows, people the world over become willing to trade the freedom of representative government for the hard fist of authoritarianism.[10]

Finally, while this is a book about politics, it is not *political*—or partisan. As coauthors, we've got the political spectrum covered. Katherine was a Democrat who now calls herself a "politically homeless centrist independent." Michael is a lifelong Massachusetts Republican. Additionally, it would be neither correct nor helpful to assign blame to one side or the other, if for no other reason than that the root problems do not revolve around political parties or politicians. We repeat: the root cause that endures across all election cycles and administrations, is the system—the politics industry—not specific people, parties, or policy.

A Guide to Reading This Book

As you read, you'll notice some new (and perhaps strange) terms we've adopted to talk about politics differently—and *think* about politics differently. For instance, we've already referred to the *duopoly*: our two major political parties who dominate the industry. Our use of this term is neutral and intended to describe the industry dynamic more precisely.

The duopoly exists within what we call the *political-industrial complex*, a term that further clarifies the industry structure by encompassing the full ecosystem that works in and around our politics, and the amalgamation of actors who interact with today's political parties and benefit at the expense of most everybody else. In this case, we are hardly neutral about it; in its current form the political-industrial complex presents dire implications for the public interest.

The duopolistic competition plays out chiefly in two arenas: elections and legislating. We've noticed that it's tempting for people to assume that these two arenas are immutable structures beyond anyone's reach. But that's not true, as will become clear. To describe these structures, we use the term *elections and legislative machinery*. Machines are designed by people to reliably deliver a product based on specifications. Today's elections and legislative machinery comprise the rules, norms, and processes that the duopoly has optimized to afford itself more control over how elections are won and how legislation is passed. This machinery has a profound and reliable impact on the outcomes our politics delivers.

Finally, when we refer to elections and legislating, we're principally talking about Congress. We've chosen this focus for a few reasons.

First, fixing Congress is at the sweet spot of powerful and achievable. Second, the Framers intended Congress to be the first branch of the US government, as established in Article 1 of the Constitution. Despite the extraordinary growth and centralization of power in the executive branch, Congress was meant to be the heart of our representative democracy. Third, Congress is where the ramifications of unhealthy competition are most evidently pervasive and destructive. At any given point in time, about half of the country approves of the White House's job, and half doesn't. But an overwhelming majority find Congress's performance to be, shall we say, lacking. Fourth, while much of our analysis and subsequent recommendations are applicable to state (and even municipal) elections and governing, national politics is what is driving us apart.

As long as Congress remains captive to the current incentives of the political-industrial complex, these challenges will only deepen. We explore these challenges and make our case for a new era of political innovation in two parts of this book.

In part 1—chapters 1 through 3—we will explore the who, what, when, where, why, and how of competition in the politics industry. In part 2—chapters 4 through 6—we focus on political innovation both through the study of American history and by translating our research and theory into a powerful and achievable game plan for breaking partisan gridlock and saving our democracy: Final-Five Voting, and a model, modern legislative machinery. In the conclusion, we describe the way forward and how to take action.

. . .

One final note: In light of this book's release date, it's quite possible that you're reading this in the summer or fall of 2020. The timing means that the roar of the presidential campaign is approaching full volume. If you picked up this book amid all this noise, it's unlikely you believe that the election machinations du jour are bringing out the best in us. We are with you.

When we started this journey, November 2020 seemed light-years away in terms of the political calendar. The theory of the politics industry first took root in 2013, and before it matured into this book, it yielded the Harvard Business School report that we took on the road to pressure-test our thinking and foster discussion. Along the way, we became keenly aware that the theory's relevance does not ebb and flow with the tides of our elections. Unless the critical political innovations we prescribe in these pages have already been embraced and implemented, it doesn't matter whether the 2020 presidential conventions are coming for you next month or already came and went. There is no better time than now for this book.

If we fail to address the fundamentals of the system, we will be forever stuck on the same, unhealthy page—yesterday, today and tomorrow. We're here to turn the page, with you.

PART ONE

Political Competition

1

A Private Industry

America's political system, an outlier in the history of nations, was once the envy of the world. It advanced the public interest and gave rise to a grand history of governing that fostered both economic and social progress. Although the distribution of that progress among all Americans has not been, by any stretch, equitable since the country's founding, Washington, D.C., hasn't always worked so hard *against* the public interest. Politicians and parties have always battled for power, but there was a time when they also produced solutions and action born from compromise, in service of today and tomorrow, and which earned broad-based citizen support—the model outcomes we should expect of our politics, as proposed in chapter 3.

As we'll explore, this legacy owes its birthright to the most American innovation in history—modern, representative democracy—and a tradition of political competition that honored the best aspects of its companion in the private sector, a free marketplace. Today, that legacy is nearly undone.

America's political system has become the primary cause of our decline and the preeminent barrier to addressing the very problems it exists to solve. Americans are resigned to political gridlock and dysfunction—or worse, are disinterested in changing it. Citizens accept as normal the system's decades-long retreat from deliberation and problem solving and its advance toward today's self-service and hyper-partisanship. We accept this new normal, in part, because we are conditioned to helplessness. We assume that our political system, warts and all, is a public institution governed by impartial laws dating back to the Constitution.

But we would be wrong. Much of what makes up today's political system has no basis in the Constitution at all. There are only six tiny paragraphs in the Constitution detailing how Congress should work, and only a few sentences describe how Congress is to be elected. Most of the rules that shape the day-to-day behavior and outcomes in the political system are perversely optimized—or even expressly designed—by and for politicians themselves as well as their allies in the larger political-industrial complex. The average American citizen today is rarely a beneficiary. Politics is the only major industry in America in which the rivals—the Democratic Party and the Republican Party—write their own rules, virtually unchecked.

The Founders were wary of political parties. President George Washington dedicated a healthy portion of his Farewell Address in 1796 to alerting the young country to the dangers of political partisanship.[1] Washington's successor, President John Adams, said, "There is nothing I dread so much as the division of the republic into two great parties, each arranged under its leader, and concerting measures in opposition to the other." Completing the Founder trifecta, President Thomas Jefferson quipped, "If I could go to heaven but with a party, I would not go there at all."[2]

Jefferson, Adams, and Washington were each badly bruised by the early politics of the republic—by opponents, political mercenaries, and even one another. There was no love lost for partisanship in their founding circle. Given that we failed to heed their advice to remain vigilant against to the dangers of unchecked party power, it's likely that not one of these men or their trusted acolytes would be shocked by the extent to which unhealthy political competition has hijacked democracy itself.

But the problem is not politicians or political parties per se. Most politicians are genuinely seeking to make a positive contribution but are trapped in a system they cannot single-handedly change. Parties in a democracy play a critical role organizing citizens around shared needs and ambition, and communicating the platforms and ideas that can help voters make informed decisions.[3] At various points during their long histories, both parties have moved the country forward. We support strong parties—provided that their strength manifests itself in their members' ability to craft and enact legislation in the public interest. This would be a stark contrast to their current ability to keep winning elections—and thwarting new competition—even when very few are satisfied with the outcomes for the country.

Today, the problem is *the nature of competition* between the parties and politicians, as well as the surrounding industry actors and organizations.[4] The American political system is perfectly designed to serve the private interests of this political-industrial complex: to grow its power and revenues and to protect itself from threats. It's not designed so well to serve citizens—those who should, by rights, be the most important customers of the industry.

The business of politics is not a public institution. It is a bona fide multibillion-dollar private industry *within* a public institution. Seeing the system from this new perspective is liberating. It allows us to understand how critical it is to reclaim the rules of elections and legislating—which rightfully belong to the public—from the influence and control of private, gain-seeking actors. The challenge is to turn the politics industry into a driver of progress, aligned with the public interest—not a predictable drag on our democracy.

As we outlined in the introduction, Politics Industry Theory is not for navel gazing but for action. We seek to motivate political innovation, and eventually, realize improved results. We must move with urgency from illuminating the true nature of America's political system to mapping its players, the power structure, and the operating incentives. To draw this map, we apply the key framework for studying industry competition: the Five Forces. In this book, we'll provide a high-level summary of our Five Forces analysis. For a comprehensive analysis, see our 2017 Harvard Business School report, "Why Competition in the Politics Industry Is Failing America."[5]

Applying the Five Forces to American Politics

The Five Forces framework was originally developed to look holistically at the forces that shape the nature of competition in for-profit industries by examining: (1) the nature of rivalry; (2) the power of buyers (channels and customers); (3) the power of suppliers; (4) the threat of substitutes; and (5) the threat of new entrants. An industry's structure is the overall configuration of these five competitive forces. This web of dynamic relationships determines how an industry competes, the value available in the industry, and who has the power to capture that value. Industry structure also helps us understand how rivals or other actors can thrive even while customers are dissatisfied—politics industry competition is singularly unhealthy.

Healthy competition is win-win. *Rivals* compete fiercely to better serve customer needs. *Customers* have the power to penalize rivals for poor products and services by choosing to take their business elsewhere. *Channels* for reaching customers reinforce healthy competition by educating customers and pressuring rivals for better products and services. *Suppliers* compete to provide better inputs that allow rivals to improve their products or services. *New entrants and substitutes* are not held back by high barriers to entry that prevent them from competing in new ways to deliver value to customers. In healthy competition, the rivals do well when the customers are satisfied.

Applying the Five Forces to politics for the first time was illuminating and it showed how American politics is an industrial-strength, nation-crippling perversion of competition. The rivals have managed over generations to entrench and enrich their duopoly while failing spectacularly to serve the customers—us. The duopoly has written its own rules and optimized others for its own gain, all while subverting the forces of healthy competition—the forces that would drive accountability for results (figure 1-1).

FIGURE 1-1

Five Forces: The Structure of the Politics Industry

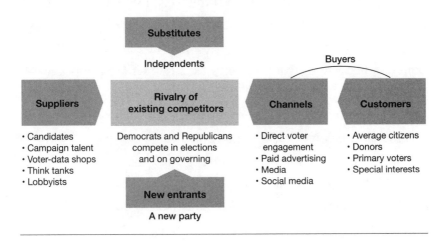

Unhealthy Competition in Politics

In the politics industry, competition takes place on two key levels—competition to win elections and competition to pass (or block) legislation. Our elections and our legislating are drowning in unhealthy *win-lose* competition: the duopoly wins and we lose. This tragic outcome is a result of the structure of the politics industry, but before we explore that structure in depth, you must understand a unique characteristic of the politics industry.

The Dual Currencies of Politics

The politics industry has *two* currencies: some customers pay with votes; some pay with money.[6] We call this dual political currency. The devastating power differential between the customers of the industry—average voters with little power; special interests, donors, and party-primary voters with tremendous power—is in no small part a result of the relative power of votes to money. Let us explain.

The currency of votes has consistently less relative value than the currency of money. The utility of votes has a limited upside (i.e., all you need to win an election is one more vote than your competitor) whereas the utility of money has no limit (i.e., more is always better—there's always something to buy in the political-industrial complex). Votes are almost always taken for granted in general elections for Congress because over 80 percent of districts aren't competitive—the winners are already decided in the primaries. Customers who deploy both currencies are especially powerful, such as special interest groups who donate dollars and get out the vote.

Said another way, money in politics gets a *great* return on investment (ROI)—votes, not so much. How can we reduce the outsized influence of money in the politics industry? By making the political currency of votes more valuable than the political currency of money—by reducing the reliability of the ROI for money and increasing the ROI for votes. As will become clear in this book, it is the structure and rules of competition in the politics industry that artificially devalue votes. The restoration of healthy and dynamic competition (the prescription for which we provide in chapter 5) will go a long way to driving a relative rise in votes-to-money value, making voters the important customers in the politics industry—as they should be—and disrupting the outsized control the current two rivals have in the industry.

Rivals: Duopoly Control

Rivals form the core of competition in any industry. It could be General Motors and Ford; or Kraft, General Mills, and Unilever. In the politics industry, the rivalry is between the duopoly, our two major political parties—the Republicans and the Democrats.

Duopolies are not inherently good or bad. But as politics is currently structured, the same two rivals are virtually guaranteed to remain in power no matter how poorly they serve the public interest. This would be a problem for customers in any industry—it's a nightmare for a democracy.

Rather than competing head-to-head for the same voters—those often described as America's "middle"—the parties divide the electorate into mutually exclusive partisan camps and prioritize on each side the highly engaged (and often single-issue or more ideological) constituencies who most dependably vote or give money. Furthermore, in a duopoly, the rivals understand that although they compete, both rivals will benefit from an "attractive" industry. From the duopoly's perspective, an attractive industry is one that strengthens and reinforces their way of competing; limits the power of suppliers, channels, and customers; and is protected by high barriers to entry.

In a duopoly, the rivals mutually take steps to enhance the attractiveness of the industry and avoid undermining it. This collusion and anticompetitive behavior has been particularly damaging because there is no independent regulator to hold the rivals accountable, and antitrust regulations conveniently don't apply. The rivals—and the political-industrial complex writ large—are free to collude as they desire to enhance their own interests.

The tacit agreement to split the electorate and target extremes makes politics polarizing. It pushes unreasonable, ideological, and emotionally charged arguments to the fore while withholding the solutions-oriented conversations citizens so desperately need—and once expected from our politics.

Customers: Power Skewed

A political system is supposed to serve the public interest, so all citizens should be its customers. But in fact, the industry does not serve all customers equally. Just as savvy businesses prioritize their most profitable customers, the duopoly prioritizes the customers who most effectively advance its own interests. In the politics industry, the most important and profitable customers are party-primary voters, special interests, and donors, because they reliably deliver the two currencies, votes and money (figure 1-2).

PARTY-PRIMARY VOTERS: These customers are the guardians at the gate. Every party candidate must pass through party-primary voters to get on the general election ballot. Primary voters are typically more politically engaged, more partisan, and further to the left or right in their respective parties. They can also be counted on to turn out in the general election.[7] In districts that reliably lean red or blue, because of either intentional gerrymandering or natural geographic

FIGURE 1-2

Customer Power in Politics

The duopoly prioritizes three overlapping groups who most reliably deliver money and votes.

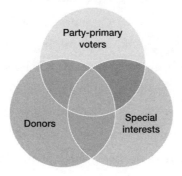

sorting, the party primary is the only election that really matters. In the 2016 general election, less than 10 percent of US House races and just 28 percent of Senate races were competitive.[8] The rest were in safe seats; the winner was decided in the primary.

As a consequence, the true influence of party-primary voters goes far beyond their low numbers. Less than 20 percent of eligible voters participate in most congressional primaries.[9] The influence of more-ideological primary voters is even greater in about half the states, where primaries are closed or semiclosed to non-party-affiliated voters. In those states, citizens who decline to register with a party aren't allowed to vote in these decisive contests.[10] The relatively small group of party-primary voters then has a disproportionate influence on who gets elected and it pushes candidates further to the left and right. We expand on the nature of primary voters and the primary system in chapter 2.

SPECIAL INTERESTS AND DONORS: These groups are incredibly powerful customers because they deliver money, or votes, or both. Special interests are organized groups—either issue-specific or industry-specific—that are heavily focused on influencing policies on particular issues in their favor. Funding from special interests comes in the form of both spending to influence elections and lobbying to influence legislation. Examples include the pharmaceutical lobby, insurance lobby, gun lobby, small business lobbies, and unions. The National Rifle Association, for example, spent $412 million on political activities in 2016, in addition to guiding its 5.5 million members on how to vote. The health-care sector funneled $268 million to influence elections and spent $1.02 billion on lobbying in the 2015–2016 election cycle.[11]

Donors are also powerful because the duopoly (and other entities in the political-industrial complex) seeks to maximize dollars raised. Large-dollar donors include wealthy individuals, organizations, and corporations, and often overlap with special interests. This money comes in the form of direct donations, which are capped and subject to oversight, as well as "independent expenditures," which are uncapped spending not donated directly to candidates or parties but used to support them (such as through supposedly independent advertising). Much of the latter is known as "dark money" because it evades disclosure and oversight.[12]

Relatively recently, small donors aggregated through online party-connected fundraising have become an increasingly powerful force, influencing policy and elections through donations and delivering votes, though they don't have the same ability to convert their collective influence into access for any specific individuals.

Some special interests also influence elected officials by offering lucrative jobs when an official leaves government. A surprising proportion of elected officials now follow this path. Of the retiring members of Congress between 2009 and 2015, some 42 percent joined a lobbying firm and about another 25 percent took a position at a company involved in lobbying.[13] These are stunning percentages—but just the tip of the iceberg. Almost half of registered lobbyists are some type of former government official, often former regulators who can influence the rule-making and enforcement process, or former congressional staffers who are instrumental in writing industry-friendly legislation.[14]

AVERAGE VOTERS: This customer group represents a substantial proportion of people who vote almost exclusively in general elections—they *don't* vote in primaries—and who are not regular donors. They tend to be less ideologically extreme and they have little power or influence in today's political influence.

The parties do pay some attention to the average voter to increase the turnout of their base or depress the turnout of the other side's base and capture swing voters. But since average voters have only two choices in most general elections, parties appeal to them marginally. The parties compete for average voters not by delivering outcomes for their benefit, but rather by seeking to be a little less disliked than—or slightly preferred over—the other party. Parties don't need to deliver solutions but only need to convince average voters to choose them as the lesser of two evils.

In a normal industry, ignoring such a large group of customers would make a competitor vulnerable to new competition. But in the politics industry, as we will discuss, new competition is not a threat, so the parties are free to concentrate on delivering value to their powerful party-primary voters, donors, and special interests.

NONVOTERS: These are the least powerful customers of all. Almost 40 percent of eligible Americans did not vote in the 2016 general election. Those who don't vote cede their customer power to the duopoly and its allies. These individuals, perhaps not surprisingly, tend to be more moderate and more independent. And, sadly, irrelevant.

. . .

Recent research supports our conclusions about customer power. For example, in 2014, researchers Martin Gilens at Princeton University and Benjamin Page at Northwestern University examined congressional action on 1,779 policy issues. Their finding: "When the preferences of economic elites and the stances of organized interest groups are controlled for, the preferences of the average American appear to have only a minuscule, near-zero, statistically non-significant impact upon public policy."[15]

Channels: Compromised

Channels exist between the rivals and the end customers. For example, warehouses and grocery stores are the channels between food manufacturers and grocery shoppers. In politics, the duopoly reaches us with information and persuasion through key channels, such as direct voter contact (the "ground game"), paid advertising, traditional independent media, and a panoply of new media channels that have remade the communications marketplace over the last few decades. Historically, channels mediated politics by taking in information directly and indirectly from the duopoly, sorting it, analyzing it, and redistributing it as unbiased news with a trusted seal of approval for the country. But the combination of market disruption—news media in free fall—and the creation or targeted capture of channels by the political-industrial complex for its own benefit have greatly diminished healthy competition.

DIRECT VOTER CONTACT: This contact takes place through face-to-face meetings, rallies, fundraisers, street teams, phone calls, and now text messages among other burgeoning digital spheres, and has always been heavily controlled by the duopoly. While this channel has not grown substantially, the duopoly has taken advantage of more sophisticated voter data to make contact much more targeted, distinguishing which voters they can bring to their sides while ignoring or suppressing turnout among the rest.[16]

PAID ADVERTISING: This channel is also controlled mostly by the duopoly and their donor allies. And it takes place on TV, radio, and, increasingly, digital media. Advertising is overwhelmingly negative and reflects and reinforces the divisive tactics deployed by the duopoly. Yet political advertising accounts for an important proportion of total revenue in election years for traditional and new media companies. Consequently, current partisan competition *works* for the media.[17]

TRADITIONAL INDEPENDENT MEDIA: Historically, traditional independent media has largely mediated information flow and persuasion efforts. Today, mainstream media is suffering declining revenues and audiences and duopoly interests are aggressively capturing particular media. What's more, the advent of new media platforms has enabled duopoly actors to bypass the mainstream media to reach customers directly. Because of changes like these, much of the media programming that was independent, influential, and widely consumed is now co-opted by political ideology, and is often nakedly partisan. Many now ignore, mistrust, or even detest it.[18]

DISRUPTIVE NEW MEDIA: These new channels, which include social media echo chambers, content aggregators, online forums, and the ever-evolving niche blogosphere, is as powerful and addictive as it is rife with ethical and influence issues on an election-tipping scale. Many of the new media players—Facebook, YouTube, Twitter, and the like— are still far younger than mainstream platforms and unregulated, albeit incredibly powerful as avenues for information and influence. Clearly we live in a dangerous era of disintermediation and confusion—an era arising in part from a sickly mainstream media's scrambling to find a viable viewership and revenue model for the twenty-first century.

. . .

The points of intersection among today's channels now appear to out-number the once-sacred separations. What constitutes news and what constitutes advertising—or, worse, propaganda—is at times a crap-shoot to decipher, especially online. What was once clear packaging for news—a story in a magazine or newspaper, or a segment on TV or radio—now comes in myriad forms, from fifteen-second videos to 280-character tweets. What was once an unbiased perspective on the local news might now be a bought-and-paid-for influencer. What was once at least moderately deliberative and balanced is now a cacophony of rhetoric and reactionaries. And few in news today can afford (or deign to budget for) good, old-fashioned editors and beat reporters.

Thomas Jefferson summarized the value of trusted media to a democracy, saying that if he had to choose between "a government without newspapers or newspapers without a government, I should not hesitate a moment to prefer the latter."[19]

The loss of confidence that many readers, viewers, and listeners once had in their understanding of issues and the truthfulness of public information is collateral damage and gut-wrenching for those of us who believe in the sanctity of the Fourth Estate. The players within the political-industrial complex can now go around the media to target, reach, and shape the points of view of the citizenry in ways that we're still struggling to understand and manage. What will it take to rebuild the common trust that underpinned our journalism?

Arthur Miller, the famous playwright of *Death of a Salesman*, once said, "A good newspaper, I suppose, is a nation talking to itself."[20] While our focus in this book is on the ins and outs of politics directly, the reestablishment of a national, moderated, and mediated conversation would be a welcome partner effort worthy of investment.

Suppliers: Captured

Suppliers provide valuable inputs that allow rivals to produce their products and services. Think, for example, of raw materials such as sugar and oil supplied to food manufacturers, or the law and accounting firms supporting corporations like these manufacturers. In the politics industry, partisan competition is reinforced and amplified by the duopoly's infiltration and capture of the key suppliers to the industry. There are five main supplier groups: candidates, specialized campaign and governance talent, voter-data shops, idea suppliers such as think tanks, and academics and lobbyists who contribute to shaping legislation or regulation and its implementation.

CANDIDATES: This group depends heavily on its party for legitimacy, funding, infrastructure, field operations, voter lists and data analytics, debate access, and other requirements of a modern campaign. Nonparty candidates face huge obstacles even to entering elections, much less winning them, given the lack of such party-supplied support. The parties also get to decide which candidates to back most aggressively—or sometimes not at all. This authority increases the duopoly's power to align individual candidate platforms—not to mention elected officials' actions—with the party line.

TALENT: The talent in politics includes campaign managers, political consultants, pollsters, public relations staff, data analysts, social media directors, ground staff, and certain legislative staff. But most talent works only for one side of the duopoly or the other.[21] You are either a Democratic pollster or a Republican pollster, a Democratic staff member or a Republican one, and so on. Working with candidates who challenge incumbents without the approval of the party or working with independents challenging both parties leads to banishment.[22] In 2013, for instance, the National Republican Senatorial Committee publicly blacklisted an advertising firm for working with a Republican challenging a Republican incumbent for the Senate.[23] In 2019, the Democratic Congressional Campaign Committee put firms on notice that they would be blacklisted if caught doing business with anyone challenging an incumbent.[24] When Greg Orman ran a highly regarded (yet unfortunately unsuccessful) independent campaign for senator in Kansas in 2014, several of his consultants could only work for him in secret.

VOTER-DATA SHOPS: These organizations are crucial to modern campaigns. Much like the exploding role of data and analytics in other industries, accumulating and analyzing the newly capturable information about people requires large, sustained investments. Candidates and elected officials depend heavily on massive voter files to efficiently cultivate supporters, raise money, decide on issues to target in campaigns, turn out the vote, and guide priorities in governing. However, such data is not available to just any candidate. Voter-data suppliers linked to the duopoly, such as NGP VAN for the Democrats, and i360 for the Republicans, have amassed the most extensive proprietary voter databases, analytics, and likely voter lists—and they keep tight control on the data they gather with agreements that ensure it all flows back to them. Partisans decide to whom such voter data is made available and at what cost. Party-supported candidates reap substantial advantages.

IDEA SUPPLIERS: These thought leaders develop and advocate for the policy ideas that are incorporated into party platforms, candidate policies, and legislation. Key idea suppliers include academics as well as an estimated 1,835 think tanks, with total budgets in the billions of dollars.[25] Idea suppliers were once independent and a significant strength of our political system, creating vigorous competition on ideas generated from diverse voices. Today, more and more idea suppliers have become closely aligned with one side of the duopoly or the other.[26] Out of the thirty-five leading US think tanks focused on public policy, about 70 percent can be identified as partisan or partisan leaning.[27] Many think tanks have moved beyond a research-only focus to create political action units.

Meanwhile, congressional staff and research support responsible for generating, reviewing, and fine-tuning ideas have been gutted. From 1985 to 2015, congressional committee staff numbers have declined by 35 percent.[28] Absent professional staff, Congress has been forced to rely more heavily on opportunistic suppliers—like lobbyists.

LOBBYISTS: These political influencers advocate for special interests by trying to influence legislation and regulation, often using leverage from significant donations. Lobbyists are employed by special interests and as part of these groups they help advance the duopoly's core customers in frontline legislating. Lobbyists have become a major vehicle for disseminating research on issues, policy ideas, and legislative support for government staffers. They are the hired guns who pitch ideas to, and even draft bills and talking points for, increasingly overstretched and under-resourced congressional staffs.[29] Lobbying has become a huge business in its own right, with reported federal lobbying spending (which significantly understates actual spending) of $3.15 billion in 2016.[30] In 2014, when lobbying expenditures reached a recent peak, companies spent more money trying to influence public policy than Congress spent on itself.[31]

Numerous studies reveal that spending on lobbying often produces a high return on investment for the spender through its influence on legislation and its success in getting adjustments or exemptions in regulation.[32] The clout of lobbyists looking out for their clients' interests, and not for the public interest, distorts legislation and sometimes blurs the line between lobbying and corruption.

Barriers to Entry and Substitutes: Colossal and Constrained

Industries that fail to serve their customers well are ripe for new entrants that improve value for customers and shake up the market. The barriers to entry determine how easy or hard it is for a new competitor to enter the fray. In the politics industry, the founding of a new party would constitute a new entrant. Substitutes and new entrants are different ways of competing—think of Uber to taxis or Amazon to brick-and-mortar retailers. In the politics industry, substitutes could be independent candidates not affiliated with a party.[33]

The barriers to entry for new competitors in the politics industry are colossal—and they dramatically constrain substitutes as well. A sure sign of the high barriers to entry is the fact that no major new party has emerged since 1854, when antislavery members of the Whig Party split off and formed the Republican Party. The Progressive Party (1912) and the Reform Party (1995) were both serious efforts but managed to elect only a few candidates and were disbanded within a decade. Today's most significant third parties, the Libertarians and the Greens, run numerous candidates every cycle but have yet to win a single congressional or gubernatorial campaign—not to mention the presidency.[34] Despite widespread and growing dissatisfaction with the existing parties, contemporary third parties continue to fare poorly. The same applies to independents, despite the high proportion of citizens who identify themselves as independents.[35]

There are myriad barriers to new competition, including economies of scale; incumbency advantages in brand recognition, relationships, expertise, and infrastructure; access to key suppliers and channels; certain election rules and practices, such as sore-loser laws; and access to funding. For example, duopoly-created fundraising rules allow a single donor to contribute $855,000 annually to a national political party (Democrats, Republicans, or both) but only $5,600 per election cycle—two years—to an independent candidate committee.[36]

Interestingly, the greatest barriers to entry are three structures that seem perfectly normal—not nefarious in any way—to us. These barriers, which were introduced earlier in the book, are (1) party primaries, (2) plurality voting—part of the elections machinery—and (3) a highly partisan legislative machinery. Later in the book, we will discuss these enormous barriers in detail and our plan for eliminating them.

Finally, unlike virtually any other industry, there is no independent regulation in the politics industry. The participants themselves dictate how they are held accountable. The only federal regulator is the Federal Election Commission (FEC), created in 1974 in the aftermath of Watergate to implement and enforce election laws. Despite its official designation as independent, the FEC is anything but that. The six-member commission is dominated by the duopoly and typically split down the middle, with three Democratic and three Republican commissioners.

Since August 2019, the Commission has been effectively neutered when the resignation of a Republican commissioner brought the number of commissioners down to three, below the legal threshold for the panel to take actions, and President Trump has not appointed a replacement. Politics is a classic example of *regulatory capture*—it's as if the US Securities and Exchange Commission were jointly run by the boards of JP Morgan Chase & Co. and Bank of America.[37]

This all sounds like a clear antitrust violation. So why hasn't the Federal Trade Commission or the Justice Department brought a case? Again, ever so conveniently, antitrust rules do not apply to the politics industry.

The "Trump Effect"?

Has the election of Donald Trump changed the structure of our political system or our analysis, conclusions, or recommendations? On the contrary, his victory validates them.

The 2016 election provided a striking indication of the level of public dissatisfaction with the status quo, as the voters clearly tried to reject the duopoly by electing someone from "outside the system." In the end, they were not successful.

Trump ran *within* the existing duopoly, recognizing that a truly independent bid would not succeed because of the high barriers to entry facing an independent or third-party candidate. He reportedly came to this conclusion in 2000, when he explored running as the Reform Party candidate. This conclusion is, not coincidentally, the same one that Michael Bloomberg reached when he considered running as an independent in 2016. That conclusion held up: Bloomberg entered the 2020 race for president as a Democrat.

Did Trump's election signal a shift in the nature of rivalry and the end of party influence? No. In fact, partisan rivalry and division have only increased, as has the capture and compromise of channels and suppliers.

President Trump can be understood as a hybrid substitute to the traditional duopoly but not as truly new competition. He ran as a Republican, albeit with mixed support from the party initially, and utilized the traditional party system and its advantages to campaign, get on the primary and general election ballots, and win. Trump's ability to win reflected a very specific personal and political context. His high brand recognition provided two great benefits: (1) unprecedented free media access because his campaign style attracted viewers and (2) his ability to go directly to the public through Twitter.[38] These two personal benefits lowered the cost of his campaign and, combined with his self-financing ability, lowered his barriers to entry.

Running as a supposed "outsider" within a party may emerge as a strategy that others imitate. However, Trump's success is likely to be more an anomaly due to his unique personal situation. Certainly, Trump's election and presidency has precipitated significant adjustments and disruption within both the Republican and the Democratic Parties. But neither the structure of the politics industry, nor its incentives, have fundamentally changed. In fact, the increased divisiveness of political competition has only increased congressional dysfunction, because Republicans who speak up for anything contrary to the Trump administration's line, or Democrats who are seen to be anything less than completely obstructionist, fear getting primaried—there's that verb again.

The Trump presidency supports our contention that the nature of the politics industry is an unhealthy pill our democracy has been forced to swallow. The fundamental failure of Washington, D.C., to address our biggest national challenges persists unaltered in the Trump administration. Yet the duopoly and the broader political-industrial complex remain intact. The need to reform our political system to create healthier competition and better outcomes remains unchanged.

A Thriving Political-Industrial Complex

In January 1961, in his farewell address, President Dwight D. Eisenhower, a Republican, warned the nation of the threat and misplaced influence of what he called the military-industrial complex: "This conjunction of an immense military establishment and a large arms industry is new in the American experience. The total influence—economic, political, even spiritual—is felt in every city, every State house, every office of the Federal government. We recognize the imperative need for this development. Yet we must not fail to comprehend its grave implications. Our toil, resources and livelihood are all involved; so is the very structure of our society. In the councils of government, we must guard against the acquisition of unwarranted influence, whether sought or unsought, by the military-industrial complex. The potential for the disastrous rise of misplaced power exists and will persist."[39]

What Eisenhower foresaw was a powerful alliance between America's military and the defense industry. He believed that if this alliance were to be left unchecked, it would perpetuate a build-buy defense-spending cycle that would outpace actual need and create products designed to serve the goals of the complex over the goals of the "customer" (which should be our national security interests). The military-industrial complex would create a supply of defense goods for supply's sake and, like many other modern American sectors, become too big and too powerful to fail.

Politics in America has mutated in much the same way. The political duopoly and its surrounding actors and interests, many of which have been co-opted and divided along partisan lines, is aptly described as a *political-industrial complex*. By nearly every measure, the complex is thriving. Campaigns are seemingly endless and put to work an immense roster of canvassers, pollsters, and staff. Top consultants are in high demand, and the media interest has never been greater. Overall spending—a normal proxy for an industry's success—continues to rise year after year.[40] Funders pour in more and more money because it works; the ROI is high.

Direct political spending at the federal level was at least $16 billion during the 2016 election cycle.[41] Roughly 40 percent of this total, or around $6 billion, was election spending by candidates, parties, PACs, super PACs, and other organizations; another 40 percent was reported for lobbying of Congress and government agencies by companies, trade associations, unions, and other special interest groups.[42] Politics is also big business for the media. At least $1.5 billion was spent on advertising during political shows on channels such as CNN, Fox News, and MSNBC.[43] The remaining balance flows to the budgets of major think tanks like the Center for American Progress or the Heritage Foundation. Together, the industry is responsible for at least nineteen thousand jobs and thousands more in consulting.[44] Keep in mind that these numbers only pertain to the federal level of the politics industry. If we were to add spending at the state level, these estimates would balloon.[45]

While these figures are staggering, they severely underestimate the total size of the industry. Because of substantial underreporting, actual direct political spending is many billions of dollars higher. Just factoring in estimates of so-called shadow lobbying, for example, would easily add another $6 billion to the total.[46] This estimate excludes politically active nonprofits and social welfare organizations, such as the National Rifle Association, the Sierra Club, the American Civil Liberties Union, and Americans for Prosperity, all of which work tirelessly to influence public policy. If we include the revenue of all these political organizations, the politics industry inflates to over $100 billion dollars per election cycle.[47]

Most importantly, the politics industry determines how the government spends an almost unimaginable amount of money—$3.9 trillion in fiscal year 2016 at the federal level alone.[48] In addition to controlling what government spends and how, the politics industry has a huge effect on the overall economy by setting policies that affect economic and social spending in every field.

By any measure, politics is big business. The mission of deliberative democracy is no longer central to the work of the key political rivals, much less to the sprawling set of supporting political entities—the core customers that fund the system, the controlled suppliers, the co-opted channels. All of this both enables unhealthy competition and feeds off it.

The politics industry is a game with one golden rule: keep the duopoly in power. It's time to write new rules. We've done it before.

2

The Rules of the Game

Depending on when you picked up this book, you may well be reading it during the run-up to the 2020 presidential election—which means it is debate season. This tradition of top party candidates facing off is must-see television, at least for some. For the networks and other major players in the political-industrial complex, 2020 means big money. During the 2016 election cycle, presidential debate viewership rivaled the Super Bowl; many millions of advertising dollars flowed to the broadcasters. CBS charged advertisers up to a quarter-million dollars for a thirty-second political slot.

Why is business so good in politics? Why does it work so well for the industry itself but not for everyone else? Only by teasing apart the key rules and practices—the machinery of elections and legislating—that have been set and optimized by the duopoly over generations can we answer these questions and devise solutions to save our democracy. But first, what exactly do we mean by rules?

Let's turn back to presidential debates. From 1976 until 1984, the debates were sponsored by the League of Women Voters. As a nonpartisan organization, the league occasionally ran into predictable conflicts with the duopoly. In 1980, for example, President Jimmy Carter boycotted the first presidential debate of that election when the league invited John Anderson, a freethinking congressman who broke with the Republican Party to run as an independent.[1] Four years later, the league condemned the campaigns of Ronald Reagan and Walter Mondale for "totally abusing the process" by trying to control what questions could be asked. By the next presidential race in 1984, the Republican National Committee (RNC) and Democratic National Committee (DNC) had begun plotting how to take over the debates themselves. The RNC chair, Frank Fahrenkopf Jr., made the reason explicit: "The two major political parties should do everything in their power to strengthen their own position."[2]

Months later, a report by the Georgetown University Center for Strategic and International Studies endorsed "turning over the sponsorship of the Presidential debates to the two major parties."[3] The report's findings, and its timing, were no coincidence. It was written by a committee packed with the industry's core constituents—politicians, political consultants, and news executives—and cochaired by a former Republican congressman and the former head of the DNC.[4] The acting DNC and RNC chairs endorsed the report. Meanwhile, Dorothy S. Ridings, the president of the League of Women Voters, issued a warning: "If future presidential forums are sponsored only by the two major parties, it stretches the imagination to think that significant independent or third-party candidates would ever be included in such debates."[5] She proved prophetic.

In 1987, the duopoly was quite pleased to follow the report's recommendation and form the Commission on Presidential Debates (CPD), initially cochaired by the heads of the DNC and RNC. At a joint news conference announcing the CPD, the new cochairs admitted that they were unlikely to allow third parties to participate in the debates.[6]

Ross Perot, a billionaire and political neophyte put this policy to the test in 1992, when he ran as the Reform Party candidate. The CPD initially planned to bar Perot from the debates. Eventually, however, he was allowed to participate after the campaigns of George H. W. Bush and Bill Clinton lobbied for his inclusion, each believing that Perot would draw more votes from the other side.[7] Perot won almost 20 percent of the vote that November, clearly proving that he was worthy of his spot on the stage.

In 1996, however, the CPD refused Perot a spot.[8] Unlike four years earlier, the two duopoly candidates now calculated that his inclusion was not in their interest. Clinton, the frontrunner, wished to make the debates nonevents, while opponent Bob Dole believed, though incorrectly, that Perot's candidacy had spoiled the last election for the Republicans. The CPD was happy to oblige. In the words of Dole's campaign chair, "the Commission does what you tell them to do."[9]

The decision to exclude was not, however, what citizens wanted. Three-quarters of eligible voters supported Perot's inclusion—and were denied the debate they wanted.[10] A *New York Times* editorial headlined "Fixing the Presidential Debates" attacked the CPD's decision, saying that "the Commission proved itself to be a tool of the two dominant parties rather than a guardian of the American interest."[11]

The CPD has since window-dressed its rules—for instance, establishing the standard that a candidate must achieve at least 15 percent support in national polls to be invited.[12] While this 15 percent rule might appear neutral, its effects are anything but. An outsider faces the nearly impossible task of reaching this threshold by the September deadline.[13] New competitors are unlikely to achieve this level of voter support without the media attention that comes with a nationally televised debate—the very platform the 15 percent rule denies them.

The duopoly succeeded in capturing the debates, a critical channel, and also managed to fortify barriers to entry—all by redesigning their own self-preserving rules of the game.

When the Players Set the Rules

In many ways, the duopoly's concerted efforts to optimize its success are no different than what we see in other industries. Players in any game hone their competitive strategies to increase profitability and adapt as the regulatory landscape shifts. Think about professional sports. When James Naismith invented basketball in 1891, every basket was worth two points, so teams prioritized high-percentage shots and sought players who could dominate near the hoop both offensively and defensively. In an effort to modernize the game and make it more exciting for fans, the National Basketball Association (NBA) adopted the three-point line in 1977. As a result, strategic priorities and team composition changed. Today's game is fast-paced, with "position-less" three-point sharpshooters and floor-spreading defenders replacing the once-dominant power forwards and bruising centers. In basketball, as elsewhere, an independent authority changed the rules and consistently monitors, and regulates, the game.

What is particularly brazen about the politics industry is that, over time, the duopoly *itself* has optimized the rules of the game and in fundamental ways. Only by pinpointing the most important of these rules and practices, and conceiving of new ones, can we devise solutions to inject healthy competition in elections and legislating.

The Machinery of Politics

Any investigative journalists worth their salt know that getting an important story off the ground almost always starts with following the money. The same guiding principle applies to investigating how the rules of the politics industry have been written over time.

Follow the money: the core currencies of the politics industry are money and votes. Consequently, the rules that dictate *how elections are won* and *how laws are written*—the arenas in which money and votes are both earned and spent—have the most impact.

A vast, arcane, but duopoly-benefiting set of rules and practices determine the structure of our nation's elections and our elected officials' lawmaking. As explained earlier, we call these rules and practices the industry's machinery. Think of this machinery as the political system's software, quietly humming in the background, out of sight and often out of mind, but powerfully shaping how candidates and lawmakers compete.

We can divide this machinery into two parts. First, how do we decide who gets placed on a ballot? How do we decide who wins? The rules that govern these questions are the industry's *elections machinery*. Second, once a candidate is sent to Washington as an elected official, how is the legislator permitted, or constrained, to draft legislation and turn bills into laws? What rules and practices determine how Congress works? These are the industry's *legislative machinery*. Together, this machinery comprises the most important rules governing competition in the politics industry—and distorting healthy competition. Let's take a look under the proverbial hood.

Elections Machinery

Today's elections machinery ensures that moderates need not apply, that those who seek compromise are punished, and that independents and third parties are locked out. Two key features of today's elections machinery are the most important in cementing unhealthy competition: party primaries and plurality voting. The duopoly did not originally create these features, but it has powerfully optimized around them.

Party Primaries

While most of us don't participate in party primaries, we are typically aware of them. Party primaries mark an election's official starting line. While all primaries narrow down the field of competition for the general election, the rules vary state by state. In states with closed primaries, only party-affiliated voters may participate in their party's primary. Independents and third-party voters are completely locked out. In states with open primaries, any registered voter may participate, regardless of political affiliation.

Party primaries go back to an early-twentieth-century innovation that ended the selection of candidates by party bosses in party conventions, instead giving citizens the power to directly choose their parties' nominees. This innovation was supposed to be a good-government reform, and it had some benefits. Today, however, party primaries have evolved to be an enemy of good government. The duopoly has learned to exploit party primaries to strengthen ideological purity and enforce party loyalty.

As discussed, in party primaries a small group of more-ideological voters (customers) become guardians at the gate. Gatekeeping authority makes this small band of partisans one of the most powerful customer segments in the politics industry. It's no coincidence that the more ideologically extreme of a voter you are, the more likely you are to think that you're able to influence government, according to recent research.[14] Party primaries can have the effect of screening out problem-solving candidates, while rewarding more extreme candidates.

When Joe Biden became vice president in 2009, it was well understood that Republican congressman Mike Castle would take Biden's seat as the next senator from Delaware.[15] Castle was elected governor in 1984 and reelected in 1988 with over 70 percent of the vote. Term limits led to a transition to D.C., where he served as Delaware's sole representative in the House for a state-record nine terms, with a reputation as a problem-solving moderate. Arriving in Congress amid Republican Speaker of the House Newt Gingrich's politics of conflict, Castle led the Republican Mainstream Partnership, a group committed to passing pragmatic policies and working across the aisle. He was integral to George W. Bush's No Child Left Behind education policy, but he broke with his party to vote in favor of the Wall Street bailout in the midst of the 2008 financial crisis.

Castle's consensus-oriented approach to politics, the so-called Delaware way, made him enormously popular in his home state and the overwhelming favorite in the 2010 election. Yet not everyone was thrilled that Castle was, at times, out of step with Republican orthodoxy. To some on the right, Castle's centrism represented a betrayal of the conservative agenda. His support for same-sex marriage, stem cell research, and gun control earned him the RINO (Republican in name only) label. In the Republican Senate primary that fall, partisan forces rallied behind Castle's opponent, Christine O'Donnell, a Tea Party Republican candidate who had twice in the prior five years run for the Senate and lost. With endorsements from national Tea Party stars and financing from conservative advocacy groups, O'Donnell pulled off a dramatic upset, defeating Castle with just 30,561 votes versus Castle's 27,021, in the low-turnout primary.[16]

It was a stunning setback, but still just the primary. If Castle were to run as an independent in the November general election, the path to victory appeared wide open. O'Donnell's was a weak candidacy bogged down by controversies, such as the accusation by her former campaign manager that O'Donnell used donations to pay her rent.[17] Castle also had the edge over the Democratic Senate nominee, Chris Coons. Even after his defeat in the primary, polls predicted that Castle would defeat Coons head-to-head by a twenty-one-point margin in the general election. In terms of American elections, that's a landslide waiting to happen.[18]

But no one has ever heard of "Senator Mike Castle." There was a problem. Delaware has what's called a sore-loser law. This ludicrous law dictates that candidates who run and lose in their party's primary are not allowed to appear on the general election ballot, even as an independent.[19] Instead, the 2010 party primary—in which less than 6 percent of the population participated and which was decided by just three thousand votes in a state of nearly one million people—denied the general-election voters the opportunity to vote for the most popular politician in the state.[20]

Because of the sore-loser law, Castle couldn't even get on the general election ballot. Coons cruised to victory over O'Donnell.

Sore-loser laws are an example of rules devised by the industry actors themselves. These rules were not invented by the Framers but gained a foothold thanks to private, gain-seeking political parties. The first sore-loser law was enacted by Mississippi in 1906. Over time, these laws gained in popularity, reaching twenty states by 1970. Another twenty-one states adopted sore-loser structures between 1976 and 1994.[21] Today, forty-four states have these wacky rules that prevent candidates from running in the general election after losing in a party primary.[22]

In the handful of states without these truly undemocratic rules, election outcomes can be dramatically different. In 2006, for example, Connecticut senator Joe Lieberman was challenged in his Democratic party primary by Ned Lamont, who outflanked Lieberman to his left by criticizing Lieberman's willingness to work with the Bush White House. With strong liberal backing, Lamont pulled off a stunning upset, defeating Lieberman by a mere ten thousand votes. If this were Delaware, it would have been the end of the road for Senator Lieberman. But because Connecticut was then one of only four states without a sore-loser law, Lieberman ran as an independent in the general election and won, proving he was the choice of the people.[23]

Sore-loser laws are just one egregious example of how democratic principles have been violated by rules designed by our parties to serve their own interests and restrict competition. Other examples abound.

For instance, biased ballot access rules in many states make it more difficult for independent and third-party candidates to get on the ballot. Candidates are required to collect a certain number of signatures, but gathering these names can be a Herculean effort, especially for new competitors who often lack the infrastructure and resources required. In Alabama, for instance, a candidate must gather signatures from at least 3 percent of voters in the last gubernatorial election. This requirement has been met just once since 1997, when the rule was created.[24]

Party primaries are the centerpiece of elections machinery. They ensure that the public interest and a person's electability do not intersect. As outlined earlier in the book, when legislators are considering a big, potentially bipartisan legislative deal, the most important question they are forced to consider is "Can I make it back through my partisan primary if I vote for this?" Today, most of the time the answer is no.

Former House Majority Leader Eric Cantor learned this the hard way.[25] He was successfully "primaried" in 2014 by a Tea Party Republican insurgent as punishment for his tentative outreach on immigration—a Republican version of the Dream Act. In this instance, even though the duopoly optimizes around and deploys these rules, it can also be victims of them—and at the highest levels, as was the case for Cantor. House Republicans have since moved even further to the right than any other time in recent history, despite little change in the ideological composition among Americans. Party primaries are a huge problem for the country, but not the only one. So, too, is a little-known system we use to tally the votes.

Plurality Voting

Many Americans are surprised to learn that our elections are not designed to ensure the election of the candidate with the broadest appeal to the most voters. In fact, politicians can easily win elections with more than two candidates *without winning a majority of votes.*

For example, in a three-way race, a candidate can win with as little as 34 percent of the vote—indicating that two-thirds of voters preferred someone else. This is precisely what happened in Maine in 2010, when Paul LePage, a Tea Party Republican candidate, won his gubernatorial primary with only 37.4 percent of the vote. He then won the governorship with only 37.6 percent. In other words, nearly two-thirds of voters—Democrats *and* Republicans—did *not* select the candidate who would now be their governor; those two-thirds preferred someone else. Despite being one of America's most unpopular governors during his tenure, LePage won a second term in 2014, again without majority support.[26] This system of voting incentivizes candidates *not* to speak to a broad cross-section of the electorate, but rather to target a just-big-enough base of partisans who can push them slightly ahead of their opponents.

But that's just the smallest impact of the pernicious plurality voting system. Plurality voting also creates "the spoiler effect." Returning to Maine, how exactly did LePage secure two terms as governor despite his unpopularity? Eliot Cutler, an independent in the race, had won more than 8 percent of the vote. Polls indicated that had Cutler not run, most of those votes would have gone to LePage's Democratic rival. In other words, Cutler *spoiled* the election, throwing it to LePage by taking votes away from the Democratic candidate.

The spoiler effect pressures voters to not vote for the candidate they like the most out of fear that they will inadvertently contribute to the election of the candidate they like the least. For example, think back to the 2016 presidential race. You weren't supposed to vote for

Jill Stein, the Green party candidate, because that would take a vote away from Hillary and spoil the election for her. On the other side, you weren't supposed to vote for Gary Johnson, the Libertarian candidate, because that would take a vote away from Trump.

Plurality voting has a bone-chilling effect on our democracy because it creates the single greatest barrier to entry for new competition in politics—the spoiler argument—which is wielded against all potential competition to the duopoly (you can't run, you'll just ruin it for [insert candidate's name]). The truth is that Eliot Cutler, the Maine independent spoiler, was an anomaly. Most potential new competitors never make it to the starting line—they can't compete when faced with the spoiler argument.

Imagine you want to run for Senate as an independent. Not only will you be heavily discouraged from running by whichever side of the duopoly views you as a threat, but the side of the industrial complex you are threatening will, without compunction, do whatever it takes to eliminate your candidacy. Think of Howard Schultz. In the spring of 2019, the former CEO of Starbucks considered an independent run for President. The outcry from Democrats was loud and often vicious because Democrats believed he would hand the 2020 election to Donald Trump. Republicans would do the same to anyone they thought would take votes from their candidate. And both sides justify their bullying, because, in our current system, the existential threat of losing to the other party is seen as great enough to excuse the bullying. That's precisely the kind of problem plurality voting creates.

If you think about it, politics is the only industry where we are regularly told that *less* competition is better for the customer. Now it doesn't matter if you think Howard Schultz would have made a great president or not—we can all still recognize that there's something profoundly unhealthy about a political system in which having more talented, successful people competing is somehow bad.

And that's not the only problem with plurality voting. Not only does it keep many potential candidates out of the race, it keeps others from success if they do get in because it creates the "wasted vote" argument. Whenever we want to vote for someone not considered to have a strong chance of winning, we are told that we're wasting our vote. Because citizens want their votes to matter, Greg Orman describes plurality voting as creating a "gravitation pull" that prevents new challengers from becoming viable.[27] How did we end up with such an unhelpful voting method? When the Constitution was written, the only electoral model in existence was the British plurality winner system. According to political scientist Lee Drutman, "None of the other more modern electoral systems had been invented yet, so none of the Framers gave congressional elections much thought." They just copied the British.[28]

The Framers did many exceptional things—but plurality voting was a mistake. Fortunately, as we describe later, we can reengineer this elections machinery. Our approach also includes reengineering its partner in unhealthy competition, legislative machinery.

Legislative Machinery

Should a candidate make it through a party primary, win at least a plurality, and head to Washington, a partisan-captured legislative machinery awaits. Like elections machinery, it is a powerful set of rules ensuring that the interests of the political-industrial complex are prioritized. Let's start with a story about budgets, brinkmanship, and a little-known rule that operates in the background of all legislation, with extraordinary ramifications.

Each year, Congress must set a budget for the federal government. If no agreement is reached before the new fiscal year begins, parts of the government are shut down. In 2013, both a divided government and increased polarization around health-care reform gripped Washington. While Democrats controlled the Senate and the White House, Republicans held the House of Representatives and were determined to repeal and replace the Affordable Care Act (ACA).[29] No Republican could survive a primary without pledging to do absolutely everything in his or her power to undo the act.[30]

In late 2013, that promise came due. As the end of the fiscal year approached, Republican forces were mobilizing for the standoff. In August, eighty House members signed a letter urging Speaker of the House John Boehner to use the budget appropriations process to defund the ACA.[31] A legion of industry interest groups fell into line. Heritage Action, the political arm of the conservative Heritage Foundation think tank, launched a multicity campaign to rally support. The political-industrial complex was activated, and forcefully.

With battle lines drawn and the deadline approaching, a back-and-forth ensued between the Republican-controlled House and the Democrat-controlled Senate—which refused to accept a budget that nullified the ACA—until the clock ran out.[32] On October 1, the government shut down. In some ways, the shutdown was just the typical story of stalled negotiations between the House of Representatives, the Senate, and the White House. House Republicans were committed to following through on their campaign promise to defund the ACA. The Senate and White House were unwilling to cave. The two sides reached an impasse until the added pressure of the debt ceiling, and an impending default on October 16, broke the stalemate and forced the House to fold.[33]

But this summary overlooks the troubling part of the story. The shutdown didn't need to last sixteen days. It didn't need to happen at all. At any time, either before the shutdown or in the sixteen intervening days, a clean spending bill would almost certainly have passed in the House *had a vote been held*.[34] Instead, the shutdown only ended when Speaker Boehner decided he would allow a bill—a bill that had already passed in the Senate and had majority support in the House—to come to the House floor for a vote. The country had been held hostage for sixteen days by using a little-known but incredibly powerful rule: the so-called Hastert Rule.

The Hastert Rule is a particularly egregious example of today's partisan legislative machinery in action.[35] Now standard practice—of Speakers of both parties—although in fact written down nowhere, the Hastert Rule dictates that the Speaker will not allow a floor vote on a bill unless a majority of the majority party—the Speaker's party—supports the bill, *even if a majority of the full House would vote to pass it.*

Unless Speakers ignore this practice—a rare occurrence—bipartisan bills that appeal to the minority party (in this example, the Democrats) and some of the majority party (the Republicans) are killed by never being introduced. Legislation supported by a majority of Americans and by a majority of the House has no chance of passing—in fact, is not even allowed to be debated—because there will never be a vote. The bill won't reach the floor. No deliberation, no amendments, no votes. No transparency. No accountability.

Effectively, this made-up rule, not found in the Constitution, not codified in law or even written in the House rules book, cements hyper-partisan control over the legislature. In the case of the 2013 shutdown, it cost the country $24 billion for a sixteen-day shutdown that 90 percent of Americans didn't want from the start.[36]

It's important to note how normal—how very "water to the fish"—this type of partisan machination has become to most of us, including journalists and editorial boards. Little was written at the time of the 2013 shutdown that illuminated the lunacy of a single person's ability (a single person elected by a small number of one party's primary voters in one district in one state) to stop a democratically elected legislature from solving a problem practically everyone in the country wanted solved. Not to mention the waste of $24 billion. This is not democracy. It is partisan oligarchy.

And it's no way to run a country. We should be outraged. And then, we should fix it (more on that in chapter 5).

The Partisan Takeover of Congress

Just like the sore-loser law in our elections, the Hastert Rule in Congress is just one of many ways in which the invisible machinery shaping our legislative process has been appropriated and self-optimized by the duopoly. To understand just how complete the partisan takeover of our nation's legislative machinery has been, let's take a step back.[37]

From World War II until the early 1970s, the way the House and Senate worked is sometimes referred to by political scientists as the "textbook Congress."[38] For those of us who are not political scientists, we may know it better as the *Schoolhouse Rock* Congress—the one portrayed in the animated musical series. In the famous song "I'm Just a Bill," the law-to-be sang about its hopes after being proposed by concerned citizens and drafted by their representative:

> *I'm just a bill. Yes I'm only a bill, and I got as far as Capitol Hill.*
> *Well, now I'm stuck in committee, and I'll sit here and wait . . .*

As an animated story made for children, it's a decent depiction of how Congress worked in the mid-twentieth century. As the song explains, the bill's fate would be decided in committee. During this time, Congress was organized around a set of strong committees spanning a range of subjects such as agriculture and foreign affairs. Bills introduced in Congress were assigned to the relevant committee. Under the leadership of the committee chair, committee members from both parties debated, offered amendments, and decided whether the bill should be sent to the floor for a vote.

Remarkably, there was no mention of Democrats or Republicans in the song—just members of Congress in committee. This reflects a key difference between the Washington of the 1950s and 1960s and Washington today. Parties had not yet gained control of the legislative process; committees were in control. The committees were insulated from the parties by a set of norms, such as the seniority system, in which committee chairs were selected according to length of service, not selected with discretion by party leadership.[39] Lacking control of personnel, party leaders had much less control over the governing process.[40] Committees were intended to be where dialogue, deliberation, and negotiation took place and where members came together to identify problems and draft solutions.[41]

By the time "I'm Just a Bill" was first aired on TV in 1976, a partisan takeover was well underway in Washington. The takeover was first led by the Democrats, who had been a permanent majority in the House of Representatives for forty years starting in 1955. It was then cemented by Republicans when they finally took the reins in 1995—reshaping Congress and setting our political system on a course toward dysfunction and gridlock.

Ground zero for the partisan takeover was the House of Representatives during the 1970s, when a Democratic majority became fed up with conservatives using committees to hold up liberal bills.[42] A liberal faction among Democrats in Congress known as the Democratic Study Group, established in 1959, had long worked to organize and strategize around liberal legislative priorities, creating "the necessary *legislative machinery* and internal party unity to guarantee action on the Democrat programs pledged in our platform."[43] The takeover started small, first by reviving the Democratic caucus. While most legislators previously had little contact with party leaders once in office, this changed in 1969, when all Democrats began holding monthly meetings in which they set agendas, devised legislative strategies, and coordinated so that all members spoke in one unified voice.[44]

The second front was an attack on committees. First, the Democrats mitigated the committee chairs' power, limiting the leaders' control over the committee agenda and transferring to party leadership the authority to appoint subcommittee heads. After the Democrats restricted what the chairs could do, the next step was to select who the chairs would be. In 1971, the Democrats announced that seniority would no longer be the only criterion used in selection.[45] Just four years later, three sitting committee chairs were ousted. While only 1.1 percent of committee chairs were not based on seniority in the 1960s, that figure had jumped to more than 15 percent by the 1970s.[46]

The message was becoming clear: ideological purity and partisan fealty (often cloaked as merit-based selection) would now be dominant factors.[47] To have a chance at securing a committee chair, members would need to demonstrate loyalty to the party leaders responsible for appointing them. Going forward, any chair who ignored party directives did so at his or her own risk.

After co-opting the committee chairs, the Democratic leadership then turned to its rank-and-file members. In 1975, the job of making committee assignments was transferred from the Ways and Means Committee to the newly formed Steering and Policy Committee, chaired by the Speaker and dominated by party leadership. Career trajectories for members now hinged on preserving good standing with party leaders.

Even with control over committee members, the Democrats were still unhappy that bipartisan committees could make key decisions. So, beginning in the 1970s, the Democrats started bypassing committees altogether, employing partisan task forces to manage policies of high importance. These task forces were staffed exclusively with Democrats selected by the Speaker to carry out the party's agenda.

To complete the creation of a fully partisan legislative machinery, the Democrats zeroed-in on the House Rules Committee, which plays a critical role as the central gatekeeper for the House's bills. After a bill leaves its committee or jurisdiction, it must go through the Rules Committee, where it's either put on the calendar for debate and a vote—or not.

The Rules Committee had traditionally prided itself as a neutral referee, making impartial decisions on which bills would move to the floor, in what order, and under which rules of debate, depending on the large bodies of proposed legislation and varying degrees of national import. In 1975, however, the Democrats commandeered the committee, giving the Speaker the power to appoint the chair and the Democratic members. Now, nothing could come to the floor without the Speaker's approval. When writing legislation, committees no longer had to think just about what the best policy would be or what would be favored by a majority in the House. Instead, a critical step was to put forward policies that could get by a cadre of partisans appointed by a party leader and in complete control of the congressional calendar.

Although the Democrats who had been in power spearheaded this first phase of turning Congress over to partisan interests, the second was carried on by the Republicans once they took control of the House in 1994 for the first time in a generation. Rather than deconstructing the partisan legislative machinery, Speaker Newt Gingrich extended it, building on the foundations established by the prior architects of partisanship. In appointing committee chairs, he bypassed senior Republicans in favor of devout loyalists.[48] In a dramatic break from tradition, he put freshmen acolytes on the most prestigious committees. With loyalists in place, he could exert more control over the work of committees—for example, forcing members of the Appropriations Committee to sign a pledge that they would cut spending.[49]

Gingrich also worked to dismantle the nonpartisan structures that had long supported the day-to-day legislative work of Congress. He cut by a third Congress's professional staff—the economists, lawyers, and investigators who work for committees, not for individual members. Meanwhile, with resources for committees dried up, resources for the Speaker's office soared.[50] Gingrich also cut by a third the staff available to the Government Accountability Office and the Congressional Research Service, two nonpartisan bodies exclusively dedicated to supporting Congress overall. And he shut down the Office of Technology Assessment, which had provided committees with nonpartisan analysis on complex science and technology issues.[51] By gutting and shutting, Gingrich effectively neutralized whatever fell outside his control as the party leader.

In addition to centralizing power over how bills were drafted by weakening committees and eliminating nonpartisan support staff, Gingrich also exerted partisan control over whether bills moved to the House floor—and even whether they were open to debate. With the groundwork laid by Gingrich's Democratic predecessors, the Rules Committee now under his thumb blocked any bills not tightly aligned with a partisan agenda by issuing an unprecedented number of "closed rules" that simply barred bills from deliberation altogether.[52] By the end of Gingrich's first year as Speaker, barely over half of the rules issued by the Rules Committee allowed for open debate.[53]

Given these steps, Gingrich is sometimes villainized as "the man who broke politics."[54] But this moniker gives Gingrich too much credit. The takeover of Congress and the creation of a partisan legislative machinery was an ongoing, multidecade project carried out by teams of partisans on both sides of the aisle.

Today, the system our legislators put in place does not promote pragmatic solutions or compromise. As was reported in late 2019, an elected official's ability to raise money and distribute it to party colleagues is incredibly meaningful in accumulating power— hitting your fundraising targets often translates to better committee assignments.[55] The system maximizes the value the parties can deliver to their core partisan and special interest customers while leaving average voters dissatisfied.

How a Bill Becomes Law Today

Congress has been carefully constructed to institutionalize partisanship and work against bipartisan solutions. To see how today's partisan legislative machinery works in action, consider the path of a bill as it travels through the House of Representatives.

Captured Committees

Once a bill is proposed, it is typically assigned to the relevant committee. As we have seen, committees are now beholden to party leaders. These individuals are motivated to be loyal soldiers and are threatened with losing their positions or being denied promotions if they stray from ideological purity.[56] Majority-party leaders have extra privileges, setting the size of committees, distributing seats and staff between the parties, and selecting the chair.[57]

The partisan chairs of congressional committees wield substantial control over big decisions, such as the committee's schedule. In 2003, for example, the Republican-controlled House Ways and Means Committee tried to rush through pension reform before the Democratic members had a chance to read the bill. When the Democrats protested, committee chair Bill Thomas called the US Capitol Police to remove Democrats from the committee library.[58]

Partisans transformed committees from havens for negotiation and problem solving into battlegrounds. Committee hearings were once used to learn from stakeholders and experts as part of deliberations. Not today. The number of committee hearings dropped by half between 1994 and 2014. And the hearings that *are* held aren't really about learning from the public. A 2016 study reviewing forty years of committee hearings found that they have been increasingly used to wage partisan warfare, not to discover sound policy solutions.[59]

If, by some fluke, this process fails to produce a satisfactory bill, party leadership reserves the right to rewrite bills after they have left committee.[60] Increasingly, however, the majority party skips the charade of bipartisanship altogether, substituting the use of committees with partisan task forces, where party leaders have more influence.[61] After retaking the House in 2006, for example, the Democrats pushed through an ambitious set of bills in their first hundred hours, with no committee involvement, no negotiations, and no compromise.[62] The House Republicans were completely cut out of the business of lawmaking. In the 113th Congress, roughly 40 percent of substantive legislation simply bypassed committees altogether.[63]

A Party-Controlled House Floor

The vast majority of bills die in committee. A few partisan proposals, however, do make it out. The next step, though, is not the House floor. Instead, the bill must make it through a small cadre of majority-party partisans on the Rules Committee. This group, just like primary voters in elections, serves as guardians at the gate, deciding whether bills can go to a vote—and if so, whether they'll be open for debate and amendments.[64] No bill goes to the floor without Rules Committee approval.[65] It's here that the Speaker can wield the Hastert Rule. Frustrated with the decline in debate on the House floor while he was in the minority, Paul Ryan promised, on becoming Speaker in 2015, to allow a more open process. Yet the partisan machinery won out. Not once in 2017 did Ryan allow open debate when considering a bill.[66] (As you can well imagine, the Senate has its own arcane approaches—worthy of at least another chapter—but the result is the same: party control.)

Partisan Conference Committees

If a bill makes it through the first two stages of the partisan legislative machinery in the House, and a similar bill overcomes the grips of Senate gridlock, then the final step is a conference committee.[67] Traditionally, these committees brought together Republicans and Democrats from the House and Senate to reconcile differences in the bills passed by the respective chambers and sent a mutually agreed upon final version to the two chambers for an up-or-down vote.

Today, conference committees are nearly extinct. In the 114th Congress, there were just eight conference reports, down from sixty-seven in the 104th Congress a decade earlier.[68] Now, when one party controls both chambers, majority leadership meets behind closed doors and then simply announces the outcome of its internal negotiation to the other side.

If a conference committee is actually held, it's staffed with leadership-appointed members who manage negotiations and undercut bipartisan deals. Before the Republican Senate voted to go to conference on the Tax Cut and Jobs Act of 2017, Democratic Senator Ron Wyden described the process: "Today the Senate is going to debate whether to go to conference with the House to resolve the differences between the two tax plans Republicans have passed. But make no mistake—the Conference Committee that will meet in the days ahead is nothing more than theater. It won't be a real effort to have an honest debate in the light of day."[69]

. . .

Today, this well-oiled machinery is so reliable that new people or new policy won't make a difference. America's top priority must therefore be to reengineer the rules of the game in politics to create healthy competition on dimensions that serve the public interest. It's both that simple and that hard. And time is short. The consequences of a political-industrial complex overrun by unhealthy competition are horrifying—and, even scarier, utterly normalized.

It is accepted as normal that only Republicans or Democrats can get on a presidential debate stage and make their case to the country.

It is accepted as normal when the Mitch McConnells and Nancy Pelosis of America—currently our most powerful members of Congress—announce publicly and proudly that their top priorities are either resisting the current president or electing more members of their own party.

It is normal that bipartisan bills are killed despite majority support.

It is normal that a "lobbying index" of companies that derive big earnings from lobbying outperforms the S&P 500 over the last decade.[70]

And it is normal that the richest country in the world—our country—has its credit downgraded as a result of partisan political gamesmanship. What could be more irresponsible?

Let's be clear: America is in decline. And it doesn't have to be.

3

Consequences
and Outcomes

The casualties of the unchecked and unbalanced politics industry are the health of our democracy, our long-term economic competitiveness, and our shared prosperity and social progress—three pillars of the American experiment. Looking carefully at these consequences connects the true nature of the politics industry to what it produces.

As you read this chapter, which is the darkest in the book, please allow yourself to feel frustrated anew about this decades-long decline—but trust that there's light at the end of the tunnel. At the close of this chapter and later in the book, we will pivot from diagnosis and dire straits to the legacy and promise of political innovation that animates our purpose. We will guide you in converting frustrated energy into targeted personal agency as we explore the strategy that will break partisan gridlock and reverse this tragic trajectory.

Consequence: Democracy in Decline

Unhealthy competition in the politics industry has resulted in five horrifying consequences for our democracy. You'll recognize these themes, as they have been explored or foreshadowed throughout the previous chapters.

Lack of Problem Solving

As we've established, there is virtually no intersection between elected officials' acting in the public interest and the likelihood of their being reelected. In our current political system, doing your job as an elected official the way we need you to will actually increase the chances that you'll lose your job. That's a ridiculous design. But it gets even worse, because, in today's system, there is actually an incentive *not* to solve problems. A true solution—with its attendant bipartisan compromises and required departures, however slight, from strict ideological purity—would no doubt disappoint some fervent supporters and reliable donors on both sides.

Conversely, keeping a problem or a divisive issue alive and festering is a proven method to attract and motivate partisan voters, special interests, and committed donors to each side, delivering both currencies—votes and money—in return. Why not solve those problems? Because the connected votes and money might disappear. Finally, even in areas where the sides agree, legislators sometimes fail to pass legislation that would represent progress. They hold out to deny the other side any claim of success before the next election.

In today's political competition, then, serious legislation is often only passed under single party control. Landmark legislation used to pass with bipartisan support, as happened with social security, highways, and civil rights. Today, important legislation is passed only along partisan lines (figure 3-1). And when the other side retakes power, it focuses not on improving, but on repealing.

Party-line legislation dominates partly because there simply aren't enough moderates remaining who can bridge the gap between the extremes of the two sides. The percentage of moderates in both the House and the Senate has declined precipitously over time—on both sides of the aisle (figure 3-2).[1]

Instead of compromise and results, we have historically high levels of gridlock.[2] Devastatingly, it's gridlock on the most important issues (figure 3-3).

No Action without a Time-Sensitive Crisis and National Debt

Congress *does* take action on substantive issues but usually does so only under two coexisting conditions: the existence of a crisis, and the use of deficit financing. When a national security crisis occurs, a

FIGURE 3-1

Declining Bipartisan Support of Landmark Legislation (1935–2017)

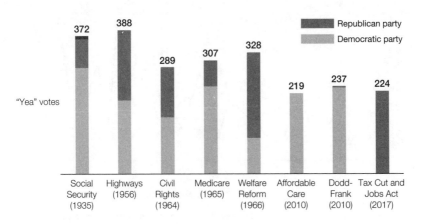

Note: The number of members of each party has fluctuated over time.

Source: GovTrack.com, accessed August 2017.

FIGURE 3-2

Disappearing Moderates of the House and Senate (1951–2018)

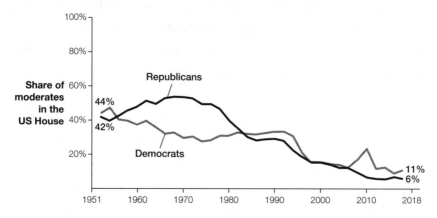

Note: Moderates within each party are defined as –0.25 to +0.25 on a left-to-right (liberal [–1] to conservative [+1]) ideological spectrum. The black line represents number of Republican moderates, and the gray line Democratic.

Source: Data from Keith Poole, University of Georgia, voteview.com, accessed August 2017.

FIGURE 3-3

Skyrocketing Congressional Gridlock on Salient Issues (1947–2016)

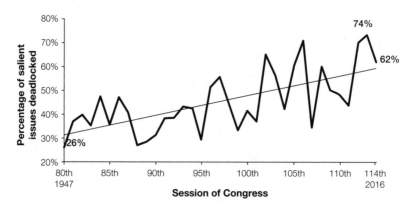

Note: Salient issues for each session of Congress based on the level of *New York Times* editorial attention. Deadlocked issues are those where Congress and the President did not take action during the session.

Source: Updated from Sarah Binder, "The Dysfunctional Congress," *Annual Review of Political Science* (2015).

national disaster hits, or a government shutdown or debt downgrade looms, Congress does take action, sometimes even swift action. But the tradeoff is that the action is virtually never paid for with current funding. Instead, Congress uses *deficit financing*, which passes the cost of the bill on to future generations by adding the spending to the national debt. Consider what typically happens with omnibus spending bills that increase spending without providing for corresponding revenue increases. In order to get these deals done, the pot is sweetened for both sides as Republicans and Democrats tuck their preferred spending and tax adjustments into such bills to please their core constituencies, while tacitly agreeing to look the other way on what the other side gets. All the while, our national debt continues to grow. There is no party standing strongly for fiscal responsibility anymore; both Republicans and Democrats have realized that in the absence of a serious competitor raising the issue (as Perot did in 1992), there's no political benefit to fiscal responsibility.

Congress is ineffective in the face of "nonurgent" crises such as our failing infrastructure. The infrastructure crisis undoubtedly has long-term implications, but there is no hard deadline like the one that Congress faces with the expiration of the debt ceiling. Nor is there a clear requirement for immediate action such as what's evident during a national security issue or natural disaster. Without a deadline forcing action, barely anything happens. Congress kicks the can down the road.

A Country More Divided

Competition is personal. It involves not only politicians, but also citizens. While party rivalry appears intense to the casual observer, it is nonetheless constrained because head-to-head competition for the middle is mutually destructive. Instead, the rivals increasingly seek to compete in ways that reinforce their differentiation and separation from one another. The political-industrial complex increasingly plays the identity-politics game, painting fellow citizens on the other side as enemies. Former Speaker of the House Paul Ryan addressed this phenomenon after he announced his retirement, describing a system that is "playing on people's divisions and exploiting people's frustrations and divisions with other people—dividing people for political gain to get a coalition that's 50 (percent) plus one."[3]

Political Disillusionment

The American public has never been more dissatisfied with the political system. Public trust in the federal government is hovering at a near sixty-year low. In 1958, three out of four Americans trusted the government.[4] By 2017, just one in five did (figure 3-4). Congressional approval ratings, meanwhile, have averaged under 20 percent every year since 2010.[5]

While there is much finger-pointing at the other side, more and more Americans know that both parties are to blame. Half of citizens today take a dim view of both the Democrats and the

FIGURE 3-4

Dwindling Public Trust in Federal Government (1964–2018)

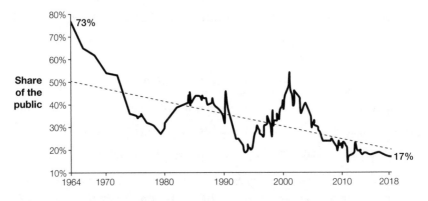

Note: Data is a moving average of individual polls.

Source: Data from "Public Trust in Government: 1958–2019," Pew Research Center, April 11, 2019, www.people-press.org/2019/04/11/public-trust-in-government-1958-2019.

Republicans, nearly equaling the record high in political disillusionment in the fallout of Watergate.[6] A growing number of Americans have expressed this discontent by dropping their party label and declaring their political independence. The percentage self-identifying as independents is at a near all-time high—41 percent, versus 30 percent as Democrats and 28 percent as Republicans (figure 3-5).[7] Nearly two-thirds of Americans think a third major party is necessary (figure 3-6).[8] It's an industry ripe for disruption—if only a candidate or party could get over the high barriers to entry.

With no other viable option, citizen discontent has been expressed through volatile swings of sentiment between the existing parties.[9] Democrats were ascendant in 2006 but quickly fell to Republicans in 2010. After Barack Obama's reelection in 2012, Democrats appeared to be back in the driver's seat, but they lost the wheel again in 2014, when Republicans retook the Senate. After Trump won the White House in 2016, Republicans were in complete command of

FIGURE 3-5

Increasing Number of Independents (2004–2019)

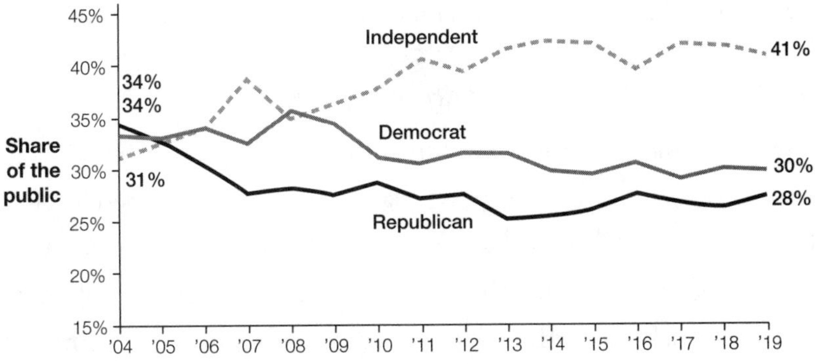

Note: Figures are annual averages calculated from a Gallup poll on party affiliation. Numbers represent the percentage of respondents who answered "Republican," "Democrat," or "independent" to the question "In politics, as of today, do you consider yourself a Republican, a Democrat or an independent?"

Source: Data from Gallup, "Party Affiliation," Gallup, Inc., https://news.gallup.com/poll/15370/party-affiliation.aspx, accessed November 2019.

FIGURE 3-6

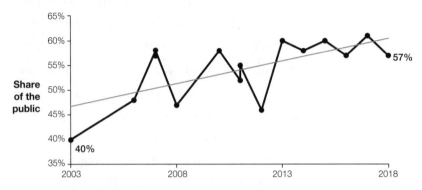

Increasing Desire for a Third Major Party (2003–2018)

Note: Circles correspond to the date of the survey. The first poll in which Gallup asked whether a third party is needed was October 10–12, 2003.

Source: Chart data from Gallup, "Majority in U.S. Still Say a Third Party Is Needed," https://news.gallup .com/poll/244094/majority-say-third-party-needed.aspx, accessed July 2019.

Washington. But unified government ended just two years later, when Democrats retook the House.

Many Americans have begun to lose faith in democracy as a system of government. Only one-third of millennials (i.e., those born between 1980 and 1996) report that it is essential to live in a country that is governed democratically. Support for authoritarianism is on the rise.[10]

Lack of Accountability

In any other industry this large—and thriving—with this much customer dissatisfaction and only two players, some entrepreneur would see it as a phenomenal business opportunity and create a new competitor responding to what the customers want. But that doesn't happen in politics, because the duopoly works really well together in one particular way—to rig the rules of the game to protect themselves from new competition. The players have erected huge barriers to entry, and the other checks and balances in healthy competition have also been neutralized, as we saw in the Five Forces analysis.

In other industries, channels or suppliers apply pressure on industry rivals to serve customers better—or abandon them. New competitors or substitutes emerge. If all else fails, an independent regulator steps in to protect the consumer. But in politics, these forces have been co-opted or eliminated. Unlike a business cycle, our political system is not in a phase; it will not self-correct.

Choosing Not to Solve Problems: The Case of Immigration

To appreciate the full suite of unhealthy competition at work, consider the contentious issue of immigration. In the past, both parties compromised on immigration to deliver real solutions and to refine immigration policies over time. In 1965, the two sides eliminated a discriminatory quota system.[11] In 1996, they returned to the table to write a bill that enhanced enforcement.[12] These actions are far from how immigration policy is made today.

Even in today's contentious times, all sides recognize that immigration policy revolves around the same clear set of issues—improving enforcement, addressing those here illegally, and refining the legal immigration system.[13] Yet, comprehensive immigration reform still appears to be a fantasy.

During George W. Bush's presidency, the door seemed open for a bipartisan deal.[14] A bill cosponsored by Senators John McCain and Ted Kennedy passed in the Senate in 2006 with the backing of almost every Democrat and nearly half of the Republicans.[15] Unfortunately, it died in the House when Republican Speaker Dennis Hastert invoked his Hastert Rule, refusing to hold a vote on the bill—already passed by the Senate—out of fear that compromising would taint the Republicans' ideological purity, disappoint their partisan and special interest bases, and reduce their chances in the midterms.[16]

Later that year when the Democrats captured Congress anyway, hope was renewed that progress could be made on immigration. The Senate took up a retooled version of the McCain-Kennedy bill in early 2007, but the proposed legislation involved compromises that upset some of each side's core constituents. Conservative radio was outraged over "amnesty" for "illegals," while the AFL-CIO protested guest-worker programs. To make it through the Senate, the bill needed to avoid amendments championed by the disgruntled groups (i.e., remain similar to what had passed only months earlier). The inclusion of these so-called poison pills would ultimately kill the bill.[17]

When the bill came to the Senate floor in June, one such poison-pill amendment was offered by then freshman Senator Obama, who had months earlier launched his campaign for president. Fortunately, the amendment was rejected.[18] But Obama quickly backed another poison pill supported by organized labor to sunset a popular Republican idea to expand the guest-worker program.[19] The amendment ultimately passed—by just one vote.[20]

Immigration reform was dead. Both parties had killed it.

While it was a major defeat for the country, the failure of immigration reform was a tactical win for Obama. In today's politics, taking ideological stands at the expense of actual legislative action can be smart strategy. Obama pandered to his Democratic base, blocked a major legislative victory for future opponent McCain, and kept a highly partisan wedge issue on the table to rally support for the elections.

Obama campaigned on a commitment to deal with immigration in his first year. Despite a Democratic supermajority in Congress during his first term, there was no action.[21] By the time the Democrats attempted immigration reform in 2013 in the Senate, the Republicans had retaken control of the House and blocked it. The Republicans followed the successful Democratic tactic employed in Bush's final years: wait for the next president, avoid compromise, and run out the clock.[22]

The duopoly has continued to fail to solve this critical issue facing the country. Today, in 2020, after more than a decade, there is still no comprehensive immigration reform. Instead, the only steps taken have been partisan decisions by executive action that are challenged by the other side in the courts. Judges have, predictably, ruled in favor of the party that appointed them.[23]

The duopoly has succeeded, however, in protecting and expanding the value of immigration as a wedge issue. A decade ago, the average Democrat and Republican reported similar feelings about whether immigrants strengthen the country. Today, their opinions wildly diverge.[24] Immigration has been politically weaponized, a surefire means to induce polarization and stir up rabid supporters. Absent the threat of new competition, there's little reason for the duopoly to aspire to consensus and problem solving.

But while the duopoly has been able to ride the waves of polarization—and even thrive—many Americans have not. Let's look at what we face.

Consequence: Deteriorating Economic Competitiveness

Competitiveness is central to the welfare of every nation. A nation is competitive if it creates the conditions for two things to occur simultaneously: businesses operating in the nation (1) compete successfully in global markets while (2) lifting the wages and living standards of the average citizen. When these occur together the nation prospers. The definition makes clear that a hallmark of any truly competitive nation is shared prosperity. A nation in which businesses thrive but most citizens struggle is not competitive. Nor is a country that pays its citizens well while its businesses fail in the marketplace. Neither of those are desirable or sustainable.

How competitive is the United States today by these standards? There is extensive evidence that the US economy is fulfilling only one-half of the definition of competitiveness. Large and midsize companies in the United States are thriving and creating prosperity for those who found, run, and invest in them. But middle- and working-class Americans are struggling, as are many small businesses. The point is that despite our current situation—126th month of the longest nonstop economic expansion in America's history with record high markets—our economy is not well positioned for the long term, and the ideal of shared prosperity is not our reality.[25]

America used to be one of the most competitive nations in the world. Our deep roster of productive, innovative, dynamic companies dominated global markets. At the same time, America boasted the best-trained workers, who commanded high and rising wages over time without undermining their companies' performances. Many citizens could flourish and reach their full potential. With such a strong track record, we came to assume that our future prosperity was assured. Not so. Over the past several decades, this illusion has been shattered as our economic performance has deteriorated on multiple key dimensions.

Since the beginning of the new century, productivity growth has fallen behind historic trends, leading to a significant drop-off in economic output and a smaller pie to divide among the population. Established firms are investing less, and our economy is becoming less dynamic as the rate of new-businesses formation has slowed. Workers—our most valuable national asset—are underutilized. Recent job gains and headlines that tout a low unemployment rate hide the millions of Americans who have been forced into part-time jobs, are not earning a living wage, or have stopped searching for work all together.

After decades of steady gains, labor-force participation has shrunk since 2000 to levels not seen since the 1980s. This falloff reflects the fact that American companies are creating fewer jobs than before. The new jobs that are created are disproportionately concentrated in low-skill sectors shielded from international competition. All these forces have combined to depress wages. The average family makes little more than it did two decades ago. As a result, too many households find themselves living paycheck to paycheck, with no financial security. The American dream is under threat. What used to be a guarantee that American children would earn more than their parents did is now just a coin toss.[26]

The era of shared prosperity has ended. For the first half of the post–World War II era, all Americans—from the most affluent to the least advantaged—saw their fortunes rise with a growing economy. Today, while middle-class Americans struggle to compete with lower-paid workers in other countries, higher-skilled Americans benefit from global markets and technological advancement. Accordingly, recent gains have been concentrated at the top of the income distribution.

The fortunes of our communities are also diverging. Regions surrounding cities like San Francisco, Boston, and New York are booming with vibrant, knowledge-based clusters. Washington, D.C., the seat of the federal government, is doing better than ever. Yet even within these oceans of affluence sit islands of hardship, where average incomes have actually declined over the past two decades. Inequality is skyrocketing, corroding social solidarity and creating a destructive zero-sum competition that pits rich against poor, haves against have-nots, workers against business, and Wall Street against Main Street.

These disturbing economic outcomes are not the lingering effects of the Great Recession, as some believe. They have been emerging since the late 1990s and were sometimes in evidence even before then.

Since 2011, as part of an effort to better understand the root causes of these dismal results, the U.S. Competitiveness Project at Harvard

Business School has conducted annual surveys of Harvard Business School alumni and the public.[27] Figure 3-7 shows the results of the alumni survey from 2016. For each dimension of competitiveness, the horizontal axis represents the US position relative to other advanced economies, and the vertical axis represents whether our performance is improving or deteriorating relative to competition. Although the United States retains some formidable strengths such as world-class universities, deep capital markets, and high-quality firm management, we are also plagued by a growing array of competitive weaknesses found in the bottom left corner. We face an astronomically expensive and unequitable health-care system; onerous and costly regulatory and legal systems; a convoluted, loophole-filled tax code; a public education system that fails to equip our children with the skills needed in the new economy; crumbling highways, railroads, and airports that are a national embarrassment. *And things are only getting worse.*

Tellingly, whereas our strengths are concentrated in areas driven by the private sector, our weaknesses tend to be in areas driven by state and federal policy. While other countries have been improving their business environments and raising the bar, our government has failed to make the necessary investments. It's not that we don't know which areas we need to address to unlock American competitiveness. We do. Nearly everyone both outside and inside Washington, D.C., agrees that we must improve our infrastructure, streamline regulations, address abuses in the international trading system, and balance the federal budget. There is a surprising amount of consensus—at least in off-the-record conversations. The problem is that consensus does not produce solutions.

In other words, it's not a policy problem. *It's a politics problem.* No wonder Harvard Business School alumni and the public consistently identified our political system as America's single greatest competitive weakness (see figure 3-7).

FIGURE 3-7

Eroding US Competitiveness Compared with Other Advanced Economies

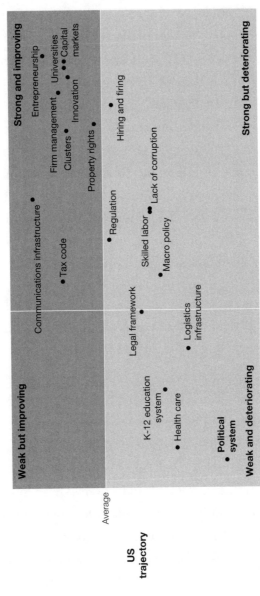

Note: Data from the 2019 survey of Harvard Business School alumni on the state of US competitiveness.

Source: Michael E. Porter et al., "A Recovery Squandered," Harvard Business School, December 2019.

Consequence: A Quality-of-Life Recession

A similar failure to make progress in economic competitiveness also afflicts our nation's quality of life. Although America has finally climbed out of the depths of the Great Recession, we remain trapped in a far more serious quality-of-life recession.[28]

We increasingly understand that the well-being of citizens is integral to a nation's competitiveness and economic opportunity. To take year-over-year stock of progress, the Social Progress Index tracks a wide range of important dimensions, including countries' performances in meeting basic human needs like nutrition, health, education, personal safety, and environmental quality, as well as measurements of freedom and inclusivity such as personal rights, political rights, and religious tolerance. Recent results are shocking.

Most Americans assume that we are the world leader on social performance—and historically we have been. We pioneered universal public education, from the first public primary schools to land grant colleges, and we led the world in bringing electricity into every home. It was our collective mission to ensure that every child born in this country had the opportunity to reach his or her full potential. Today, however, we are falling well short of these goals. According to objective bench-marking, *America has fallen to twenty-sixth place overall in social progress.*[29] This ranking places the United States behind far less advanced and affluent countries such as Portugal and Slovenia. Even more disturbing is that while other countries are improving, the United States is the only advanced country where social performance continues to decline.

Table 3-1 shows how the United States ranks among the thirty-six countries in the Organisation for Economic Co-operation and Development (OECD) on a select group of key indicators. The OECD is comprised of advanced democratic nations with market economies like Germany, Japan, and the United Kingdom, but also countries

TABLE 3-1

Eroding US Social Performance, Compared with Organisation for Economic Co-operation and Development (OECD) Countries

Indicator	US Rank*	Indicator	US Rank*
Education		**Personal safety**	
Access to quality education	33	Traffic deaths	35
Secondary school enrollment	22	Homicide rate	35
Environment		Political killings and torture	29
Access to basic drinking water	31	**Inclusiveness**	
Greenhouse gas emissions	29	Discrimination or violence against minorities	26
Biome protection	34	Acceptance of gays and lesbians	16
Health		Equality of political power by socioeconomic group	34
Maternal mortality rate	35	Equality of political power by gender	24
Child mortality rate	33	**Rights and freedoms**	
Premature deaths from noncommunicable diseases	28	Freedom of expression	23
Life expectancy at 60	27	Access to justice	27
		Freedom of religion	21
		Property rights for women	29

*Rank among the thirty-six OECD countries.

Source: Data from "Social Progress Index 2019."

that are not typically thought of as top-tier performers, like Greece, Turkey, Hungary, and Mexico.

In secondary school enrollment, a mainspring for citizen opportunity, we are 22nd out of 36. Beyond the OECD, we're on par with Serbia, which has one-quarter of America's economic prosperity.

Despite spending far more than any other nation on its health-care system, the United States is 35th in maternal mortality and 33rd in child mortality. Beyond the OECD, overall health outcomes are comparable to Jordan or Panama, and our life expectancy has actually fallen in recent years.

Our homicide rate has skyrocketed to 35th, and we are a disturbing 26th in discrimination and violence against minorities in the OECD. American citizens often lack access to the most basic essentials—America ranks 31st on access to basic drinking water—and our communities are increasingly unsafe. Globally, in personal safety, we have fallen behind countries like Indonesia, Ghana, and Sierra Leone.

Core rights enshrined in our Constitution are also under threat. Our performance has declined significantly since 2014. We now register a lowly 32nd out of 36 on political rights, 23rd on freedom of expression, 27th on access to justice, and 21st on religious freedom. Our inclusiveness is not far below Hungary, an OECD country whose leader, Viktor Orbán, has declared that he intends to build an "illiberal state."[30]

We are no longer the country we like to think we are.

Our society is fracturing. Quality of life in America is declining for many. Key American accomplishments that were once thought to be rock-solid are now on shaky ground. As one casual observer once said to us, "It's simple. We [our government] used to be able to solve problems, and now we can't." Meanwhile, the politics industry continues to grow and prosper—despite its dismal, even life-threatening results—outcomes that diverge dramatically from the public interest.

Modern Outcomes: What Our Democracy Must Deliver

As we have just seen, competition in our political system is delivering outcomes that diverge from the public interest. Before we consider the causes, we need clarity on what the desired outcomes look like. In business, the key desired outcomes are clear: profit and growth. But what essential outcomes should citizens expect from our elected officials?

Despite the fundamental importance of this question, there is surprisingly little discussion of outcomes in politics, much less any consensus on which outcomes we want. Instead, there is endless commentary on the drama of politics and who did what to whom. This lack of attention to outcomes has created a vacuum that has allowed political actors to define success in ways that fit their own purposes. To remedy this, we propose five key outcomes for a healthy democratic political system.

Solutions

Solutions are policies that address important problems or expand opportunities for citizens. A solution is a policy approach that actually works and makes things better in practice. While the importance of solutions seems obvious, solutions are almost nonexistent in America's political system today. What do we know about the nature of effective policy solutions? Although there is no simple way to determine the best solution—and there are many opinions—a solution has essential characteristics.

Effective solutions address real problems, not ideology. Effective solutions rarely arise from applying stylized ideological principles; doing so can often make things worse. Effective solutions are seldom purely right or purely left. For example, the question is not "Big government or small government?" but how to strike the right balance across the various roles that government must play. Similarly, the issue is not "regulation or no regulation," but how to create regulations that deliver the desired social or economic benefits (e.g., less pollution) without inflicting unnecessary cost on the stakeholders being regulated, or on citizens, who ultimately have to pay for it.

Practical and sustainable solutions are not unidimensional. They are nuanced and integrate the range of relevant and important considerations. These solutions must weigh and balance points of view across constituencies and make sound tradeoffs in integrating them. Solutions usually require compromise and bipartisanship.

Good solutions are fair and acceptable to the greatest number of people possible. The challenge is that not everyone can get everything they want from government, especially in a democracy. The tradeoffs involved in good solutions mean that some individuals or groups will benefit more than others from a given policy, and some will shoulder more (or less) of the cost. Yet the overall outcome needs to be perceived, over time, as balanced and fair. Good solutions are often achieved when no group or faction gets everything it wants.

Finally, good solutions make real progress, but rarely achieve everything at once. The key test is this: "Have we made things better?" Effective solutions often initially require partial steps in the right direction, with iterative improvements over time.

The Social Security Act is a textbook example of an effective solution. Before the program was created in 1935, retired Americans were forced to rely on family and friends for support. Yet as the economy modernized, more and more citizens lost their safety nets and struggled to support themselves in old age. This trend was only exacerbated by the Great Depression. Searching for an answer, President Franklin D. Roosevelt created the Committee for Economic Security (CES), which brought together leaders in government, business, academia, and civil society to develop a plan that would balance the interests of all those affected. For six months, the CES studied pension systems around the world and engaged constituents to discover what would work best. Using these findings, Democrats and Republicans then worked together to create a social insurance program that continues to this day.[31]

That we should expect solutions to our nation's most salient problems to be born from compromise seems almost painfully obvious. Yet many Americans have become so used to partisan ideology and political theater instead of real progress that we have altered our expectations of the kind of solutions our political system was intended to deliver.

Action

Our system today often delivers gridlock, not action. But we need our politicians to enact and implement substantive legislation. Yet politicians have little incentive to put the public interest first if they believe that blocking legislation is rewarded by their party and if inaction is not penalized by voters. Unrealistic promises and talk without action are worthless, but in today's unhealthy system that's what passes for progress.

At the signing of the Social Security Act, President Roosevelt acknowledged that "this law, too, represents a cornerstone in a structure which is being built but is by no means complete."[32] Since the law's passage, presidents from Lyndon Johnson to Ronald Reagan have worked to improve the program, expanding coverage, and scaling back costs when necessary.

Today's political-industrial complex views action as a threat. What if a powerful customer base—say, a provoked special interest—reacts poorly? Or what if a key channel, like a partisan media outlet, penalizes the action in front of millions of viewers? The vast majority of promises made by candidates and political leaders on both sides never get acted on because the promises were unrealistic in the first place, and compromise, which would produce action, is vilified. As such, serious legislation is rarely advanced, much less passed and implemented.

Blocking, grandstanding, and making empty gestures are rewarded; action is avoided. Consider the Affordable Care Act (ACA), passed by the Senate in 2010 on a 60-to-39 vote.[33] Every Democratic senator voted in favor of the bill, and every Republican senator voted against it. The process was so divisive that there was no subsequent desire to improve the bill. Instead, the Republicans spent the next seven years trying to kill the ACA, with more than fifty votes to repeal or eliminate key parts of the law rather than working with the Democrats to find common ground and improve it.[34]

Except they weren't actually trying to kill the bill. The Republicans knew they could never repeal the ACA while Obama was in office. These were show votes to signal to their base that they were fighting the good fight.[35] The display was a sham that did nothing but waste time.[36] Once the sideshow was over and the Republicans regained unified control of Congress and the presidency in 2017, it became clear that they had no actual health-care agenda to implement. They couldn't even muster enough votes to repeal the ACA, despite years of empty promises, drama, and meaningless votes.[37] In commenting on the situation, Republican Speaker Paul Ryan remarked, "We were a 10-year opposition party. You just had to be against it. Now . . . we tried to go to a governing party where we actually had to get 216 people to agree with each other on how we do things." To no one's surprise, being a real "governing party" is more difficult than just being the party of no.[38]

Broad-Based Buy-in over Time

Good solutions should be able to gain, over time, reasonably broad-based acceptance and consensus across the population. While there will never be 100 percent support for any policy, true solutions, which most often involve bipartisanship, can be accepted by a range of constituents across the political spectrum. Citizens can accept a solution when political dialogue helps them understand the realities of policy options and the rational compromises needed for them to work.

This is not to say that elected officials should only respond to public opinion. Political leadership is required and must—at times—be ahead of popular opinion to move the country forward or to do the right thing (that's why it's called leadership).

Our nation's history is replete with political leaders who have risen above political noise to actually advance the country—from James Madison convincing a young nation that a stronger constitution was needed, to Abraham Lincoln preaching unity and forgiveness after secession and bloodshed. True political leadership advances policies that reflect the overall public interest. It helps articulate the common interest and allows progress and policy continuity even when the balance of power shifts from party to party. At its healthiest, political competition should educate, unite, and inspire citizens.

A Balance of Short- and Long-Term Needs

Good outcomes also involve legislation that balances the needs and interests of both current and future generations. This balance makes solutions sustainable, rather than giving rise to future crises that ultimately require radical policy shifts and that penalize citizens who had little say in the original policies. When devising social security, Democrats and Republicans agreed that pensions had to be funded out of current payroll checks, not from the government's general revenue or by taking on debt. This foresight has been essential to the program's long-term viability.

Today's story is markedly different. Simpson-Bowles, a bipartisan effort to create a sustainable federal budget, provides a telling example.[39] In 2010, President Obama established the National Commission on Fiscal Responsibility and Reform—most often referred to by the last names of its cochairs, former Senators Alan Simpson and Erskine Bowles. The product of their work was a sound report with a well-crafted compromise solution that balanced the interests of current and future citizens. The preamble to the report says: "The President and the leaders of both parties in both chambers of

Congress asked us to address the nation's fiscal challenges in this decade and beyond. We have worked to offer an aggressive, fair, balanced, and bipartisan proposal—a proposal as serious as the problems we face. None of us likes every element of our plan, and each of us had to tolerate provisions we previously or presently oppose in order to reach a principled compromise. We were willing to put our differences aside to forge a plan because our nation will certainly be lost without one."[40] But Simpson-Bowles was never enacted. Neither party was willing to go against its party orthodoxy or bite the hand of special interests. Instead, Simpson-Bowles died a bipartisan death.[41] Representative Paul Ryan, who served on the commission, voted against it. President Obama, who created the commission, declined to forcefully support it. No other legislators jumped in to save it (though some from both parties were courageous enough to voice public support). Most legislators were unwilling to go against their party line and risk a primary challenge.

Simpson-Bowles also demonstrates another important reality: the duopoly controlling today's political competition has no accountability for results. Neither Representative Ryan nor President Obama nor Congress paid a political price for failing to deliver a solution to this pressing national problem. President Obama won a second term, Representative Ryan became Speaker of the House, and the re-election rate in Congress was 90 percent.[42]

Instead of sustainability, our political leaders today regularly devise short-term measures that they themselves admit just kick the can down the road.

Fidelity to the Constitution

This last outcome, we realize, is quite basic. But it's always worth coming back to—especially when we see elected officials tempted to push the boundaries of our framing document. The beautifully unique American commitment to a unifying framework of self-government, with all that it requires of us, will always be more important—and will unite us—more than any expeditious search for easy solutions.

From Unhealthy Competition to Political Innovation

A successful political system finds solutions, acts on and improves them, generates citizen buy-in over time, and balances the needs of current and future generations, all while honoring the Constitution. With healthy competition, these outcomes are possible.

You might still be skeptical. Maybe the important realities of the politics industry are now clear, but the prospect of fixing this system may feel as farfetched as it ever has. And that's fair; the consequences of this work are too great to accept anything at face value. But this book isn't an industry think tank in Washington, D.C.; we like to think it's closer to Steve Jobs's garage and we're inviting you to come inside and review our blueprints. We are inviting you to think *different*.

If you need more inspiration or proof that political innovation is possible, consider this: America has done it before. As you'll read in chapter 4, a little more than a century ago America was in a similar crisis. With a politics industry failing to deliver for its citizens, many Americans were left asking themselves, what has gone wrong? The answer they came to is the same answer for our questions today: it's a systems problem.

A little more than a century ago, Americans saw the water. And they changed it.

PART TWO

Political Innovation

4

An American Legacy

On September 19, 1796, as the end of his second term approached, George Washington published a farewell address—a series of prescient warnings for a young nation learning to stand on its own two feet.[1] In the address, Washington foresaw the danger of two powerful political parties, or the "alternate domination" of one party over the other, as Republicans and Federalists developed into vicious adversaries. He cautioned against the accumulation of the national debt "ungenerously throwing upon posterity the burden which we ourselves ought to bear." And he implored Americans to resist factionalism. With the North pitted against the South and the East against the West, he reminded citizens that they were all, by "birth or choice," American.

The address is appropriately celebrated for Washington's uncanny insight into the future. Parties, the national debt, and factionalism remain center stage in the United States over two centuries later. But the address also stood for something even more profound. It wasn't just what the address said—it's that it existed at all. The original title, "The Address of Gen. Washington to the People of America on His Declining the Presidency of the United States," was big news: after two terms, Washington would not be seeking reelection. As historian Harry Rubenstein observed, "In that time and era, politicians would gain power, or kings would stay in office, until they die."[2] When Washington published his address, he was introducing a radical innovation: stepping down from power.

Unlike today, there was no norm or expectation that a president—especially one as popular as Washington—would be beholden to term limits. If he had decided to seek a third term, he would almost certainly have won. But instead, Washington grasped the danger of an entrenched executive and so established the limited-term tradition. In 1797 John Adams assumed the presidency in a peaceful transfer of power, setting us apart from much of the world.

From our nation's infancy, the American project has depended on a series of innovations. The innovations of each generation illustrate a very American commitment to the idea that our politics is never a given and that changes to our system of government are not only possible, but also essential—such as ensuring a regular turnover of our commander in chief.

In fact, the very idea of American democracy was itself a revolutionary innovation. Democracy as a form of government, one in which power is vested with the people, has ancient origins. But representative democracy in the modern era, a system in which people elect representatives who make decisions on their behalf, was ushered onto the world stage by the American Revolution. After the Americans defeated Great Britain, the Founders rightly feared the kind of monarchical rule they had recently rejected. But they also feared direct democracy, or a "tyranny of the majority," where the people would directly decide policies. Their solution was to devise a system of intermediaries—of legislators and government leaders whom we hire and fire to do the work of governing. Electing our representatives may seem intuitive and obvious now, but it certainly wasn't always the case.

The list of innovative elements in our heritage goes on. The US Constitution provided the first formal blueprint for democracy. It codified a system of government that was nothing short of an outlier among nations, enshrining an elaborate structure of checks and balances that limited the power of any particular branch and prioritized the role of citizens in the revolutionary concept of self-government. It is today the world's longest-surviving written charter of government—a gift from framers who established firm principles but allowed for amendments and evolution as the nation itself evolved. Indeed, each amendment that came after ratification tells the story of a national debate that fundamentally altered our political system. Political innovation is an American legacy.

But simply "keeping" our democracy has never been enough. Instead, it has required constant reinvention. Neither the Founders nor the Framers delivered a perfect government that needed only our protection, but instead one that was designed to evolve and adapt. What came out of that Constitutional Convention was both extraordinary and deeply flawed. Long, hard-fought struggles to improve our founding document came—and must still come—from a legacy of belief in big, system-level change. Over time, powerful, principled ideas competed for the nation's attention as reformers made their cases and worked to change hearts and minds. Thomas Jefferson captured this ethos well. As the circumstances change, he wrote, our "institutions must advance also, and keep pace with the times."[3]

Today, most Americans can be forgiven for thinking that the current system is beyond repair. With a politics industry optimized for the benefit of an entrenched duopoly, and the deck stacked against citizens, it's easy to believe that our political problems are insoluble. Calls and promises for change are made every election cycle but go nowhere. But despite what many think, we as citizens have the power to reform politics in America and restore our democracy.

History proves it.

The Gilded Age: Political Dysfunction Spurs Americans to Take Back Their Democracy

On February 10, 1897, amid an economic recession, Bradley and Cornelia Martin, elite New York City socialites, invited eight hundred friends and associates to the Waldorf Astoria Hotel for a costume ball. Guests were to arrive dressed as royalty: kings and queens bedazzled in embroidered gowns and finery. In today's dollars, the ball racked up a bill of nearly $10 million. Meanwhile, the average American was taking home around $400 a year.[4] The lavish affair became a symbol of an era known as the Gilded Age. Inequality soared, as did polarization. Corruption and gridlock defined Washington. The very survivability of democracy seemed to be on the line. Sound familiar?

The challenges of the twenty-first century are serious. But America has been here before. This is not the first time our political system has fallen into disrepair and failed to tackle the nation's most pressing problems. While polarization, for instance, has spiked to dangerous levels, they are not unprecedented. In fact, as shown in figure 4-1, polarization was just as high in the late 1800s, when the Martins were entertaining their guests.[5]

During the Gilded Age, America was plagued by many of the same diseases we suffer from today. Republicans and Democrats competed as a dominant duopoly, serving their own interests and special interests rather than the needs of average citizens. Then, as now, the duopoly rigged the rules of politics in its favor, competed by dividing citizens, and infiltrated powerful areas of government to expand its influence. The resulting partisan rancor, governmental dysfunction,

FIGURE 4-1

Political Polarization in the United States, 1880–2019

Current ideological gaps between the parties are at levels unseen since the Gilded Age.

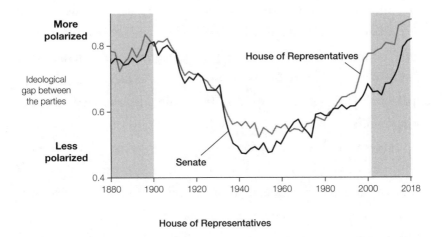

House of Representatives

and inaction took a heavy toll on America. By the end of the nineteenth century, America was on the cusp of unraveling. But as we now know, the country emerged from this chapter with our democracy made stronger, thanks to groups of determined Americans who spawned a generation of political innovation.

By the late 1880s, American citizens had had enough. From 1890 to 1920, political reformers who emerged across the country took action to restore our democracy in a period that became known as the Progressive Era. Not *progressive* in today's sense of being on the left, but progressive in moving the country forward through structural reform of the system.

The Progressives understood that to get beyond partisan loyalty, they had to actively reshape the rules of the game in politics. Though not all potential areas for improvement were addressed; the Progressives changed the direction of the country and left a long-lasting imprint on our democracy.

Progressive reforms have produced myriad benefits for our democracy. Candidates today are chosen in primaries, not by party bosses in smoked-filled rooms. US senators are selected by popular vote, not by partisans in state legislatures. Today we cast a single private ballot in elections instead of separate party ballots that invited coercion and bribery. And businesses can no longer give unlimited contributions to politicians without reporting them. Finally, ballot measures in twenty-four states make it possible for citizens to bypass politicians if they want to by passing legislation from the voting booth.

Progressive reforms ushered in an era of problem solving in our democracy that yielded sustained American progress in spite of two brutal world wars and periodic economic downturns. The systemic changes, coupled with economic growth and postwar expansion, enabled America to become not only the world's richest and most powerful nation, but also a country with an ability to forge compromise and set policies that expanded citizen opportunity and shared prosperity.

The Progressive movement also carries important lessons about how our urgent need for political innovation could be realized today. First, no matter how bad things get, we as citizens retain control of our government—if we exercise it. We citizens have the power to shift the nature of politics and shape the architecture of our democracy if we can create a widespread understanding of how our political system actually works and galvanize action accordingly. The Progressive Era also illustrates the need for reform advocates to band together, regardless of ideology, and not allow partisan or policy preferences to deter or divide them on issues of political innovation. And finally, the Progressive movement shows us why we can never take our democracy for granted. There will always be incentives for the political-industrial complex to distort the system in its favor. Citizens are the only ones who can prevent it. It's up to us.

Precursors of Political Dysfunction

Mark Twain coined the late nineteenth century as the Gilded Age, an era in which there was a thin veneer of gold-plated opulence but mounting strife and corruption. Economic and social disruptions gave rise to tensions, social divisions, and ethnic prejudice. This loss of unity provided an opening for political actors to divide citizens and shape the system in their favor.

Economic factors were important catalysts. Agriculture, an economic and social bedrock of many communities, was upended by mechanization.[6] As the broader economy industrialized, self-contained local economies were disrupted by increasingly national competition. Railroads and the telegraphs connected previously separate communities and markets, and large national companies grew up to supplant many smaller, localized businesses.[7] For example, brick-and-mortar local retailers were disrupted not by e-commerce as they are today, but by huge mail-order companies like Sears.

Companies such as Campbell's, Quaker Oats, Procter & Gamble, Kodak, Singer, and General Electric became household names as the first truly national business enterprises.[8] Industry concentration increased, and competition was blunted even further as companies merged entire industries into monopoly trusts led by infamous robber barons with names like Vanderbilt, Carnegie, Rockefeller, and Morgan.[9] These titans of industry came to dominate not only markets but also politics, using their vast resources to gain undue government influence, distort policy, and extract special favors.

As America was remade into a modern industrial nation, many felt left behind.[10] While consumers benefited from new products and lower prices, many communities suffered, and existing ways of life were lost.[11] Many small businesses shuttered their doors, and employees were forced to search for work in jobs for which they had little training. Workers abandoned farms and local factories in droves in search of opportunity in cities but arrived to find millions of immigrants competing for jobs.[12] Battles arose over what it meant to be American.[13] Americans who were once immigrants themselves claimed that newly arrived immigrants—many from southern and eastern Europe—would be unable to assimilate into American society. Anti-immigration sentiment soared, the Ku Klux Klan was revitalized, and many argued that citizenship should be restricted according to race or creed.[14] Anti-immigration sentiment also found its way into the law. In 1882, Congress passed the Chinese Exclusion Act—the first time the United States would flatly bar an entire group from immigrating. Violence against Chinese communities followed.[15]

Wages rose, but inequality skyrocketed.[16] By the time of the Waldorf Astoria costume ball, the four thousand richest families in America had as much wealth as did all other families combined.[17] Rapid industrialization led to robust economic growth but also far more economic volatility with vicious booms and busts.[18] Deep depressions in the 1870s and 1890s threw millions into poverty, with no social safety net in place for support.[19]

The new economic and social challenges were different from anything the country had faced before, requiring more than local community action. But just when Americans needed effective government to address growing needs, the same pressures and division that were facing citizens gave rise to political partisanship and fractured government. As policy gridlock set in, legislators spent most of their time not creating policy solutions but waging partisan battles that had begun soon after the last shot of the Civil War.

How Political Competition Was Undermined

The year 1876 marked the nation's centennial. Instead of celebrating American democracy, what took place soon thereafter was an abrupt end to Reconstruction and a stunning display of how self-interested political organizations could subvert the Framers' vision.[20]

After the Civil War, formerly enslaved African Americans vigorously engaged in the democratic process, organizing voters and electing black candidates to local, state, and federal offices. More-egalitarian state constitutions were written, public education was introduced across the South, and the Fourteenth and Fifteenth Amendments—ensuring equal protection under the law and enshrining the right to vote regardless of race—were passed by Congress. After the extraordinary destruction of the Civil War came a brief period of zealous democratic activity.

Southern whites responded with intimidation and violence, mobilizing a determined resistance to Reconstruction. The result was the rollback of newly formed democratic gains through voter suppression, electoral fraud, and undemocratic changes to state constitutions. Poll taxes and literacy tests prevented black citizens from voting, while the advent of "white primaries" flatly barred black voters altogether. The tactics worked. From 1876 to 1898, the number of African Americans registered to vote plummeted by 97 percent in South Carolina and 93 percent in Mississippi, with similar declines elsewhere across the South.[21] Sound familiar?

This turn of events was the consequence of a backroom deal made by the duopoly. In a bitter presidential race between Republican Rutherford B. Hayes and Democrat Samuel Tilden in 1876, each candidate lobbed negative attacks to rally his base. Hayes supporters painted Democrats as disloyal Southerners. Tilden supporters claimed that Republicans were punishing the Democratic South for the Civil War.

With voters divided, the election came down to three Republican-controlled states—Louisiana, South Carolina, and Florida. Partisan officials in charge of the vote count declared Hayes the winner. Tilden, who had won the popular vote, protested. A constitutional crisis ensued until the parties struck a backroom deal. Hayes was declared president. In return for forfeiting the election, the Democrats were rewarded with patronage, subsidies, government contracts for their special interests, and, most consequentially, the removal of federal troops from the South. After the Civil War, the federal government had kept troops in Southern states to protect the newly formed Republican state governments. But with the troops removed, the road was cleared for Southern whites to reestablish governments that barred black citizens from political participation. In 1898, a state constitutional convention was convened in Louisiana for the express purpose of establishing "the supremacy of the white race." In 1896, there were 130,344 blacks registered to vote in Louisiana. By 1900, the first year after adoption of the new constitution, there were 5,230.[22] Collusion between the parties ended Reconstruction and inaugurated a period of black disenfranchisement known as Jim Crow.[23]

Both sides of the duopoly got what they wanted out of this deal, but the country lost. This battle was a harbinger of the unhealthy competition that would come to define politics in the Gilded Age and that we face again today.

The Five Forces of the Politics Industry in the Gilded Age

To understand how political dysfunction rose during the Gilded Age, we can apply the same politics-industry analysis we employed to understand today's political dysfunction. The Five Forces analysis that clarifies industry structure can also explain how the rivals could thrive while abdicating their responsibilities to the public interest.

Intense Rivalry but on the Wrong Dimensions

Today's duopoly, the Democrats and the Republicans, emerged out of the Civil War. Rivalry between the parties was intense, but they were not competing to advance the public interest. Instead, by the early 1870s the duopoly began reshaping the politics industry through new rules and new ways of accumulating power while ignoring the needs of citizens who should have been its customers.[24]

Average Citizens' Lack of Customer Power

The parties sought out potential supporters for their ability to deliver money and votes, just as the duopoly does today. Average citizens had little influence.[25] Money, meanwhile, rose in importance as campaign expenses ballooned and party finances were constrained by efforts to reduce the patronage system and restrict the sale of government jobs to citizens.[26] Republican National Committee chair, Mark Hanna, remarked in 1895: "There are two things that are important in politics. The first thing is money, and I can't remember what the second one is."[27]

To attract more money, the parties turned to the new corporate special interests. The parties offered an attractive value proposition that included lucrative government policies, such as subsidies, land grants, and tariff protections.[28] Just as it is today, this transactional mix of business and politics was toxic, distorting competition in both arenas.

Co-opted Channels

The parties also co-opted the channels for reaching voters much as parties do this today. If today's press seems polarized, the Gilded Age was even more so. Newspapers did not even pretend to be independent or fair and balanced. Most towns had two party-backed papers—one Democratic and the other Republican.[29] Each paper promoted its own party platform while smearing the opposition. Loyal editors were rewarded with government posts.[30]

This era also saw the emergence of aggressive organizations aimed at direct voter outreach. Local party organizations hosted huge rallies. They also distributed campaign literature partly subsidized by the taxpayers in the form of free postal privileges.[31]

Control of Suppliers

As the economy industrialized, so did politics. A large political-industrial complex emerged, known during this period as "the political machines." These included powerful party bosses, political operatives, and loyal foot soldiers who controlled nominations, doled out government posts, enforced party discipline in governing, and ran major election organizations that bribed voters for their support.[32] The machines cultivated future candidates, polled with rising precision, and built sophisticated get-out-the-vote apparatus to ensure that their target voters reached the polls.[33] With politics heavily localized, there were not yet many Washington think tanks or lobbyists. But party control over the election infrastructure made it almost impossible for nonparty competitors to break into the industry.

Barriers to Entry

Dismal political outcomes left many Americans grasping for alternatives. In response, new entrants were continuously trying to break in.[34] In the 1870s and 1880s, the Greenback Labor Party emerged on the left. On the right, the Republican "Mugwumps" broke away from their party out of disgust with corruption. These anticorruption activists became a critical swing vote, credited with putting Democrat Grover Cleveland into the White House. In the 1890s, the Populist Party emerged, claiming to represent the interests of workers and farmers. While the Populists failed to establish a viable new party, they did create a base within the Democratic Party. Yet the barriers to entry for a new party were too great to overcome. Some barriers, like economies of scale, were natural. Others, like tying up channels and suppliers, were artificial, cultivated by the duopoly for its own benefit.

How the Parties Competed in the Gilded Age

As discussed, industry structure determines the nature of competition, providing insight into how rivals compete, and why. At the center of the politics industry in the Gilded Age was the duopoly, which predictably embraced a two-pronged strategy familiar to us today: collude to rig the rules and compete on division.

Colluding to Rig the Rules

With no independent regulator, not even an ineffective one like today's FEC, parties struck deals with each other in both elections and governing rules to further entrench their power. In elections, the duopoly instituted and optimized a slew of anticompetitive rules and practices, some of which remain in effect to this day. With plurality voting already in place since the nation's founding, new entrants were attacked as spoilers. Although gerrymandering dates even further back in time, Gilded Age parties were experts at drawing congressional districts to maximize partisan advantage.[35] In fact, they didn't content themselves with districts; they gerrymandered whole states. The divide between North and South Dakota, for example, is a legacy of Republicans' carving up what was a single territory in 1889 to create two more safe Senate seats.[36]

Other rules in this period now seem extreme even by today's standards. Nominees for office were selected in party conventions increasingly dominated by party bosses, who picked only loyalists. Parties designed the ballots, and voters going to the polls would receive separate and clearly distinct ballots distributed by each party, which included only that party's candidates.[37] Split-ticket voting was nearly impossible. Partisan ballots were often printed on different-colored paper so that onlookers could easily see for whom citizens had voted. Votes were cast under the watchful eye of party officials, who coerced and bribed citizens for support. New competitors who lacked the resources to print and distribute ballots at every voting station faced even higher barriers to entry.

On Capitol Hill, the legislative machinery of the day already gave party leaders tight control of the governing process. Under the so-called Reed Rules, adopted in 1890 by Republican Speaker Thomas Reed, the Speaker appointed all members and chairs of the standing committees and wielded complete power over the congressional agenda by chairing the House Rules Committee himself. Then, as now, bills and amendments that were not favored by the Speaker were denied a vote.[38] Czar Reed, as he became known, summed up his view of how Congress should operate: "The best system is to have one party govern and the other party watch."[39]

Competing on Division

Like today's duopoly, neither party during the Gilded Age competed for the political middle, avoiding the accountability produced by head-to-head competition. Although the parties were less ideologically distinct than they are today, they accentuated their differences. Each party divided voters into separate groups along racial, religious, and ethnic lines.[40] Republicans served Protestants, Nordic immigrants, and African Americans. Democrats targeted Catholics, German immigrants, and Southern whites.[41] Democrats depicted Republicans as enemies of liberty, as evidenced by the Republicans' promotion of tariffs and prohibition. Democrats also accused Republicans of corruption and punishing the South for the Civil War. Republicans smeared Democratic immigrant communities, fueling an ugly backlash against new Americans. Such sharp divisions turned party affiliation into a central part of citizens' identity. Politics became tribal. To switch parties was to betray one's group or community.

Campaign rhetoric made it appear as if the nation would be at grave risk if the other party took power.[42] Once a party was in office, there was little working together. Moderates became an endangered species on Capitol Hill, paralleling today's circumstances. Dedicated party loyalists did not dare to work with the other side on forging solutions. Compromise became a dirty word. With voters evenly divided, one party rarely dominated all branches of government. The result was gridlock.[43]

Then, as now, the parties not only differentiated themselves through partisanship, but also delivered value to core supporters by infiltrating government agencies. They accomplished this infiltration primarily by doling out government positions to party supporters, irrespective of qualifications, in what was known as the *spoils system*.[44]

The outcome was predictable: the parties failed to deliver solutions. Public outrage, together with failed attempts at regulation by individual states, produced a few pieces of significant legislation. For example, the Interstate Commerce Act of 1887 was designed to regulate the railroad monopolies, and the Sherman Antitrust Act of 1890 empowered the federal government to combat anticompetitive business practices. Overall, however, the legislative process ground to a halt—and the nation suffered.[45]

Markets went unregulated, leading to free-for-alls and destructive competition. With no policies in place to moderate the business cycle, wildly oscillating economic conditions ensued.[46] Farmers struggled to stay afloat as crop prices plummeted and costs soared, with no real agricultural policies to address the economic difficulties.[47]

In the 1880s alone, businesses and their workers clashed in thousands of often-bloody strikes, with no collective bargaining rules or government mediators.[48] Public schools failed to equip students with the skills needed for the new economy.[49] Crime-ridden cities lacked basic services and infrastructure. Streets were lined with unlivable tenements and unsafe factories.[50] Racial progress after the Civil War was largely undone. Reconstruction was rolled back and replaced with backward Jim Crow laws that reinforced segregation and disenfranchised black Americans.

All the while, our elected representatives stood idly by, delivering favors to their partisans and special interests while accumulating resources for themselves.[51] Faith in government waned. Washington was seen as a swamp where big business and the trusts pulled the strings and where the average citizen had no voice. Historian Henry Adams captured the popular sentiment of the day: "One might search the whole list of the Congress, the Judiciary, and the Executive during the twenty-five years from 1870 to 1895 and find little but damaged reputations."[52]

Consensus grew that the country could not sustain itself with government as it was operating. But the problem was not one of just policies or politicians. It was a systems problem.

The Progressive Movement: Americans Fight Back

At the beginning of the twentieth century, America emerged from the Gilded Age a divided nation, torn apart by divisive politics and unresolved economic and social challenges.[53] Ethnic communities squared off. Farmers clashed with industrialists. Workers clashed with management. Some workers, like Eugene Debs, renounced capitalism in favor of socialism. An American trade unionist and five-time candidate for president, Debs led nationwide strikes against the railroads. Other observers questioned the very foundations of the republic, wondering whether a democracy built around the idea of decentralized power across states could survive economic concentration. Decades after the Civil War, America was again on the verge of fracturing.

But instead of accepting this divisiveness as inevitable, citizens came together around a shared goal: restoring democracy.[54] From 1890 until 1920, reformers across America mobilized, devoting the time and resources necessary to change how politics worked and its results. The resulting major shift in political competition was powerful in the same way it would be today.

A bold vision for reform emerged, but not a starry-eyed one. The movement began with a shared recognition that the country was on the wrong track. Important to this acknowledgment were changes in the media. The party-owned papers of the Gilded Age gave way to what has been termed a golden age of journalism. Reform-minded journalists, known as muckrakers, spotlighted the corruption of corporate monopolies and political machines, laying the foundation for what would become investigative journalism.[55] A deep depression and violent labor clashes increased the sense of urgency. Whatever their divisions, Americans found unity in their disgust with the status quo and their optimism that the future could be better.[56]

Progressives were idealists, but not ideologues. As individuals, they were pragmatists, willing to try different approaches to see what worked. They erected a big tent, unlike earlier reform efforts like those of the Populists, who had divided citizens into distinct social classes. Progressives engaged citizens of all persuasions, even if the citizens disagreed on tactics or even policy.[57] This embrace of ideological diversity was essential to the movement's ability to achieve a critical mass and eventual success.

The Progressive movement began as an uncoordinated effort involving hundreds of community organizations aimed at addressing state and local issues.[58] Interestingly, we are seeing such decentralized efforts emerging today. Progressive reformers at the turn of the old century soon recognized the limits of a piecemeal approach, however, refocusing their efforts on transforming the political system itself and restoring good government. They recognized that effective government was also a prerequisite for success.[59] A new form of political engagement emerged. It worked not through parties or ballot boxes, but by creating a wide coalition of concerned citizens and civil society actors setting out to change the rules of the political game.

There was never a single, national Progressive movement.[60] Reform was city or state based, spearheaded by local coordinating organizations that loosely stitched together diverse constituencies. The Progressives did build some national infrastructure, including groups like the National Municipal League and the Direct Legislation League, both of which advocated model reforms. A nucleus of prominent reformers—including Teddy Roosevelt and Wisconsin's Robert La Follette—joined in, providing much-needed hope, energy, and direction. The Progressives targeted not just reform-oriented journals, but also major national publications like *McClure's Magazine*, a leader in muckraking journalism. As the movement's profile rose rapidly, Progressivism transformed America's political system in just three short decades.

The Progressive Reform Strategy

The Progressives advanced a series of structural innovations to make politics work for the people, not for political actors—a radical idea at the time. Reforms changed the way citizens cast their ballots. Voters now had the power to select their candidates in primaries. Senators were chosen in popular elections, not by party caucuses. Progressive reforms placed limits on money in politics and vested more power in citizens to influence policy through direct democracy. And the legislative machinery was reengineered through a revolt in Congress.

Ballot Reform

Innovation was kick-started in 1888, when a band of reformers from an elite Boston social club toppled the anticompetitive partisan-ballot system.[61] Massachusetts became the first state to adopt the so-called Australian ballot, which was modeled after a system pioneered in Australia and replicated in several European countries.[62] Government, not the parties, provided a single ballot that listed all candidates regardless of party—voters could select their favorite candidates in secret, without fear of coercion.[63] Other states soon followed, and in just five years, the Australian ballot had spread across the country.[64] Ballot reform was what energized the Progressive movement. The corrupt nomination system became the next target.[65]

Direct Primaries

Gilded Age candidates were handpicked by party bosses at party conventions.[66] This setup began breaking down in the early 1890s once the parties' dominant role in the political system became known to all because of the new government-issued ballots.[67] A round of primary reforms kicked off in 1898 with the National Conference on Practical Reform in Primary Elections, held in New York City.[68] In the crowd was La Follette, who two years later made primary reform a pillar of his successful bid to become governor of Wisconsin. Under his leadership, Wisconsin became, in 1904, the first state to endorse a direct primary, determining party nominations by popular vote. One year later, Oregon followed, with six more states joining the next year. Direct primaries for congressional and state races became the law of the land in most states within a decade.[69]

Still, direct primaries weren't perfect. In previous chapters we have described the unintended consequences evident today. However, for a time, direct primaries were effective in curing the runaway power of party bosses and the political machines of the day.

Direct Democracy

The rapid spread of primary reform was aided by another Progressive innovation: direct democracy. Inspired by Switzerland's election format, James Sullivan published *Direct Legislation by the Citizenship through the Initiative and Referendum* in 1892. Sullivan advocated giving Americans the ability to bypass a corrupt legislative system to directly shape policy.[70] The book inspired the creation of the Direct Legislation League and led to Oregon's becoming the first state where citizens could vote directly on bills at the ballot box, starting in 1902.[71] Over the next fifteen years, twenty-two states followed suit.[72] By 1912, direct democracy was a centerpiece of Teddy Roosevelt's third-party campaign for president.[73] It also became the preferred instrument to enact further political innovations.[74]

Direct Election of Senators

US senators were originally selected by state legislators instead of voters, as was specified in the Constitution. This unpopular practice survived attempts at a constitutional amendment; the efforts were routinely defeated in Congress.[75] By 1913, however, the Seventeenth Amendment was ratified, giving citizens the power to pick their senators. In part, this breakthrough was spurred by David Graham Phillips's exposition of corruption in "The Treason of the Senate," a series of articles that exposed how various senators championed policies favorable to wealthy families like the Rockefellers and Vanderbilts in exchange for bribes and campaign contributions. But it was also made possible by the ability of citizens to circumvent Congress through their use of direct democracy, an expanded toolkit.[76]

In 1901, Oregon held a "primary" in which voters picked their preferred senators.[77] A ballot measure in Oregon required candidates for the state legislature to indicate whether they would respect the primary results. Almost all signed on, transforming the primary into the Senate election in all but name.[78] Other states soon followed. By the time the Seventeenth Amendment passed, it was less a radical transformation and more a recognition of an emerging reality.[79]

Changing the Legislative Machinery

The electoral reforms changed incentives in Congress, prompting members in 1910 to rebel against Speaker Joseph Cannon in what became known as the Cannon Revolt. Tired of oppressive partisan control, Progressive Republicans and Democrats, led by Rep. George Norris of Nebraska, united to strip away the Speaker's power over the Rules Committee and decentralize control to committees made more independent by a new seniority system.[80] This transition from a Congress built for partisans to one constructed around bipartisan committees was the first step toward a sensible governing structure reflected in the "textbook Congress" discussed earlier. The process culminated in the Legislative Reorganization Act of 1946, which reinforced a committee-centric legislative machinery designed for problem solving. It also professionalized Congress by increasing staffing and more sensibly dividing legislative work among committees.[81] This system lasted until partisan forces rose up again in the 1970s to undermine it, as we described in chapter two.[82]

Regulating Money in Politics

Rules changes for elections and governing encouraged stronger regulation of money in politics. During the Gilded Age, big business spent large sums on campaigns and lobbying to advance its special interests.[83] Citizens decried money's pernicious influence but were skeptical that politicians would ever cut off their own funding sources. After the electoral changes were implemented, and after countless news stories of corruption, Congress itself finally took action. In 1907, it banned corporate contributions to campaigns. Four years later, other legislation required disclosure of all campaign contributions.[84] Money in politics was tamed—though later unleashed again starting in the 1970s.

. . .

The Progressives transformed political competition.[85] Polarization and partisanship declined, and compromise became the norm, allowing critical legislative solutions to be drawn up and passed. Badly needed regulatory agencies were formed, including the Federal Reserve System, which stabilized the capital markets, and the US Food and Drug Administration, which began regulating consumer products. Thanks to the Sherman Antitrust Act, the government reopened competition by breaking up monopolies, like Standard Oil, and created the Federal Trade Commission to improve its enforcement of fair business practices. The government also took steps to protect the most vulnerable by instituting workplace safety rules, restricting child labor, and improving public health. But it didn't stop there. By changing the structure of the politics industry, Progressives set the stage for other landmark legislation in subsequent decades, from the Social Security Act in the 1930s to Medicare in the 1960s.

Progressives were not perfect. Some of their efforts came with serious unintended consequences, like the establishment of party primaries. And neither side got everything it wanted. Those on the left chastised Progressives for not doing more to protect the poor.[86] Those on the right bemoaned the expansion of government.

But this is what progress looks like. Refinements are always needed. Importantly, progress cannot be driven by ideology. It isn't all-or-nothing. It's not either-or. Progress is about compromise and problem solving to steadily move the country forward. The legacy of the Progressives' nonpartisan structural innovations allowed the nation to tackle our big challenges and ushered in what would become known as the American Century.[87]

Fertile Ground for Political Innovation

As was seen during the Gilded Age, economic and social disruption can provide fertile ground for political dysfunction—and innovation. Once again, we are living in an age of disruption. Digital transformations have shaken up virtually every industry, rendering old ways of competing obsolete. Just as these changes create possibilities for new companies, they also destabilize communities and companies alike.

Industrialization has given way to deindustrialization. Rather than the displacement of farmers and the creation of large-scale national companies by mechanization, automation creates concerns about where jobs will come from and the future of work. As new technology and skills grow in importance, economic gains have disproportionately flowed to the top, again fueling rightful fears of runaway inequality. Many citizens today are left to wonder whether there is a place for them in the economy of tomorrow.

Instead of the nationalization of competition that took place during the Gilded Age, we now have globalization. The years following World War II inaugurated a new era of global commerce and investment. Policy makers in nations across the world prioritized reducing barriers to trade, harmonizing intellectual property laws, and reducing capital controls. Efforts to economically integrate were successful: world exports as a share of gross world product climbed to 8.5 percent in 1970 and then to 16.2 percent by 2001.[88] But as markets and competition have become increasingly global, companies and jobs that have been sources of opportunity and good wages—such as traditional small businesses (small shops, restaurants, personal services, etc.)—have come under threat. The net result has been that economic prosperity is increasingly uneven. While parts of urban America are booming, other urban communities face economic distress. Many rural communities are stuck in a secular recession. Workforce participation has declined, and many working Americans are not earning a living wage. And so there is, all too predictably, pushback against a free-market system that works well for some— and barely works at all for many.

At the same time that such divisive forces are altering the American economy, a new wave of immigration and the concurrent growing diversity are again putting strains on society and sparking another wave of anti-immigration sentiment.[89] Since 1965, the absolute number of immigrants in the United States has more than quadrupled.[90] While the economic consequences are not in dispute—immigration generates more innovation and greater economic productivity, with a net positive effect on public budgets—the social consequences are messier.[91] Change instigates shifts in culture and a community's sense of continuity and security. Together, economic and social changes create greater demands on government to innovate in public policy and to ensure that business and other systems incorporate the interests of all groups, not just a special few.

As in the Gilded Age, the divisions created by the economic and social changes of the last fifty years have again been used in the politics industry to create political division, harden partisanship, and block the kind of compromise-based policy solutions we now need more than ever. Ineffective government makes problems worse, which opens the door for further political division. Political dysfunction then feeds off itself.

Only we citizens can break this cycle.

5

New Rules of the Game

Rules are not glamorous. They are not necessarily fun to consider or create, and they can be even less fun to enforce—just ask a Little League umpire. But as we have explained, rules are ground zero in politics. They are universally and unequivocally the only way to change the game. Rules determine not only *how* a game is played, but also *who* the players are and *what* outcomes the game can—and cannot—deliver. Add a three-point line in the NBA, and watch as dominant dunkers are unsympathetically supplanted by eagle-eyed shooters in a fast-paced, high-scoring game.

Change the rules, change the game. That is *the* rule.

The game of politics is not exempt. The rules around American elections and lawmaking—the machinery we dissected in chapter 2—largely determine how the politics industry works, who gets elected, what they do while in office, and the outcomes they do—or do not—deliver. Today's rules pervert the forces of healthy competition. That is self-evident. They favor ideology over solutions and gridlock over action. Partisanship pays, compromise costs. But placing all of the blame for bad outcomes at the feet of the players—the individual politicians—is at best unfair and misdirected. Like any human being in a profession, a politician is beholden to the incentives and rules that determine success and failure in their industry.

The incentives driving members of Congress are largely a function of the electoral dynamics they face, such as the outsized influence of special interest groups and ideologically extreme voters. And between elections, legislating is a zero-sum game held captive by the next party primary. Just as today's duopoly has cemented its market power in elections, it has also cemented its grip over lawmaking by capturing Congress and devising rules in its favor—particularly in leadership's favor—and often at the expense of effective problem solving in the public interest. As a result of these corruptions of electoral and lawmaking rules, there is virtually no intersection between an elected official acting in the public interest and the likelihood of getting reelected (figure 5-1). So we don't get the results we need.

Because there's rigged competition in the political marketplace—and virtually no possibility of *new* competition—there's no account-

FIGURE 5-1

Unhealthy Competition in Politics

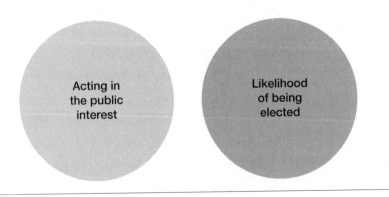

ability. We are caught in a vicious, unhealthy cycle of electoral and legislative dysfunction: no results and no accountability for their absence. To break this cycle we must change the rules of the game and restore healthy competition. But how?

Consider a real-life example of the potential power of healthy competition. Ross Perot, the independent candidate for president in 1992, may not have won the election, but he won tangible results for the country. By altering the political conversation with his charts and graphs about debt and deficits that were emblematic of his candidacy, he introduced elements of competition. And the voters responded, giving him 19 percent of their votes on that first Tuesday in November. As such, the duopoly was forced to respond in turn.

Before Perot, fiscal responsibility wasn't a top campaign priority for either party. After Perot, both parties knew that 19 percent were motivated by fiscal discipline and could be influenced by it in subsequent cycles. This competitive pressure meant that neither the Democrats nor the Republicans—neither President Clinton nor later Speaker Gingrich—would ignore this group of voters while governing. This awareness contributed to balanced budgets and even surpluses. Of course, the booming economy created rising revenues, but absent Perot's competitive threat, it's most likely that Washington would have squandered those revenues. It's far easier to pass the buck to the next generation.

Yet Perot's run—a blip of healthy competition and its benefits—was, unfortunately, an anomaly enabled by his tremendous personal wealth that allowed him to force his charts and graphs into the debate. In the nearly thirty years since, the duopoly's hold on the national conversation remains the status quo. The cycle continues. But the Perot example signifies what's possible.

By revolutionizing how elections are contested and laws are made, we can break the cycle and change the nature of the positions politicians take, the customers they aim to please, who is elected, how they govern, and the voting public's ability to hold elected officials accountable. Given the interdependence between the electoral and legislative arenas, we must address them both. Fixing one alone is far less powerful than fixing them in combination; releasing one choke point on the interstate only ensures you'll get to the next bottleneck sooner.

Elections machinery is the first bottleneck, and must come first, for one simple reason: our elections are the on-ramps to the interstate of governing. When our leaders enter through an unhealthy process, they carry that burden—that threat—into everything they do. Because they are beholden to the partisan elections machinery that put them in office and to the leadership of their respective sides of the duopoly, changing the nature of the legislative machinery is a pipe dream unless and until the elections machinery is changed. It is not that our elected officials aren't empowered to change the rules and practices of legislating—quite the contrary. According to the Constitution, "Each House may determine the Rules of its Proceedings." Changing our legislative machinery is as easy—or as hard—as getting a majority of legislators onboard. The main hurdle is the nature of their accession to office, and whether they are liberated to serve the public interest or still in the pocket of unhealthy election influencers and party leadership—not to mention the normalcy of the current legislative machinery. Elected officials currently serving are either benefiting from or subservient to the current rules of the game and wouldn't be very likely to cast the necessary change votes. After transforming the elections machinery, our collective voice as citizens will ring louder. Instead of being prisoners to ideology, our representatives will be more accountable and responsive to our demands, and perhaps also emboldened to hope for better themselves—including the redesign of how Congress goes about its business by creating a modern, model legislative machinery.

Let's be clear: transforming the legislative machinery *would be* powerful now, but such a change only passes the achievability bar *after* the electoral incentives change. In fact, we saw this exact sequencing during the Progressive Era. Electoral innovations in ballot reform, primaries, and direct democracy preceded the Cannon Revolt that in 1910 stripped the legislative power on Capitol Hill from party leaders and gave it to bipartisan committees.

If we take care of our elections, they will take care of us.

Reengineering Electoral Machinery: The Final-Five Voting System

Election rules determine the types of politicians who seek and hold public office and how they govern once elected. Today's partisan elections machinery ensures that moderates need not apply, those who seek compromise are punished, and independents and third parties are locked out. From sore-loser laws to biased campaign-finance rules, the elections machinery ensures that the duopoly remains powerful and prosperous even while failing to produce results for voters.

But not every rule is equally important in determining the outcomes the system delivers. As discussed earlier, two dimensions of our election machinery have the greatest impact on the unhealthy competition to win elections and make laws: party primaries and plurality voting. To revive our democracy, we must address both through what we call Final-Five Voting.

Final-Five Voting will change the very nature of our elections. It realigns the incentives that drive the elected officials who lead us and it forces open the gates of our elections to new competition. The ballot will finally become the accountability mechanism it should be, rather than the limiting mechanism it has become. Final-Five Voting is how we change the game.

Final-Five Voting consists of two parts—open, single-ballot, non-partisan primaries in which the top-five candidates qualify for the general elections (*top-five primaries*) and ranked-choice voting (RCV) in general elections. These two changes will dramatically impact the competitive nature of our Congressional elections by stripping away party control and ending the drawbacks of plurality voting. Final-Five Voting constitutes a powerful and achievable transformation of the election incentives that loom over every decision our legislators make. As noted, a Final-Five Voting system requires two changes—one in primary elections and one in general elections. It's critical to make both changes together for maximum impact.

Nonpartisan Top-Five Primaries

As discussed earlier in the book, party primaries have dramatically distorted competition in our Congressional elections. They empower partisan gatekeepers at the expense of most voters, which perverts the behavior of our elected officials while they are in office. To repeat, party primaries create an eye of the needle through which no problem-solving politician can pass.

So, let's get rid of them. We propose top-five primaries.

In a top-five primary, you will no longer vote in a Democratic primary or a Republican primary. Instead, there will be a single, open, nonpartisan primary. Every candidate from any party as well as independents appear on this single ballot (with a partisan affiliation next to their name if they so choose). All voters are eligible to vote in the primary (unlike party primaries, which, depending on state rules, often exclude independents and third-party supporters). The top five finishers, regardless of their partisan affiliation, advance to the general election. Instead of one Democrat and one Republican facing off in a head-to-head matchup in November, the general election could become a contest between *three* Republicans and *two* Democrats; or

one Republican, *one* Democrat, and *three* independents; *one* Democrat, *one* Republican, *one* Libertarian, *one* Green, and *one* independent. Top-five primaries create a new way of determining who gets
to compete and sets up a broader competitive field of five candidates
for the general election.

While the top-five proposal hasn't yet been implemented, some
single ballot, nonpartisan primary pioneers are paving the way. California and Washington have implemented top-two primaries, in
which the top two finishers advance to the general election, regardless of party affiliation. The results are telling. Before California
introduced top-two primaries in 2012, some 79 percent of its state and
congressional races were deemed "uncompetitive," with the results
all but guaranteed.[1] Partisan primaries, combined with pervasive gerrymandering, meant that once candidates won their primaries, they
faced no real challenge in the general election. For example, in a district that's overwhelmingly represented by Democrats, the primary
effectively determined the ultimate winner: whoever the Democrats
nominated would sail to victory over a Republican in November. The
results of the general elections were all but ensured. The only real
competition occurred during the low-turnout primaries, where candidates would appeal to their more extreme base of primary voters to
secure their reelection.

Uncompetitive general elections preceded by highly partisan primaries had serious effects on California politics. Consisting of hyper-
partisan politicians who had little reason to worry about the safety
of their seats, the state legislature regularly ranked among the most
dysfunctional in the country.[2]

But top-two primaries changed that calculus—significantly. After
implementing top-two primaries, the number of races evaluated as
competitive across the state immediately doubled. Landslide victories decreased, and the number of incumbents who began to lose

in the general election increased. Research shows that many of the candidates who now win the general election—who appeal to a broader cross-section of the electorate—would have lost under the old system's closed primaries.[3] Just four years after implementing this innovation, California was ranked among the most electorally competitive states in the country.[4]

When elections change, governing changes. California's notorious gridlock began to loosen as voters began electing more politicians committed to solving problems. By 2016, the approval rating for California's legislature hit 50 percent, up from a dismal 10 percent in 2010.[5]

Despite these results, the top-two approach has faced some pushback (led, not surprisingly, by leadership on both sides of the duopoly). Leading up to California's primary elections in 2018, House majority leader Kevin McCarthy (R-CA) said, "I hate the top-two." The then House minority leader Nancy Pelosi (D-CA) said California's top-two system "is not a reform. It is terrible." But in response, former Republican governor Arnold Schwarzenegger and Representative Ro Khanna (D-CA) wrote: "Their bipartisan response should tell you everything you need to know: Political parties hate top-two, so voters should love it."[6]

But top-two doesn't go far enough to fully inject healthy competition into our elections. Only allowing for two candidates in the general election still limits voter choice and opens little opportunity for new challengers outside the duopoly. It can also generate unintended consequences. In 2012, voters in California's Thirty-First Congressional District had the choice between two conservative Republicans—even though a majority of the district voted Democrat. Vote splitting across a large number of Democratic candidates had allowed the Republican Party to squeeze two candidates through to the general election—hardly the intention of a reform designed to improve representation.

While there is no perfect number, we believe top-five is optimal for three main reasons.* First, the additional slots in the general election make it highly unlikely that a single party will capture all five spots. Second, top-five ensures that more voters are likely to have a choice they support come November. Third, more choice means more competition, for candidates and ideas, and more competition means more elected officials who are more accountable to citizens—and more accountability in an industry means better results. Always.

There's a reason that the Final Four, the National Collegiate Athletic Association's famous yearly basketball tournament, is such a resounding success: starting with a field of sixty-four teams from around the nation, the tournament is known for its upsets and Cinderella stories—the unknown teams from far-flung conferences who find their way to the highest levels of hoops competition. Would this tournament be as healthy if it *only* allowed powerhouse teams like Duke and North Carolina, Wisconsin and Michigan, or Kentucky and Louisville to compete? It absolutely would not. In politics, offering five spots on the general election ballot not only fosters opportunity for everyone, and creates space for new ideas, but also makes it harder for the duopoly to game the competition.

Will some races fail to utilize all five spots? Yes. But there's no real downside to that; having unused, empty spots is far superior for the health of our democracy than not having options at all. Opportunity is an American cornerstone. Our elections must become embodiments of opportunity. It is our birthright. It is liberty in practice.

Most importantly, the top-five approach alters the calculus for legislators. They know they won't automatically lose their seat if they

---

*While our recommendation is five slots, we wholeheartedly support top-four efforts, like the one underway in Alaska.

vote yes on a bipartisan landmark bill that violates party orthodoxy. The party-primary eye of the needle, through which no problem-solving politician can pass, disintegrates.

Ranked-Choice Voting General Elections

As we have discussed, plurality voting—and the resulting spoiler effect and wasted-vote arguments—is the greatest structural barrier to new competition in the politics industry. Plurality voting also creates incentives for negative campaigning and dividing voters, and sometimes creates the undemocratic situation in which a majority of voters do not support the winner.

So, let's get rid of it. We propose ranked-choice voting (RCV) in general elections.

The idea is simple. Whereas plurality voting can elect candidates without majority support, RCV does the opposite. For candidates to win, they *must* pass the 50 percent threshold.

Here's how RCV works in practice. When you arrive at the polling station on Election Day, you receive a ballot with the names of the five nonpartisan primary winners. In a hypothetical election between the Founding Fathers (and a Founding Mother), you would receive the ballot shown in figure 5-2. As always, you pick your favorite—in this case, Alexander Hamilton, who is running a young, scrappy, and hungry campaign.* But you can also pick the candidate you like second best (Abigail Adams), third best (George Washington), fourth best (Thomas Jefferson), and fifth best (John Adams).

After the polls close, the first-place votes are counted. If one candidate receives more than 50 percent of the first-place votes (a true majority), then the election is over. Hamilton might get a whopping 65 percent

---

*Shout-out to Lin-Manuel Miranda.

FIGURE 5-2

Sample Ranked-Choice Voting (RCV) Ballot

This sample ballot shows how a voter might rank five theoretical candidates, with the first choice being Alexander Hamilton and the fifth choice John Adams.

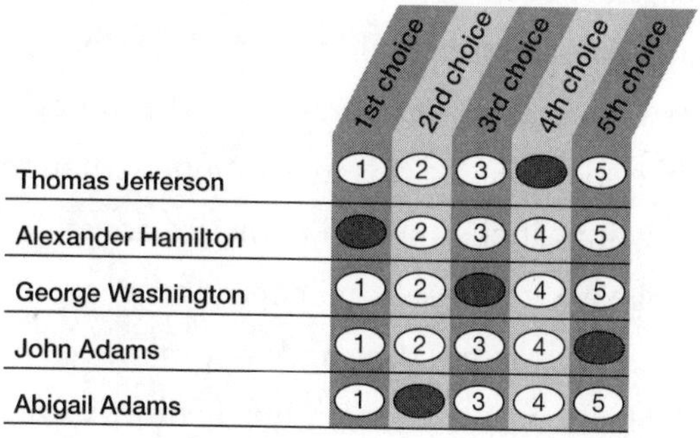

of the vote, in which case, he wins. But what if Hamilton only gets 33 percent—less than a majority—and Abigail Adams gets 32 percent? In plurality voting, Hamilton would still win, despite only having the support of a third of voters. But not with RCV—at least not yet.

If no candidate gets a true majority (50 percent plus one), the candidate in last place is eliminated. In this case, Thomas Jefferson. But votes cast for Jefferson aren't wasted, because voters who selected him as their first choice have their ballots automatically transferred to their second choices. Let's say that most of Jefferson's supporters have Washington as their second choice: when the ballots for Jefferson are redistributed to Washington, he is pushed over the 50 percent threshold. Hamilton would have won under plurality voting by securing the turnout of a strong base (just 33 percent), but Washington wins by garnering a higher level of popular support through RCV.

While most Americans have not yet heard of RCV, it is far from a new idea. In 2002, Senator John McCain recorded a robocall urging Alaskans to support a ballot measure to adopt RCV, stating that it would "lead to good government because voters will elect leaders who have the support of a majority."[7] That same year, McCain's future opponent, then Illinois State Senator Barack Obama sponsored Illinois Senate Bill 1789 for RCV in state and congressional primaries. Although both proposals were ahead of their time and neither of them passed, in 2018 Maine became the first state in the nation to adopt RCV, and Massachusetts will vote on RCV in November 2020.

The potential benefits of RCV aren't just theoretical. Cities across the country have spearheaded this innovation, with nineteen municipalities such as Minneapolis and San Francisco adopting RCV to elect municipal officials. With these local experiments producing promising results, momentum is building and we can see the benefits in real time. A 2017 evaluation of seven US municipalities using RCV to elect various city officials found that voters were much more likely than those in plurality-voting cities to report that candidates focused on the issues of the campaign rather than denigrating their opponents.[8] After San Francisco implemented RCV, research found that campaign materials—like the mailers sent to voters' homes—focused more on "valuable information" like positions on policy, and less on attacking other candidates.[9] If candidates need to win second-place (or third- or fourth-place) votes to make it over the 50 percent threshold, campaigning by simply attacking your opponents will have limited utility.

RCV ensures that the winner will always have support from the broadest possible portion of the electorate. Most importantly, RCV eliminates the enormous barrier to entry that plurality voting creates. Combined with nonpartisan top-five primaries to create Final-Five Voting, it's transformational.

The Benefits of Final-Five Voting

Earlier in the book, we asked you to imagine yourself as a politician stifled by the self-interested rules of the politics industry and stuck between a rock and a hard place. Let's put your politician hat back on, but this time you don't need to think like a renegade or challenge the rules and practices of the politics industry in order to legislate with the public interest as your top priority. This time, things are different; the rules of the game have changed. Your decision on how to vote on a bill is no longer threatened by the special interests, or hyper-partisan primary voters, or party leadership who controlled your fate—and lorded over your vote—on legislation. This time, back at your desk in Congress sits that same bipartisan bill. But now, with your team of whip-smart and passionate staffers, you are free to debate the bill's official particulars and crosswalk them with the goals of your constituency, the goals of your party, and the broader goals and needs of the country at large. You're free to vote yes without the fear of career-ending retribution. The questions guiding your decision will finally be the right questions: Is this a good idea? Will this improve the lives of a broad base of my constituents? Is this the right policy for the country?

Instead of a perverse incentive structure that penalizes elected officials for challenging the entrenched culture of the politics industry, there's a new guiding principle etched above your doorway: acting in the public interest intersects with and contributes to the likelihood of your being reelected (figure 5-3). Your constituents can expect results and hold you accountable for those results. Amen to that.

FIGURE 5-3

Healthy Competition in Politics—with Final-Five Voting

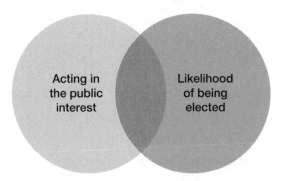

To create healthy competition that incentivizes results and accountability is more than enough of a reason to push Final-Five through. But there's more. The following pages describe additional facets and layers of the benefits connected to Final-Five Voting in the politics industry.

Realigned Customer (Voter) Power

Voters become the most important customer—as they should be. The general election replaces the primary as the most important election—as it should be. The winning candidate will have the broadest appeal to the most voters. Candidates will be incentivized to appeal to a larger group of voters than they did when the competition was in the primary. Every voter in the district is potentially valuable to more candidates. With five spots, it's likely that most voters—not just a minority faction—will see a candidate they like on the November ballot. And with RCV, citizens can vote their actual preferences among all five candidates without fear that their vote will be wasted or that they may help elect the candidate they like the least. This liberates citizens to vote for the candidates they actually favor, instead of the duopoly candidate they are told they should support for strategic reasons. Finally, by making the currency of votes rise in value relative to the currency of money (because the outcome of the general election will, in more cases, no longer be certain), Final-Five Voting takes us in the right direction where money in politics is concerned.

Barriers to Entry Lowered Dramatically

Final-Five Voting nullifies both the spoiler effect and the wasted-vote argument that discourage competitors from within the major parties and outside of them from running. Five slots ensure a broader slate of candidates, allowing candidates typically eliminated upstream in party primaries to make their case to the general electorate. The media is motivated to cover all five candidates with all-important "earned media" because each candidate has a potential impact on the outcome.

Incentives to Divide Citizens Diminished

It's not just first-place votes from partisans that count. Depending on the election, candidates will have to compete to be the second or even third choice of a much broader set of voters. Gratuitous and false negative attack ads that alienate citizens become potential liabilities, not roads to victory. A candidate can less easily afford to ignore swaths of the electorate when he or she needs to gain support from more than 50 percent of voters.

Of course, Final-Five Voting won't magically make campaigns wholesome and collegial; elections will remain tough and cutthroat, and candidates will—and should—draw legitimate distinctions between each other and often still do so in sensational ways. But the newly increased power of every vote will act as a counterweight to the mudslinging and boundless negativity that has become customary. Candidates in winner-take-all plurality elections commonly deploy this negative strategy, often with impunity, because as long as you attract one more vote than your competitor does, it doesn't matter how many other voters you alienate along the way. Final-Five reorients the playbook of campaign managers around a new calculus: differentiation without alienation.

More Innovation. More Diversity. More Ideas.

We believe that moderate, compromise-oriented politicians have an important value in creating and delivering solutions to the nation's problems. We are not suggesting, however, that moderates are the only valuable type of elected officials. They are not. Historically, transformational changes in the United States—from emancipation and women's suffrage to social security and civil rights—have often begun at the "fringes," in what were decidedly nonmoderate camps. Eventually, however, change must be enacted by a majority in democratically elected public bodies. It is here that cross-partisan, problem-solving, consensus-seeking moderates are crucial for delivering practical solutions. It is precisely this type of behavior that our current political competition has rendered almost extinct.

Imagine the impact of having five candidates in every general election. Imagine the impact on elected officials who see double-digit first-round vote totals for the candidate running on a platform of national debt reduction (like Perot in 1992) or running on climate change (like Jay Inslee in the 2020 Democratic primary). The potential for innovative ideas to become part of the public debate is increased. The lowered barriers apply to what may originally appear as the "fringes" too. Final-Five Voting gives us the best of both worlds.

Better Jobs for Legislators

Final-Five Voting will empower legislators to do what they came to Washington to do: make a difference. People pulled to public service who are brave enough to run and win can practically accomplish their goals because the new system incentivizes action, not duck-and-cover leadership. The system will make better use of existing talent and attract more smart and talented people because the jobs are satisfying and the campaigns are not a lesser-of-two-evils game. As Lee Drutman, a senior fellow in the political reform program at New America, says, ". . . elected officials today are also sick and tired of the status quo. They bellyache constantly about the partisan rancor. They don't like how the centralization of power in Congress that flows from toxic politics has rendered many of them marginal players. Almost every retiring member of Congress complains about how bad it is to be an elected official these days, how the partisanship has gotten so much worse, and how this was not what they thought they were signing up for when they eagerly first came to Washington."[10] Final-Five Voting won't just be better for voters—it will mean better jobs for most legislators.

Achievable Modern Outcomes (Sooner Than We Might Think)

As we outlined in chapter 3, elected officials should be measured on their ability to deliver our desired outcomes: solutions, action, and broad-based consensus over time, while balancing the short- and long-term needs of the country. Unless we change the incentives that currently make doing their jobs in service of these outcomes risky, we'll continue to see gridlock instead of compromise. And here's something particularly exciting and encouraging: we don't need fifty states to change the rules in order to start changing D.C. If just ten states sent delegations to Washington who were elected through Final-Five Voting we would immediately have twenty senators and approximately one hundred representatives who could serve as a new, vital fulcrum—solving problems, compromising, and bucking a partisan stranglehold on governing. It only takes a few states to begin to improve the possibilities for desired outcomes for the entire nation—and the first state to adopt (almost) this exact package might be Alaska, which will see an initiative for Final-Four Voting on their ballot in November 2020.

. . .

The Constitution's Framers were silent on the kind of voting systems used to elect our politicians, delegating those decisions to the states. From Alabama to Wyoming, the choice is ours. Final-Five Voting will represent a giant leap toward better outcomes for America and open the door for further political innovation. As we saw during the Progressive Era, political innovations can be contagious and build on one another. Innovation begets innovation, and the next frontier for newly liberated elected officials—and the newly empowered voters holding them accountable—is legislative machinery. Final-Five Voting will be a powerful start, but its incentives for results and accountability will be increased when paired with an effective legislative process.

Reengineering Legislative Machinery:
Model, Modern Lawmaking

In 2010, an intrepid reporter from the *New York Times* named Robert Pear visited with Stanley A. Feder, the president of a plant that produced several tons of sausage links every year. Pear was investigating a quotation attributed to Otto von Bismarck, which is used with impunity by elected officials to excuse their much-maligned legislative process: "If you like laws and sausages, you should never watch either one being made." Going to the source where actual meat is encased, Pear got the skinny, saying, "But a visit to a sausage factory here, about ten miles from the Capitol, suggests that Bismarck and today's politicians are mistaken. In many ways, that quotation is offensive to sausage makers."[11]

It's time to make our legislative process better. As we've shown, the rules and practices of Congress are far from effective. The legislative machinery has been carefully constructed over time for the duopoly's benefit and is designed to serve partisan purposes, not to solve problems. The end product of this partisan legislative assembly line is often the ideological, unbalanced, and unsustainable laws passed by just one party over the opposition of the other. With each new Congress comes promises of repeal and replace, rather than implement and improve—or, more often, complete gridlock and inaction. Again: it doesn't have to be this way.

So let's get rid of it. We propose a model, modern (and nonpartisan) legislative machinery.

Remember, there are just six short paragraphs in the Constitution about how the House and the Senate should work, but the House and the Senate rulebooks have multiple hundreds of pages each—and they wrote them all. We accept this as rational, that the parties are free to write their own process and accountability mechanisms. And because the product of that design and optimization process is slow, arcane, and ceremonial, and, well, painfully boring at times, it creates convenient cover for the unhealthy competition it fosters. *It's the water we swim in.*

Even many veteran members of Congress are so used to the day-to-day dysfunction that they become blind, or at least completely resigned, to the degree to which party-optimized rules smother the legislative process. Most members are too busy blaming the other side instead of spotlighting how the vast machinery shapes political behavior. But fresh faces can see the dilemma clearly. Rep. Mike Gallagher (R-WI) saw early on in his first term that the rules of Capitol Hill needed to change. "Until we fix the processes and the structures of power within Congress," Gallagher acknowledged, "we should expect more of the same—polarization, vitriol, and demagoguery. Every two years, candidates will inveigh against the status quo in the swamp, and then promptly get swallowed by it. A great country such as ours deserves a functional legislature—and only structural reforms can deliver it."[12]

If we want better results for the American public, we must redesign Capitol Hill to create a truly nonpartisan legislative machinery, one designed to solve problems, not to serve partisans. The Constitution doesn't prescribe the inner workings of Congress. Instead, it directs each chamber to "determine the rules of its proceedings." In other words, we can push our officials to create something different. In fact, it's our job as citizens to be as concerned about this as we are about our elections. What's the point of healthy elections without healthy lawmaking?

So, what exactly does reengineering our legislative machinery involve?

Here's the theory of change: Use a proven management practice to reimagine the legislative machinery from scratch: zero-based budgeting. With this method of budgeting, used by organizations across the private and public sectors, all expenses must be justified and approved according to anticipated value, not history. Developed by Peter Pyhrr in the 1970s, zero-based budgeting starts from zero at the beginning of every budget period, analyzing the needs and costs of every function within an organization, and allocating funds accordingly—regardless of how much money has previously been budgeted to any given line item. Similarly, zero-based design eliminates constraints on thinking and opens new possibilities for problem solving.

Our prescription for changing Congress: *zero-based rule making.* Put aside the Rules of the House of Representatives, the Standing Rules of the Senate, the Authority and Rules of Senate Committees, the Rules Adopted by the Committees of the House of Representatives, and the Rules of the Committee on Rules—the volume of rules upon rules optimized and weaponized over the decades. Put aside the informal rules, too—practices such as the Hastert Rule. And put aside customs that create separate podiums, separate cloakrooms, and separate dining rooms for Democrats and Republicans and that seat the chamber according to party. Put it all aside. And then, reimagine from a clear, white space.

We may find that many of the current rules and practices perform an important purpose. Let's pull those into the future. But critically, we should also be free to acknowledge what *hasn't* worked and begin the imaginative process of creating something new.

Organizations often fall short of the goals of zero-based budgeting, but that's not the point. What matters is that we give ourselves license not to tinker at the edges, but to instead begin imagining a model, modern legislative body designed to deliver results for the citizens it serves—a big, audacious, and necessary goal.

A Legislative Machinery Innovation Commission

Such a goal is going to take time—perhaps three to five years of design, preceding the time required to pass it on Capitol Hill—so we need to get started now. We propose the establishment of a

Legislative Machinery Innovation Commission, an independent and nonpartisan effort to design a model, modern legislature built to produce real results by adopting the best practices for state-of-the-state negotiation, communication, and problem solving. When the commission's work is complete, they will deliver their body of work to the two chambers of Congress for consideration. When Congress finally has enough members elected under the problem-solving incentives of Final-Five Voting, they will be in a position to reject the past partisan legislative machinery and adopt a new legislative machinery designed to solve problems (and, at the same time, make their jobs more doable and more satisfying for them and their constituents).

Here's the question for the commission: assume you have 435 people in one legislative chamber and 100 people in another chamber, with different backgrounds, perspectives, ideologies, and electoral directives from their constituents. Despite their differences, they love their country and want to deliver good outcomes and create a strong record to run on in their next election. They have to reach agreement on bills to send to the president for signature. How should they organize their work? What processes would you recommend? What staff? What methods? What physical structures? What communications mechanisms? What technological and data support? What best practices for collaboration and negotiation can be implemented? To summarize, what would a modern, model legislative machinery look like?

In this spirit, the commission will mobilize a nonpartisan consortium of leading experts representing a diversity of disciplines and organizations to propose a reengineered legislative machinery fit for tackling the nation's biggest challenges. There are already many ideas toward transforming Congress into a place of deliberation, negotiation, and compromise—such as those being developed by the 2019 bipartisan Select Committee on the Modernization of Congress. But that committee—and other similar efforts—doesn't have a zero-based mandate (not to mention that they are beholden to forces within the very institution they are attempting to change). Improving a terribly broken system is immensely challenging. Imagine our potential for progress if we didn't constrain ourselves with the misplaced notion that things must remain the way they are and that, at best, we can only adjust at the margins. Ridiculous.

Functions of an Innovation Commission

The Legislative Machinery Innovation Commission will serve three principal functions. First, it will use the zero-based approach to produce a blueprint for a model, modern legislature. The commission will create a large tent—a space for much-needed collaboration between political scientists and scholars who have long studied the inner workings of Congress, current and former senators and representatives, together with experts from fields typically far away from Capitol Hill. With expertise in areas such as behavioral science, conflict resolution, negotiations, technology, and organizational management, the diverse team will enjoy the benefits of groundbreaking research in fields with much to contribute to the design of a model problem-solving body. It's time not just to impugn the many egregious rules and practices we have discussed here, but also to leverage a vast and growing body of knowledge that holds promise for restoring true problem solving to Congress.

Second, the commission will make its findings public, shining a national spotlight on a legislative machinery that presently works for partisan interests—not ours. The Legislative Reorganization Act of 1946 faced fierce pushback from those whose interests in Congress were threatened. But with public pressure for change at a high, the act passed with bipartisan majorities. Indeed, such change rarely happens unless the public demands it. By widely publicizing its work, the new commission would help bring clarity to the hidden machinery responsible for congressional dysfunction, galvanizing Americans around the need for big change.

Third, the commission will join with legislators dedicated to building a better problem-solving body—perhaps a then-current Select Committee on the Modernization of Congress. Ultimately, change will only happen if Congress makes it happen, adopting and adapting a new playbook for how the institution works. Congress rarely, if ever, simply adopts something wholesale. Instead, external proposals can serve as a major contribution to institutional innovation—especially when lawmakers are part of the process from the beginning. As the American Political Science Association's Committee on Congress— more on this in a moment—demonstrates, when a group of committed lawmakers champion big internal change, institutional change is possible. A commission external to Congress must work with lawmakers to supply ideas and channel public pressure for taking bold actions.

We expect many legislators, especially those elected under Final-Five Voting, will welcome a new legislative machinery because in many ways, the transformation we advocate is about underused talent and misspent opportunity. Better rules mean smoother and more effective work. And better work creates more interesting opportunities for talented people. These are the same magnetic principles that draw Americans to Silicon Valley, Wall Street, or any other professional frontier marked by healthy competition. Good rules are great for business. Good rules will be great for legislating—and for legislators—too.

Successful Models from the Past

Commissions like the one we propose have been used to instigate large-scale change within Congress in the past.[13] In the late New Deal era, as concern was mounting about the rapid expansion of executive power and as public dissatisfaction with Congress was hitting historic lows, a group of political scientists working across universities, think tanks, and government agencies began discussing the possibility of big congressional reform.[14] In January 1941, the American Political Science Association (APSA)—a prestigious professional society founded at the turn of the century—formalized these discussions by creating a Committee on Congress.[15] Led by an independent group of nonpartisan experts, the committee assigned itself the audacious task of scrutinizing "the machinery and methods" of Congress and recommending an operational overhaul.[16]

Most members of the committee were already bringing to the table a career's worth of research. So rather than produce yet more research, the committee saw itself primarily as a "catalytic agency." Its members met with lawmakers throughout Congress to document problems firsthand and to mobilize support for new thinking. They solicited input from academic peers across the country. And, perhaps most importantly, they initiated a national discussion—across radio programs, public forums, and newspaper editorials.[17] The committee's work culminated in a short report of big ideas.[18] With ideas such as reorganizing the committee system, requiring the registration of lobbyists, and dramatically increasing staff capacity so that lawmakers could do their jobs effectively, their vision was nothing short of a transformation of Congress.

Of course, it would have been easy for the report to find itself collecting dust on a shelf. But the committee had thought ahead. It collaborated early on with reform-minded legislators who came from both parties and were gravely concerned about the institution's health.[19] In 1945, these legislators took the baton from the APSA to create the Joint Committee on the Reorganization of Congress.[20] Less than two years later, Congress passed the Legislative Reorganization Act of 1946, reflecting much of the APSA's recommendations. Congress's once sprawling and unwieldly landscape of committees, which had become personal fiefdoms for powerful chairs, were reduced from thirty-three to fifteen in the Senate and from forty-eight to nineteen in the House. For the first time, Congress delineated clear jurisdictions for these committees, and the institution could now meaningfully invest in hiring expert staff to aid it in complex policy making.[21] These changes arguably amounted to the most sweeping reorganization of Congress in American history.[22]

A Reinvigorated Democracy

There is no one optimal set of rules that will create a democratic utopia. As Winston Churchill famously said: "It has been said that democracy is the worst form of government, except for all those other forms that have been tried from time to time." Democracy is messy and hard. It will remain so. Ideas will be debated. Groups will disagree. No single group or side will get everything it wants. The definition of utopia for democracy? Still messy and hard, but with good outcomes to show for it. That must be our collective aspiration.

Reengineered elections machinery—Final-Five Voting—and reengineered legislative machinery—model and modern lawmaking—is a powerful combination. It is our best opportunity to move off our present course of self-destruction and step onto a new path toward progress and shared prosperity. It's exciting to realize we don't have to accept the status quo of our politics. It is now our job as citizens to execute—to transform this vision of healthy political competition that serves the public into a reality. The good news is that across the country, from Maine to California, progress is already being made. And keep your eye on Alaska!

6

Laboratories and Principles

In the depths of the Great Depression, the Supreme Court heard a case contesting an Oklahoma law requiring companies to have a license to sell ice. It was an unremarkable legal proceeding and would have soon been forgotten by history were it not for Justice Louis Brandeis's opining on the benefits of federalism in his dissent. He wrote: "It is one of the happy incidents of the federal system that a single courageous state may, if its citizens choose, serve as a laboratory."[1]

Through individual states, America can experiment with new rules and processes to see what works best, particularly toward our first priority: electoral innovation. In the early twentieth century, the inventiveness of Thomas Edison's fabled Menlo Park was rivaled by the Progressive Era's "laboratories of democracy," which patented a line of political innovations that included secret ballots, direct democracy, regulations on campaign donations, and many more.

Today, from coast to coast, the states are reinvigorated yet again, churning out twenty-first-century innovations that address the problematic structures of the politics industry—plurality voting and the partisan primaries—that are stifling our democracy, our economy, and our quality of life. On the legislative-machinery front, while the avenue for innovation runs directly through Congress, there are lesser-known, torchbearer examples of legislative innovation from the states worth studying, along with a glimmer of activity in our nation's capital.

This chapter explores and connects the efforts of these early innovators and draws from their impressive victories—and crucial failures—to inform guiding principles and nonnegotiables for electoral and legislative innovation. As you read, keep in mind that the number of activated American laboratories will only increase over the coming years. Additionally, the guiding principles and nonnegotiables we have created and outlined in this chapter are also embryonic; best practices must evolve and grow with the movement itself.

Electoral Innovation Laboratories: From Washington to Maine

As we said earlier, the Constitution delegates to the states the authority to make most of the rules governing elections—even congressional elections. Of course, in the case of Final-Five Voting, if Congress were so inclined, it could change the rules for its own elections.[2] Not surprisingly, we do not rate this action as highly likely, so we take our movement to the states, tailoring and sequencing our tactics to the conditions on the ground.[*] (As you'll see later in this chapter, an important guiding principle is "localize, localize, localize.")

Depending on the unique circumstances of each state, two major approaches—legislative action and ballot measures—can be used to achieve political innovation around elections:

- *Legislative action:* In every state, political innovation can be achieved through legislative action. Like any law, legislation to restructure the political rules of the game must be drafted, passed by the state legislature, and then signed by the governor. While state politicians may be reluctant to upend the system that elected them, they ultimately work for us. If enough citizens across powerful constituencies demand change, elected officials will be forced to respond. And because many officials agree that Washington is broken and the prospect of a more doable and enjoyable job is appealing, the action becomes more viable as the volume of support increases.

- *Ballot initiatives or referenda:* In twenty-four states, there is an extra tool for political innovation: direct democracy, another Progressive Era accomplishment.[3] With direct democracy, citizens can bypass politicians and directly vote on legislation. The process is straightforward. First, a proposal is placed on the ballot in one of two ways. With ballot *referenda*, a bill is first proposed by a representative in the state legislature. But rather than vote on the bill themselves, legislators can opt to refer the proposal to the ballot box for citizens to decide whether it will become law. With ballot *initiatives*, citizens themselves draft the proposal and place it on the ballot, most often through a signature collection process.[4] Second, once a proposal has been placed on the ballot, voters on Election Day

---

*We do hope that there comes a time, perhaps when half the states have already acted on their own, when Congress decides to finish the job and adopt this innovation for federal elections in every state—which is in their power to do.

are asked not only to vote for the candidates they favor, but also to vote for or against the proposal. If a proposal receives majority support, it becomes law. Most ballot measures deal with particular policies, like California's 1978 Proposition 13, which placed a limit on property taxes. Ballot measures are currently the leading tool to pass structural political innovations.

A handful of states have already won major electoral-machinery victories around voting-system reforms.[5] As explained earlier, although top-five primaries (half of our recommended package) have yet to be implemented, two states, Washington and California, have taken the first step by moving to top-two nonpartisan, single primaries. Their efforts mirror our proposal but with only the top two candidates advancing to the general election.[6]

Washington: The First Mover

The State of Washington's electoral innovation started early on when it created the *blanket primary* in 1935.[7] Just like partisan primaries, under the blanket-primary system, the top vote-getter of each party advanced to the general election as his or her party's nominee. But unlike closed partisan primaries, voters were not restricted to choosing only Democrats or Republicans. Instead, if they wanted, citizens could vote for a Republican in the gubernatorial primary and a Democrat in the Senate primary, or a Democrat in their state assembly primary and a Republican in the US House primary.

But in 2003, after the system was in use for nearly seventy years, the courts used a recent precedent to strike down Washington's primary system, in *Democratic Party of Washington v. Reed*.[8] Facing a return to closed, partisan primaries, Washington devised a workaround. Rather than have the top finisher from each party advance to the general election, the state created a new system in which the top two finishers would move forward, regardless of party. Top-two primaries were created.[9]

The first top-two bill passed in the Washington state Senate but stalled in the House, where the Speaker of the state House refused to hold a vote. Then, in 2004, the bill made it through both chambers of the state legislature, only to be vetoed by the Democratic governor on April 1. Hearing news of the veto, supporters of top-two initially thought it must be an April Fools' joke.[10] But it wasn't funny at all.

Thankfully, citizens took charge, first by passing the reform via a ballot initiative and then by successfully defending it against a lawsuit backed by the duopoly (*Washington State Grange v. Washington State Republican Party*).[11] In 2008, the US Supreme Court cemented Washington's victory, ruling that top-two primaries did not violate the parties' asserted right to pick their own nominees. In the majority opinion, Justice Clarence Thomas attacked the parties' argument, writing that to strike down primary reform would be an "extraordinary and precipitous nullification of the will of the people."[12] With that decision, the path was paved for top-two primaries to travel down the Pacific Coast Highway to the most populous state in the union: California.

California: Better Electoral Incentives

The State of California was in crisis throughout the 2000s. Government was failing to solve the state's mounting problems. Unemployment was rampant, infrastructure was crumbling, deficits ballooned, the state's bonds were rated the worst in the nation, and the state was plagued with power outages. All the while, the legislature regularly failed to perform the basic task of reaching a budget deal to keep the government's lights on, because of a deadly mix of ideological polarization and hyper-partisanship.

During this period, the California legislature ranked among the most polarized in the country.[13] The memory of compromise faded as party-line votes became the norm.[14] Partisan rancor reached such an extreme that a small working group of solutions-oriented Democratic and Republican assembly members who wanted to work together to solve the state's mounting challenges was forced to meet in secret.[15] Fearing punishment from party leadership and primary voters, no one wanted to be seen conspiring with the enemy. Citizens suffered as a result. Pew Charitable Trusts' Governmental Performance Project ranked the California legislature as the worst in the nation.[16] By 2010, its approval hit a record low of 14 percent.[17] Los Angeles mayor Antonio Villaraigosa called California "ungovernable."[18]

It *was* ungovernable, given the rules of the game. After the 2000 census, the two parties drew electoral maps that protected incumbents and eliminated real competition. Districts had been so packed full of members of one party or the other that the winners in nearly 80 percent of races were completely decided in the low-turnout partisan primaries that were put in place after the US Supreme Court struck down the blanket-primary system.[19] Election Day in November was little more than a coronation. Under this system, politicians were pushed to the fringes as the views of extreme primary voters were all that counted. Average citizens had no power. Despite the dismal outcomes and public disgust, just two incumbents across all state legislative and congressional races were defeated between 2002 and 2010.[20]

So, Californians changed the rules. Following Washington's lead, the state mobilized an effort to eliminate its new party-primary system. After an initial attempt to enact top-two primaries through a ballot initiative failed in 2004 by a vote of 54 to 46 percent, a Sacramento group that was part of the Independent Voter Project launched a multiyear study of what had gone wrong.[21] Determined not to make the same mistakes again, it began the push for a new initiative in 2008.

While getting on the ballot through signatures could be a lengthy and costly process, the group had an ally with political leverage. When budget negotiations broke down yet again in 2009, the Democratic majority courted moderate Republican state senator Abel Maldonado, who promised to support the budget deal only if Democrats in the legislature referred primary reform to the upcoming ballot in exchange, thereby mitigating the need to collect signatures. Desperate, they agreed.[22]

It seemed a small price to pay. The ballot measure, they thought, was destined to fail. And although the *Economist* was supportive of Maldonado's efforts, in early 2009 the publication predicted: "His initiative is probably doomed. Every special interest group that benefits from the current system, of which there are many, [will] fund the campaign against it."[23] The hurdles were no doubt high. Yet this political calculus overlooked the champions of the public interest on the other side of the ledger. As the campaign kicked off, the Independent Voter Project started a voter education effort targeting unaffiliated independents, who had often been overlooked, particularly in California's closed primary elections, where they could not even vote. Prominent current and former politicians came out in support, including then Republican governor Arnold Schwarzenegger and former Democratic governor Gray Davis. Major media outlets such as the *Los Angeles Times* and the *San Francisco Chronicle* endorsed top-two primaries. Civic groups, including the California branches of the Chamber of Commerce, American Association of Retired Persons, and Common Cause lent a hand. All their support was needed, as the Democratic and Republican Parties united in opposition. Through public pronouncements and backroom maneuvers, the duopoly tried to sabotage reform.

In June 2010, when all the votes were counted, the percentages were the same as they had been six years earlier: 54 to 46 percent.[24] But this time, the script was flipped. The measure had passed. Since its passage, the duopoly has not warmed to the idea of nonpartisan primaries.

Voters have taken a different view. As discussed in chapter five, support for nonpartisan primaries has only grown as its benefits have become clear.[25] After the reform, California elections ranked among the most competitive in the country.[26] In previously uncompetitive red and blue districts, numerous incumbents have lost to their own respective party members who placed second in the nonpartisan primary and won in November by reaching beyond their party's base.[27] In the first use of the new primary system, for example, incumbent Democrat Michael Allen was unseated by fellow Democrat Marc Levine, whose moderate platform allowed him to cobble together a winning coalition of Democrats, Republicans, and independents.[28]

Changing who is elected, however, is less important than changing what politicians get done while in office. Here, the impact has been dramatic. By shifting incentives, top-two primaries combined with nonpartisan redistricting reform and the emergent fulcrum of solutions-oriented candidates backed by Govern for California have altered behavior in Sacramento. While states across the country continued to become more polarized, ideological extremism and party-line voting has declined in California.[29] New electoral incentives have opened the door for bipartisan deals on emissions standards, gun violence, immigration reform, and more.[30] "It's given more courage to my Republican colleagues," said a Republican legislator reflecting on the difference that primary reform has made. "They were afraid of getting primaried. Now, it's not just their [partisan] base they have to appeal to."[31]

The *New York Times* reported, "Democrats may also be changing. The state Chamber of Commerce reported last month that thirty-nine of the forty bills it had described as 'job-killing'—regulatory legislation that typically was supported by Democrats—had been defeated this year. 'In the freshman class, a lot of the folks had moderate voting records,' said Anthony Rendon, a Democrat who was elected to the State Assembly last year, evidence of the need for many legislators to appeal beyond the Democratic base."[32]

Yet political innovators in California know their work is not finished. A new effort is under way to implement a close version of our Final-Five Voting package; supporters are hoping to get this on the ballot in 2024.[33]

Maine: Battling Political-Industrial Complex Roadblocks

The State of Maine has a long track record of eschewing partisan politics in favor of iconoclastic moderates such as George Mitchell and Olympia Snowe, and independents such as Angus King. But plurality voting has created problems for Maine, too. Nine out of the last eleven governors failed to win 50 percent support.[34] These numbers include the pugnacious Paul LePage, who was first elected governor in 2010 with less than 38 percent of the vote and was reelected in 2014 while again failing to win a majority.[35]

In response to this affront to the democratic principle of majority rule, reformers regularly proposed ranked-choice voting (RCV) legislation in the state assembly, but to no avail. In 2010, Maine's *Sun Journal* lamented that "the ranked-choice system is an interesting alternative that stands virtually no chance of approval in a Legislature dominated by the two traditional parties . . . [E]xpect our winner-take-all, minority-rule system with all its warts to be around for a long time to come."[36]

A depressing prediction, but one that overlooked the full democratic tool set available to the citizens of Maine. Before polls had closed on LePage's reelection bid, Cara Brown McCormick, a political operative turned political innovator, had decided that enough was enough. She convened a team of campaign professionals, local leaders, and average citizens across the ideological spectrum. Together, they collected over sixty thousand signatures to put RCV on the 2016 ballot.[37]

McCormick's group, the Chamberlain Project, worked alongside a grassroots organization called the Committee for Ranked Choice Voting to gather endorsements from hundreds of current and former politicians from all sides, as well as business, religious, and academic leaders. Even former Vermont governor and onetime presidential hopeful Howard Dean came out in support, writing in the *New York Times*, "It is fitting that Maine's motto is 'the way life should be.' I believe ranked-choice voting represents what democracy will be. It's a solution to the problem of how to uphold majority rule and give more voice to voters by presenting them with more than two options."[38] Backed by this groundswell of popular support, Maine citizens passed the ballot measure in 2016, making Maine the first state to adopt RCV.

The people of Maine had pulled off a democratic coup against the political-industrial complex, but the parties didn't take defeat lying down. A counterattack soon began. Maine's secretary of state Matthew Dunlap, a Democrat, railed against RCV and predicted that it would lead to "cars burning the streets"—even though he had to know that Maine's largest city, Portland, had switched to RCV years earlier, and citizens there overwhelmingly support it—while he worked behind the scenes to block its implementation.[39] In February 2017, the Republican-controlled state Senate asked the Maine Supreme Judicial Court to review and provide an advisory opinion on whether RCV violated the state constitution, pointing to a provision that precisely stated that officials were elected with a "plurality."[40] This rule had its roots in Gilded Age mayhem, when partisan militias nearly plunged the state into civil war after the Democrats in charge refused to certify the election of a Republican who had won a plurality of more than 49 percent of the vote in a three-way gubernatorial race.[41] Now, in the modern age of partisan turmoil, this rule was called on to protect the duopoly from the Mainers the legislators were supposed to represent.

The court responded to the request with a nonbinding ruling that state races could not be conducted using RCV. This opinion was a godsend for the duopoly. Rather than amend the state constitution to preserve the citizens' decision to implement RCV, the advisory opinion was used as political cover to override the people of Maine.

Four months after the legislative session had ended, Maine's entire state legislature reconvened on October 23 for a sneaky late-night special session. Only one issue was on the docket: delaying the implementation of RCV and mandating that it be repealed entirely if a constitutional amendment were not passed before the end of 2021.[42] The bill targeted not just state races, but all races, even though primaries and congressional races posed no constitutional problem. At roll call, these politicians voted to overrule the public and essentially repeal RCV. It was a blatant partisan power grab and an affront to McCormick, who watched from the gallery as years of work and the votes of hundreds of thousands of Maine's citizens were nullified in a matter of minutes by a few dozen partisans.

But McCormick and her colleagues didn't admit defeat. They doubled down and launched a People's Veto campaign taking advantage of a Progressive innovation that allows Maine citizens to veto a law passed by their legislators.[43] McCormick actually drafted the press release announcing the People's Veto from the gallery only moments after watching the law pass.

The first step was to collect sixty-one thousand signatures over the next ninety days to get RCV back on the ballot. In Maine, petitioners are allowed to collect signatures at polling places, prime venues where citizens show up in droves ready to engage with politics. If a ballot initiative in Maine wasn't organized in time to begin the collection of signatures on Election Day, it was often dead in the water.

There was just one problem for the People's Veto. The timing of the state legislature's special session was not random, but instead had been planned to leave citizens little time to respond. Election Day was just two weeks away and the People's Veto still needed to be drafted and certified by the secretary of state. After frantic scrambling to launch the effort as soon as possible, Secretary Dunlap dragged his feet, waiting until 4:45 p.m. the night before Election Day to approve the measure. The clock was ticking. The polls opened in just fourteen hours.[44]

What happened next, in McCormick's words, "was magic." That night, her team distributed the petition to copy centers throughout the state, driving hours to pass out signature pages at turnpikes and ferry docks to ensure that the team reached every polling place by morning. By the time polls closed the next day, a remarkable thirty-three thousand signatures had been collected.[45]

But this was only half of the signatures needed. For the next three months, almost two thousand volunteers braved frigid conditions as they stood outside grocery stores and shopping malls collecting signatures. But by February, these volunteers had collected over eighty thousand, more than enough to put the People's Veto on the June primary ballot.[46]

Again, the duopoly fought back with all its power. Secretary Dunlap wrote an impossibly convoluted ballot measure designed to confuse voters. He was even sued for violating the law by stating his intention to refuse to use RCV in the June primary. Meanwhile, the Maine Republican Party filed its own lawsuits in both state and federal court to block implementation. In the final hours of the campaign, just as citizens were set to vote, Governor LePage called RCV "the most horrific thing in the world" and threatened not to certify the result.[47] The duopoly's tactics were so outrageous that a local newspaper that had initially opposed RCV published an editorial in May lambasting the parties: "There's nothing wicked about opposing ranked choice voting. It's a complex issue. But enough's enough. The people . . . have spoken."[48]

Enough was enough. The time had come for RCV. Many Nobel Prize–winning economists endorsed the People's Veto, as did the *New York Times*. Social media was flooded with ads featuring popular actor Jennifer Lawrence urging support.[49] On June 13, 2018, Maine voters used RCV to vote on candidates for the first time, and passed the RCV measure (again) by a margin of 54 to 46 percent, the same as California's margin and twice the margin the measure had received in Maine two years earlier.[50]

The impact was immediate. In the first election using RCV, the initial vote in Maine's Second Congressional District showed that the incumbent had won a plurality. Under the old rules, the election would have ended and the incumbent would be headed back to Washington despite the fact most voters had backed someone else. Under the new rules, the election proceeded to a second round, where the thirty-six-year-old Marine Corps veteran Jared Golden was elected with a majority of support.[51] In one last-ditch effort, opponents unsuccessfully appealed the outcome of the election in federal courts. After they were defeated, Governor LePage was forced to begrudgingly certify the outcome of what he called a "stolen election."[52] Perhaps the election was stolen from the duopoly, but democracy had been restored by Maine's citizens. Magical.

The magnitude of the nonpartisan victory was captured by Stanford University political scientist Larry Diamond: "Rarely in recent American history has a political struggle so clearly exposed the gulf between a two-party duopoly that does not want more electoral choice and a public that craves it . . . Many reforms are needed, but ranked choice voting can be the Archimedean lever of change, enabling a small force to move a great weight."[53]

As goes Maine, so goes the nation? Early returns are encouraging. Momentum is building. And as we have seen, momentum is a powerful force in political innovation. Efforts to expand RCV are already under way across the country.[54] Six states plan to use RCV to select the Democratic presidential nominee in the 2020 primaries.[55] Maine was the first, but it won't be the last.

By examining the successes and setbacks in the states of Maine, California, and Washington, we can start to understand the bucking bronco of political innovation—and how to wrangle it. Ideally, early innovators in the states would provide a checklist that an aspiring innovator could follow. But as many of the players in the political-change space know well, what works in Minnesota won't necessarily work in Oklahoma, let alone California. The individual personalities and histories of America's states are great strengths, but if each state's unique situation isn't considered and appreciated, nothing lasting can be accomplished. Some states already have strong track records of political reform. Others are just getting started. In some states, Democrats and Republicans are locked in a never-ending battle. In others, one side of the duopoly has complete control.

In spite of these state-to-state nuances, a set of overarching principles for how to execute Final-Five Voting is worth proposing. These principles do not dictate what to do in every case but rather frame the order of things—from big decisions to key tactics with the best odds of moving the ball downfield. We aren't dropping these principles down from a 30,000-foot view, either. We've got boots of our own on the ground: Katherine is cofounder and cochair of the cross-partisan Democracy Found, a Wisconsin-based initiative committed to achieving Final-Five Voting. We're not just recommending these principles; we're fighting to implement them, on a daily basis.

Guiding Principles for Electoral Innovation

We define the efficient frontier of political innovation as the maximum amount of *power* you can deliver without sacrificing *achievability*. That's where you'll want to be, on every decision, and the specifics of the efficient frontier are different from state to state. As we've learned, having the right innovation agenda—the right *ideas*—isn't enough; you need to know what to do with them and attract a critical mass of support. To that end, we recommend three guiding principles for electoral innovation.

Keep It Cross-Partisan

The death knell for political innovation is partisanship anywhere, be it in the leadership teams, staff members, boards of directors, or funders, not to mention your innovation agenda itself. Do the work to engage Republicans, Democrats, and independents—don't count anybody out. And don't add partisan agenda items to the nonpartisan Final-Five Voting package.

In May 2018, Katherine and a group of prominent Milwaukee-area leaders from across the political spectrum hosted an event. After the presentation on the need to change the rules of the game in politics, Lynde Uihlein and Andy Nunemaker took the stage. A lifelong Democrat, Uihlein is one of Wisconsin's most prominent supporters of liberal causes and candidates. A diehard Republican, Nunemaker hosted the only fundraiser for Donald Trump in Wisconsin during the 2016 election. "We have differing opinions on ballots, on policy, on elections," Uihlein acknowledged that night, "and Andy and I haven't changed our minds about what is of value to us, and what's important, and how we're going to vote."

Nunemaker added, "But we do agree on this: our current system does not do justice to the United States and our great country. It doesn't deliver long-term solutions to our greatest political challenges, and it divides us."

Uihlein and Nunemaker declared to the almost four hundred people in attendance that they were working together to change these election rules in Wisconsin. And they're still at it—as is every member of the original (and now much larger) group.

An early Colorado innovator and a CEO of a *Fortune* 500 company, Kent Thiry credits his success to his Noah's Ark approach.[56] When Thiry began his campaign to create an independent redistricting commission in Colorado, not only did he bring in both right-leaning and left-leaning organizations, but he also followed a simple rule: for every Republican who joined the campaign, he recruited a Democrat. This balance helped him navigate the choppy political waters and ensure that voters viewed redistricting reform not as one party's attempt to gain an edge over the other, but as the people's wresting back control from the political-industrial complex. Political innovation is designed to support a political system that is a stronger force for uniting than dividing, and the process of delivering those innovations should do that as well—right from the start.

Localize, Localize, Localize

Changes to the many rules of our democracy belong to the states— and to the people in that state. At the heart of any successful state effort is a nucleus of dedicated citizens living in, and committed to, the state they're working to change. These can be both seasoned political operatives, like Cara McCormick in Maine, and new grassroots leaders, like Katie Fahey in Michigan. The leadership group must understand the local terrain and have ties to the communities across the state, engaging and motivating diverse constituencies.

Again, the unique personalities and histories of our fifty states are some of America's greatest strengths, but this individuality can and will bite back if not respected. Additionally, the broader localism movement is taking root in communities and neighborhoods across the country, a bottom-up movement that's also the by-product of the self-interested and dysfunctional politics industry. As *New York Times* columnist David Brooks wrote, "Localism is also thriving these days because many cities have more coherent identities than the nation as a whole. It is thriving because while national politics takes place through the filter of the media circus, local politics by and large does not. It is thriving because we're in an era of low social trust. People really have faith only in the relationships right around them, the change agents who are right on the ground."[57]

How should local leaders organize? While we don't recommend a wholesale outsourcing of state-based innovation efforts to national reform groups, some national groups have state chapters that can offer established, reputable platforms that local leaders can utilize, especially for startup operations, guidance, and fundraising. For example, Common Cause California was an important force behind the state's redistricting reform. That said, other local leaders have opted to create new organizations that may then collaborate with national experts and organizers.

Build a Four-Constituency Coalition

Winning coalitions must include four key constituencies:

Grassroots members: organized local volunteers on the ground

Grass-tops supporters: donors, business and civic leaders, and national organizations that provide financial capital, infrastructure, expert advice, and connections

Political leaders: people who can provide credibility and help navigate legislative and legal hurdles

Prominent opinion leaders: groups (e.g., editorial boards) or individuals who can raise a campaign's profile and endorse it

Breaking through the inertia and political noise can be a challenge but it is possible if each of the four constituencies plays their part. While ballot initiatives and legislative campaigns appear radically different on the ground, they share common threads. Successful campaigns manage to stitch together broad coalitions either to persuade and motivate voters, in the case of ballot initiatives, or to lobby elected officials, in the case of legislative action.

Finally, and this observation is less a guiding principle of electoral innovation than it is a certainty of life, expect pushback from the powerful. Political innovations disrupt unhealthy competition and the partisan profit machines the political-industrial complex has created. Not surprisingly, then, many in the duopoly will do everything in their power to block this work. Nevertheless, there is also a benefit from the compelling leadership of some current and former elected officials who know how dysfunctional the system is and who courageously choose to say, in effect, that the emperor has no clothes.

Expecting pushback means, more often than not, committing to building and running an A-campaign. To achieve our goals, we have to work harder and smarter, because the opposition has so many advantages, they can't even be documented fully in this book. And if we succeed, passage of an electoral innovation is just the first step. The case of Maine shows that implementation is a completely different story—and Maine was no anomaly. In state after state, the duopoly has taken legal and legislative action to repeal innovations and suppress the will of the people. Every campaign must be prepared for this protracted battle that can continue for years after the initial campaign has ended. And yet, it's not entirely inevitable. Thiry's Colorado-successful referenda were not challenged by the duopoly after the fact. The work he and his collaborators did proactively to include elected officials from all sides right from the start prevented that kind of opposition from developing. So, while we should plan for pushback, the best plan includes first trying to avoid it by building buy-in within the political system.

Legislative Machinery: Under Construction

Millions of citizens have taken action to restructure elections, with increasing success. Our priority is to accelerate this movement, focus it on Final-Five Voting, and open an enormous bottleneck on the gridlocked interstate of democracy. Then what? As we've described, political innovation feeds on itself, pushing more ideas into the powerful and achievable sweet spot. Although we have earmarked legislative machinery as the next chapter of political innovation, few citizens know much about how Congress conducts its business, partly because the process is opaque (and assumed boring) compared with the public spectacle of campaigns.

But a once-in-a-generation window to changing the rules of the legislative game is opening. And once we've got a new legion of officials elected via Final-Five Voting, our energy will shift to motivating and supporting a new crop of "procedural entrepreneurs" to ride the next wave of congressional innovation.

As political scientist Roger Davidson observes, "In every era, at least a few members of Congress cultivate a lively interest in the institution itself: how Congress works, how its virtues can be nurtured, how its effectiveness can be improved. Such members might be called 'procedural entrepreneurs.'"[58] Whereas most legislators find themselves trapped within an institution's ways of working and accept the status quo for what it is—learning to play the game as best they can by the constraints of the current rules—others become intent on changing them. Most of the time, these internal change agents fail. Congress is littered with the remains of well-intentioned efforts that failed to translate good ideas into action: committees and commissions that elevated big problems but found themselves stuck in gridlock or saw their reports shelved and gathering dust.

One such effort to make inroads began in 2019. Established in January of that year, the Select Committee on the Modernization of Congress was established to investigate why the institution had been failing Americans so badly and what to do about it. As a *Washington Post* article reported, "It's one of the most important committees in Congress, yet it has only temporary office space. It has just two full-time legislative staff members. And it borrows other committees' rooms to hold hearings." And yet, the piece continued, "against those odds, the Select Committee on the Modernization of Congress is pushing ahead with a bipartisan approach that could produce some of the most important work of the 116th Congress."[59]

A bipartisan-backed mandate has given this temporary committee broad latitude to spotlight the rules and processes handicapping the legislature's ability to deliver real results for the country. So far the committee has produced nearly four dozen unanimous recommendations, including basic organizational best practices on issues like payroll, staff training, and administrative efficiencies, along with more ambitious proposals like investing in new capacities at the Congressional Research Service and reestablishing the Office of Technology Assessment—legislative support bodies that suffered under Speaker Newt Gingrich's dismantling of Congress's nonpartisan infrastructure. Taken together, the recommendations represent an effort to find common ground on issues that affect the ability of all members, regardless of party, to do their jobs well.

The Select Committee is laudable in that it proves, if nothing else, that legislative-machinery innovation is *theoretically possible*, and we support most of its recommendations—although none of them have yet been adopted as of this writing. But we should not expect the committee to reengineer the legislative machinery in any transformative way. It represents a modest effort driven by a cadre of reform-oriented lawmakers, not the culmination of an institution-wide movement to rewrite Congress's playbook. The committee's very existence was the result of internal bargaining, not a recognition from party leaders—today's ultimate power holders in Congress—that our partisan legislative machinery needs to fundamentally change. While the modern movement to streamline legislative machinery is still in its infancy, we can learn from, and be encouraged by, the very existence of these contemporary procedural entrepreneurs. We can also learn and take inspiration from torch-bearing mavericks, like Nebraska's George Norris, who long ago demanded something better—at both federal and state levels—than the corrupt legislative machinery he experienced.

Nearing the end of his decade of service in the House in 1910, Progressive insurgent Senator Norris led the so-called Cannon Revolt that dismantled the partisan legislative machinery of his time (see chapter 4). The effort was later memorialized in the pages of John F. Kennedy's best-selling *Profiles in Courage*.[60] In its place, Norris built the foundations of a new legislative machinery designed around bipartisan committees insulated from party pressure through a seniority system. This structure was refined over the next several decades to create the textbook Congress (which is perhaps better understood as the *Schoolhouse Rock* Congress discussed earlier in the book).

During his three decades in the Senate, from 1913 to 1943, Norris continued his push for good-government reform, not just in Washington, D.C., but also in his home state of Nebraska.[61] For decades, Cornhuskers had tried and failed to reorganize their legislature to peel partisanship from the governing process.[62] When public dissatisfaction hit new heights during the Great Depression in the 1930s, however, Norris returned home to lead the campaign.[63] Working with a group of prominent citizens from across the state who had banded together to create the Model Legislature Committee, Norris drafted the blueprint for a new legislative body for the state.[64] Despite widespread opposition from prominent groups like the American Bar Association and American Bankers Association, past and present legislatures, and most of the mainstream press, the measure passed in a ballot initiative in November 1934.[65] The revolutionary but sensible design remains in place to this day.

Most of us know little about Nebraska state politics. Why would we? (Unless, of course, we live in Nebraska.) The Nebraska state legislature has just one chamber, the Nebraska Unicameral Legislature. Norris saw this single-house system as essential, believing that closed-door conference committees to reconcile differences between the two chambers had become hotbeds for special interests.

But for us its unicameral structure is not the most interesting thing about the Nebraska legislature. The real innovation is that it features nonpartisan legislative machinery.[66] Rather than divide elected officials into majority and minority parties, all officials serve as one body of equals. Just as in the US Congress, there are Republicans and Democrats in the Unicameral.[67] But unlike Congress, the legislative machinery is not designed around these divisions. There are no recognized party leaders or whips.[68] Committee positions and chairs are determined not by partisan steering committees but by a nonpartisan Committee on Committees.[69] And the Speaker is not a partisan official carrying out the majority party's agenda but is an agent of all members.[70] Charles Warner, the first Speaker of the Unicameral, said, "We owe no allegiance to any party or to any group. Our responsibility is to the whole people of Nebraska."[71] This is a far cry from what we see in Washington today.

This unique structure has bred better results. Party-line votes are far less common in Nebraska than in other states.[72] Instead, cross-party coalitions tend to form on an issue-by-issue basis.[73] It is not unusual for legislators to break from their party on bills.[74] In 2014, for example, despite the fact that a majority of members of the Unicameral were registered Republicans, they overrode the Republican governor's veto of a budget deal.[75] In 2015, they overrode his veto on a bill repealing the death penalty.[76] And in 2016, they overrode a veto of a bill allowing undocumented immigrants to receive professional licenses.[77] Fed up with the lack of partisan fealty, the governor called on voters to elect more partisan "platform Republicans." Legislators from both parties responded in a joint statement in which they affirmed that they "support the Nebraska Constitution and not any particular political party."[78]

Our job now as citizens is to bring this ethos and structure back to Washington, D.C., similarly reengineering the federal legislative machinery to eliminate partisan control and create processes that promote solutions that serve the public interest. And we shouldn't stop there. After following Nebraska's lead and eliminating partisan control of governing, we need to go further, redesigning Congress to put in place the best practices of problem solving. As we proposed in chapter 5, this redesign will require a new commission similar to Nebraska's Model Legislature Committee to draw a fresh blueprint for Capitol Hill.[79]

Beginning America Over Again

In a slim pamphlet titled *Common Sense* and published in Philadelphia in 1776, Thomas Paine captured the spirit of his era: "We have it in our power to begin the world over again." Were it not for the chord his proposals struck with the people of the colonies and the action that followed, Paine's bold ideas might have been remembered as little else but aspirational—if they were to be remembered at all.

Almost 250 years later, the spirit of American revolution still reverberates for many of us, and the successes of initiatives in states such as Maine and California reinvigorate the democratic renegade in our marrow. But skepticism is bound to creep in. You might be asking, If Final-Five Voting were really so powerful, wouldn't we have long ago figured that out and accomplished it? Or wouldn't I have at least heard of it? But that's not how innovation works, in politics or in any industry. There is a moment when the idea germinates, but often a great deal of time passes before something takes root. At some point early on, the startup that becomes Apple or Google first consisted of a few people in a garage or dorm. And in the case of political innovation, there is an entrenched political-industrial complex engineered to quash any new ideas before they spread.

Think back to the Progressive Era. Innovations eventually spread quickly, but only after achieving some momentum. Success was built on the sustained efforts of dedicated citizens who formed groups, disseminated information, pushed through initiatives, and lobbied politicians.

Ideas alone aren't enough. We need to get to work.

We must now spread the ideas of Final-Five Voting, scaling a few early innovators into a coast-to-coast campaign of universal adoption and action. Thanks to the upstart laboratories of democracy that have shown us the way (in victory and defeat), we know that action is getting results. And it will continue to be difficult, especially in the face of an entrenched duopoly. The transformation requires smart decisions and sustained effort from multiple actors across multiple states, each with its own unique history, political climate, party loyalties, and democratic rules. But transformational political innovation can be achieved whether a state is big or small, red or blue. There are fifty states in this union, and many are still waiting for the political innovation spark to be lit.

Will you do it?

Lighting that spark requires shaking away learned helplessness about politics, and trading skepticism for leadership. We are not powerless in our democracy. We are not bystanders. We are the makers. Former Wisconsin Senator Robert "Fighting Bob" La Follette put it best: "America is not made but is in the making. There is an unending struggle to make and keep government representative. Mere passive citizenship is not enough. Men must be aggressive for what is right if government is to be saved from those who are aggressive for what is wrong."[80]

We the people had the audacity to reject taxation without representation from across the pond and to create a new nation founded on the radical idea that all are created equal. Whether they were a single voice in a town hall or a chanting chorus on the National Mall, citizens have rallied to make America anew, time and again. The product of our making is—in the stirring words of John McCain—this "big, boisterous, brawling, intemperate, striving, daring, beautiful, bountiful, brave, magnificent country."[81]

Today, we are called on to remake American democracy once more. The energy for the movement is out there, vibrating in a citizenry fed up with the status quo. Today, we often see scattered, impulsive reactions to problems rather than a unified movement with a targeted strategy. This approach must change. We must direct this energy toward addressing the root cause of the problem—a political system festering with unhealthy competition. The first priority is Final-Five Voting—to change how we vote and thus alter the nature of competition.

It's often said that we do not have an American government by the majority but have government by the majority *who participate*. Traditionally, most of us have thought we should participate by voting. Some of us have gone a step further by contributing to candidates. And a still smaller fraction became vocal advocates of particular candidates or policies. But it turns out that none of that is enough. We must also participate in the design of the rules of the game itself.

Today, our shared challenge is to reform our political system to restore healthy competition in the public interest. We cannot retreat into our partisan corners or exit the political arena altogether. We must fight for our democracy. As we have seen, this fight requires concerted effort across multiple constituencies.

Time to invest.

Conclusion

Invest in Political Innovation

We started this book by describing some key distinctions, first and foremost that the political-industrial complex is a private industry within a public institution. Such a distinction reveals the root causes of the situation in which we find ourselves—no longer confident in the "shining city on a hill." No longer believing the American dream is possible for all. No longer certain the great American experiment will endure.

And yet, we are still in love. In love with America. With being American. With our fellow Americans. With the idea of America. With the possibility of America—imperfect yet striving.

What do we do with this love of our breaking country? We put it to work.

We start with elections-machinery innovations. Pass legislation for Final-Five Voting in every state in the country. This action will again make our federal elected officials accountable to us and restore the connection between getting results in the public interest and getting reelected. Next, we must reinvent from scratch a healthy, nonpartisan congressional legislative system—a model, modern legislature—that advances compromise and problem solving. Together, these political innovations will return healthy competition and compromise to politics, realign our system with democratic principles, and unlock the critical outcomes we all desperately need. I like to call it "free-market politics."

But there's another distinction to make before we conclude (and call you to action). Although the American politics industry as currently engineered is a problem for most Americans, nearly every citizen lacks the personal agency to fix it—at least at the outset. To have agency is to have the ability and the access to change the structures that surround you. Social scientists have long argued about which is the chicken and which is the egg—does agency dictate structure, or structure dictate agency? But putting this question aside, we know that decades of democratic, economic, and social decline have widened not only America's wealth gaps and opportunity gaps, but also our *agency* gaps.

Many Americans live hard-fought lives. Rare are the citizens able to risk their livelihoods by deploying their agency to challenge the institutionalized structures towering around them. And for those with enough nerve, tickets to the arenas in which agency and action can actually be converted to tangible change are now the most prohibitively expensive in town.

But maybe not for you.

In hearing from the followers of our work, Michael and I have a sense of who you are, dear readers. Whatever your career trajectories, be they business or technology or philanthropy or even politics, you probably have at your fingertips actionable levels of agency *and* access—some combination of time, expertise, resources, or network, through which you already influence the world around you. More than likely, your active investments of agency are predicated on some expectation of a return: an increased graduation rate, a decreased carbon footprint, a modern regulation implemented, or an outdated one retired—something tangible that validates your commitment.

Historically, most people have not viewed politics as an attractive investment. Those who do view it this way often invest in the people and parties of the entrenched duopoly (or, to a much lesser degree and symbolically, in the spoilers and independents stuck in political purgatory). Some investors play the game and see their investments materialize into "wins"—you get your tax cuts, or your judges, or your new social programs. Other investors in politics commit a portion of their agency to good-government reform efforts, many of which we support, at least in principle.

But as this book makes clear, many of these popular good-government reforms are either not powerful enough, not achievable, or both. And such policy "wins" should be at best cold comfort, because in the aggregate, we're all losing.

You have a choice to make. You can continue applying your agency elsewhere, indirectly perpetuating the political-industrial complex that undermines the very causes you are prioritizing separately (and nobly, to be sure). Or you can redirect your agency to further catalyze a twenty-first-century wave of political innovation to break partisan gridlock and save our democracy; in which case you're advancing *every* cause. Without a sea change, our political system will continue to do more harm to education, the environment, the economy—you name it. A transformation of the politics industry can do more than we can do on our own to help those sacred corners of America.

"From those to whom much is given, much is expected," my father started telling me when I was a young girl in Wisconsin watching him a build the company that I would someday run. For so many Americans, barely enough opportunity is given. Barely enough to foster neighborhoods and families. Barely enough to lead this fight. For most Americans, the consequences of our runaway, behemoth political system are faits accomplis. The livelihoods and futures of the moms and dads and sons and daughters and friends and coworkers who make up the great, multicolored fabric of America are the only justification for the years we have put into this work. But asking them to redirect their limited personal agency to catalyze political innovation is as unfair as it is impractical.

It is *your* agency we hope to redirect.

When I first redirected mine, people would ask me about my plans. After describing for them the contours of my political-innovation agenda, I'd often get a similar tongue-in-cheek response: "Good luck with that." And it was easy to laugh along with them; the water of resigned acceptance is warm for those of us with means.

But this work is deadly serious, generations-of-socioeconomic-failure serious, national-security serious, global-trajectory serious. If talking about and fighting for political innovation is too risky, I'm sure our soldiers overseas, our teachers and firefighters and single moms with two jobs who are the backbone of every city in America might have something to say to me about risk—not to mention suffering critics.

So would Teddy Roosevelt, after whom I named my son, who slept newborn on my lap for weeks as I typed the last words of our first report on politics in the summer of 2017: "It is not the critic who counts; not the man who points out how the strong man stumbles, or where the doer of deeds could have done them better. The credit belongs to the man who is actually in the arena, whose face is marred by dust and sweat and blood . . . who spends himself in a worthy cause; who at the best knows in the end the triumph of high achievement, and who at the worst, if he fails, at least fails while daring greatly, so that his place shall never be with those cold and timid souls who neither know victory nor defeat."

I am calling on you to answer a simple question: will the dysfunctional politics industry continue to determine the health, prosperity, and security of America, or will you? If the answer is *you*—and I hope, almost desperately, that it is—consider how best to enter the arena and invest your agency in political innovation.

How to Invest: Evangelize, Join, Found—and Fund

Investing in political innovation begins by *evangelizing* its benefits. It grows to *joining* innovation campaigns in your state. If no effort is under way, you can take the critical step in *founding* one yourself.

Evangelize

This book drops a stone in the political waters. For the message to ripple, you need to drop one, too—especially around the powerful individuals to whom you have access. If you know your governor, hand this book to her. If you know the editor of your local newspaper, submit an op-ed in support of Final-Five Voting. If you donate to candidates, tell them the money stops unless they fight for political innovation.

Many people are disgusted by politics but wrongly think they can't do anything about it. You need to tell them there's a solution. Whenever politics comes up in conversation—which happens more and more as the crisis worsens—speak up and say that it doesn't have to be this way, that the dysfunction has been engineered, and that we have the power to design a new system that delivers better outcomes. Talk, tweet, email, repeat. Visit www.political-innovation.org, and share anything and everything we provide, from articles to podcasts to videos.

You must not be muted by the fear of being politically correct. Perversely, political correctness now protects *against* political conversation itself. Remember that the aversion to political discussion is based on the polarization the political-industrial complex creates.

Your words are antidotes. And your evangelism will have more impact than any book could ever have on its own.

Consider this: if you had a close friend or family member in a terrible situation, and you became aware of a solution, you would stop at nothing to deliver it for them. Our democracy demands the same passion. It's time to talk politics again at family gatherings, business events, cocktail parties—everywhere, really. I have a 100 percent success rate (almost) with every airplane seat neighbor in the last year. Don't let a captive audience pass you by.

Join

If you live in one of the twenty-four states in which direct democracy is an option, you can throw your support behind nonpartisan ballot measures to adopt top-five primaries and ranked-choice voting in general elections as soon as the next election cycle. If you live in one of the other twenty-four states, you can organize a coalition and lobbying effort using collective citizen power to demand that officials pass these reforms legislatively.

You will not be alone. After years of important work that many of us have known little about, a political-innovation industry has formed and continues to grow. On our website, you can find a resource guide detailing the array of incredible organizations working nonstop across the country to implement these innovations. Michael and I are associated with several of them, including Unite America, Leadership Now, Business for America, and Democracy Found. Many of the larger groups have state chapters, so innovators are likely to already be at work in your community. This nascent political-innovation industry is remarkably fluid, with new organizations and new campaigns popping up all the time. To keep up to date with the latest developments, to identify organizations that work in your state, to find ways to get involved, and for a robust and evolving FAQ, visit us at www.political-innovation.org.

Found

If your state does not have an active campaign for Final-Five Voting—which is likely because we're at the early stages here—create one yourself. As we discussed earlier, every campaign must start with a group of dedicated local leaders. You can be that local leader. As a motivated citizen, you are more powerful than the political-industrial complex would lead you to believe. Many of the national reform organizations, such as Open Primaries, FairVote, and RepresentUs are happy to provide support to startup efforts. An increasing number of individuals and organizations, such as the Unite America Fund (on whose board I sit) and the Arnold Foundation, are actively looking for political-innovation campaigns in which to invest. Just remember the words of Margaret Mead: "Never doubt that a small group of thoughtful, committed citizens can change the world; indeed, it's the only thing that ever has." Connect with us at www.political-innovation.org and we can help you get started.

Fund

America has a great philanthropic tradition. Since Warren Buffett and Bill and Melinda Gates created the Giving Pledge, hundreds of the world's wealthiest individuals have pledged to donate at least half of their wealth to charitable causes, adding up to hundreds of billions of dollars. And that's just the tip of the iceberg. Annual charitable donations from all Americans reached $410 billion in 2017—and that doesn't count the time and energy Americans volunteered to countless causes tackling a wide array of social challenges. But as substantial and heartwarming as philanthropy is, it's a pittance compared with federal and state government spending. Together they spent nearly the same amount—roughly $405 billion—every four weeks during the 2017 fiscal year.[1] Philanthropy is no substitute for effective government.

Melinda Gates, who runs the largest charitable foundation in the world, has experienced this firsthand. "One of the first lessons we learned when we started our foundation," she said, "was a humbling one: Our resources are only a drop in the bucket compared with the needs around the world, and only a small percentage of what governments spend each year to help meet those needs."[2] Just how small of a percentage? To put this into perspective, the Bill & Melinda Gates Foundation has an endowment of over $50 billion. This seems like a lot of money, but as Bill Gates notes, "California spends more than our entire endowment just to run its public-school system for one year."[3]

Today, our political system is the single greatest impediment to achieving economic and social progress in America. As problems mount and we fall further into division and crisis, we can't rely on the same old approaches. We need a new kind of philanthropy—*political philanthropy*. Political philanthropy offers the greatest potential return on investment available today. The reason is simple: huge leverage.

Any good hedge-fund manager will tell you that leverage is a force multiplier. Rather than breaking our backs trying to solve all of society's problems with private donations alone, we need to leverage our limited resources by using political philanthropy to unlock better government outcomes. As David Crane, cofounder of Govern for California, argues, improving government operations, policy choices, and policy implementation would make spending far more effective. These improvements would have a major impact on the country's progress in health care, public education, antipoverty efforts, and countless other areas that make a real difference in citizens' lives.[4] Now is the time for concerned donors to redirect a portion of their philanthropic resources to the cause of revitalizing our democracy.

Now is *also* the time for business leaders to stand up and be counted in this cause.

The irony is that just as businesses feel the negative effects of declining US competitiveness, the public often blames business for this decline. But let's not let business off too easily. Many in business have contributed to the national decline by playing both sides of this partisan game.

But here's the thing: a functioning, healthy democracy is a public resource greater in its value than our infrastructure, education system, or the environment, because each of these critical dimensions of the American experience rise and fall with the trajectory of our politics. Businesses and business leaders are uniquely positioned to grapple with this critical relationship and help protect this sickly public resource.

Who better than business to evangelize for innovation? Who better to understand the power of healthy competition—and the perils of the inverse—and convert that expertise into agency? Who better to vouch for the value of organizational practices designed to support problem solving and accountability?

Business leaders who may have believed, before reading this book, that the most they could hope for from Washington, D.C., was a favorable line item in the omnibus bill, might now have a different view. We hope they now know that they can play another role—a more inspiring and transformational role of founding, leading, and funding campaigns for political innovation.

The best news is that by publicly and energetically supporting the structural political innovations proposed in this book, and by joining the burgeoning coalition for corporate civic responsibility—a movement for new standards and best practices that we are also encouraging—business leaders can simultaneously help fix our broken politics for the good of all citizens, improve the overall business environment, and confront the popular consensus that business-owned special interests are the root cause of our problems.

It is time for a new role for American business, one that moves away from single bottom-line thinking and toward a more holistic balance sheet that includes the health of our great nation, writ large.

And business leaders and political philanthropists need not limit themselves to their own states' efforts. As discussed earlier, the benefits of Final-Five Voting will materialize long before it is implemented in all fifty states. It only takes a handful of states restoring healthy competition to create a fulcrum of congressional problem solvers who can shift the outcomes our political system produces. Political philanthropists can add their resources to the national fund at Unite America or look elsewhere across the country for the most promising political-innovation campaigns, and join the local residents to fund them. As they say, put your money where the movement is.

Everybody asks me what it's going to take. It is an important question. I believe that political philanthropy—a "special interest for the general interest"—offers the absolute best potential return on investment of any philanthropic investment out there today, in part because the dollars actually aren't prohibitive.[5]

Let's scale the investment. The cost to deliver Final-Five Voting runs anywhere from approximately $5 million for legislative action in a small state to $20 to $25 million for a ballot initiative in larger state like California. An aggressive average of $15 million across twenty states gives us $300 million. This $300 million is less than five percent of the billions spent in the 2016 federal elections. And $300 million to spread Final-Five Voting is far more likely to sustainably impact the effectiveness of $4 trillion of total government spending and transform the trajectory of our democracy. That's powerful and achievable. If you're interested in becoming a political-innovation philanthropist, let me know at katherine@katherinegehl.com.

. . .

I am so excited for the future. Our laboratories of democracy will prove these ideas right—or prove what needs to change to make them right. And we will create the system changes needed to help our government achieve the results that we Americans deserve. My enthusiasm for the future aside, I can't help but reflect on another period of critical American innovation in our past.

In the summer of 1787, dozens of delegates gathered in a hall in Philadelphia, where just a decade earlier many of them had declared our nation's independence. Although the location was the same, the mood was different. America, having only a decade prior accomplished the impossible and triumphed over Britain, was now on the brink of disintegration.

Our federal government was broke, and there was no process for raising the money needed to pay off the debts that had been accumulated to finance the war. The states faced similar crises. Some tried issuing new money and inflating away their liabilities, but that ended up creating chaos instead of prosperity. Other states increased taxes and were met with armed insurrections. As problems mounted, more and more states raised the drawbridges and blocked trade with their neighbors. Protectionism within America only deepened the depression, which was even worse than the Great Depression it preceded. Whether the young nation would survive was an open question.

The delegates to the Constitutional Convention knew that the problems lay in the design of the political system. The Articles of Confederation, hastily drafted in the midst of the Revolutionary War, were failing to keep the colonies together, let alone move the new nation forward. For four months in a sweltering Philadelphia summer, the Framers debated, fought, and compromised.

As the final draft of our Constitution was signed that September, Benjamin Franklin, the convention's oldest delegate, gazed on the engraving of the sun on the back of the arm chair where George Washington had sat. Franklin remarked, "I have . . . often looked at that behind the president without being able to tell whether it was rising or setting. But now at length I have the happiness to know it is a rising and not a setting sun."[6]

Franklin knew, though, that unlike the morning sun, America's continued rise was no sure thing. After the ceremonies ended, Franklin, crippled by gout, limped out of Independence Hall, where a crowd of onlookers had assembled to get a first glimpse of their new Constitution, which had been written under a veil of secrecy. A woman asked, "Well, Doctor, what have we got—a republic or a monarchy?" Slow on his feet but quick with his wit, Franklin replied, "A republic—if you can keep it."[7]

Can we? That is the challenge of our time.

Together, we must meet it. Michael and I are all in.

Are you?

—Katherine Gehl

Notes

Authors' Note

1. "158 Million Americans Told to Stay Home, but Trump Pledges to Keep It Short," The Coronavirus Outbreak, *New York Times*, March 23, 2020, https://www.nytimes.com/2020/03/23/world/coronavirus-news.html.

2. Josh Mitchell and Josh Zumbrun, "Coronavirus-Triggered Downturn Could Cost Five Million U.S. Jobs," *Wall Street Journal*, March 21, 2020, https://www.wsj.com/articles/coronavirus-triggered-downturn-could-cost-5-million-u-s-jobs-11584783001.

Preface

1. Appreciation to Greg Orman for the idea of learned helplessness.

Introduction

1. David Foster Wallace, "This Is Water," commencement address at Kenyon College, Gambier, OH, May 21, 2005, audio and transcript available on *Farnam Street*, https://fs.blog/2012/04/david-foster-wallace-this-is-water.

2. The numbers are based on author analysis of data from 2019 Social Progress Index, https://www.socialprogress.org/assets/downloads/resources/2019/2019-Social-Progress-Index-executive-summary-v2.0.pdf.

3. Mickey Edwards, *The Parties Versus the People: How to Turn Republicans and Democrats into Americans* (New Haven: Yale University Press, 2012).

4. Use of the term "political-industrial complex" in US contexts appears in several prior works. See, for example, Gerald Sussman, *Global Electioneering: Campaign Consulting, Communications, and Corporate Financing* (Lanham, MD: Rowman & Littlefield Publishers, 2005); Gerald Sussman and Lawrence Galizio, "The Global Reproduction of American Politics," *Political Communication* 20, no. 3 (July 2003): 309–328; and "Political-Industrial Complex," *Wall Street Journal*, March 28, 1990, A14.

5. Robert Boatright traces the origins of the use of "to primary" to the rise of groups like the Club for Growth on the right and MoveOn.Org on the left in the mid-2000s, writing that: "During the 2004 and 2006 elections, a new word entered the American political lexicon: the verb 'to primary,' meaning to mount a primary campaign against an incumbent member of Congress . . . these incumbents were (often) criticized for being insufficiently partisan." See Robert G. Boatright, *Getting Primaried: The Changing Politics of Congressional Primary Challenges* (Ann Arbor, MI: University of Michigan Press, 2013).

6. In accordance with the emergence of the verb "to primary" in 2004, since then, ideological challenges have become increasingly common, reaching an apex of twenty-five in the 2014 election. In the six election cycles of the past decade (2006–2016), there were more ideological primary challenges (seventy-eight) than in the previous eighteen elections of the preceding three and a half decades (sixty-nine). As with other types of primary challenges, ideological challenges are rarely successful. Even among the "significant" ideological challenges (i.e., those primaries in which the incumbent received less than 75 percent of the vote), the challenger still only defeated the incumbent in 8 percent of races in the House of Representatives, for a total of twelve successful ideological primary challenges since 1970. Thus, while stories such as Eric Cantor's

defeat in the 2014 Republican primary capture national headlines, they are exceptional. However, looking at the time series of these successful challenges is revealing. Nine of the twelve successful challenges have taken place since 2006, showing that while successful ideological challenges are still rare, they are becoming more common and likely force incumbents to "outflank" their challengers on ideology. Almost all of this increase in primary challenges has come from the Republican Party. Data provided by Robert Boatright, analysis extended from "The 2014 Congressional Primaries in Context" to include the 2016 cycle ("The 2014 Congressional Primaries in Context," paper presented September 30, 2014, http://www.cfinst.org/pdf/papers /Boatright_2014_Primaries_in_Context_9-30-14.pdf).

7. Samuel F. Toth, "The Political Duopoly: Antitrust Applicability to Political Parties and the Commission on Presidential Debates," *Case Western Reserve Law Review* 64, no. 1 (2013).

8. For a more detailed explanation of the concept of industry structure, see Michael E. Porter, *Competitive Strategy: Techniques for Analyzing Industries and Competitors* (New York: Free Press, 1980). See also Michael E. Porter, "The Five Competitive Forces That Shape Strategy," *Harvard Business Review,* January 2008.

9. This phrase, "more choice, more voice, better results" builds on the "more choice, more voice" slogan created by Maine's successful campaign for ranked-choice voting. https://www .morevoice.org/.

10. As brilliantly described by Yascha Mounk in *The People vs. Democracy: Why Our Freedom Is in Danger and How to Save It* (Cambridge, MA: Harvard University Press, 2018).

Chapter 1

1. "Washington's Farewell Address 1796," The Avalon Project, September 19, 1796, http:// avalon.law.yale.edu/18th_century/washing.asp.

2. "Founders Online: From Thomas Jefferson to Francis Hopkinson, 13 March 1789," National Archives and Records Administration, March 13, 1789, https://founders.archives.gov/ documents/Jefferson/01-14-02-0402.

3. For a discussion on the importance of strong parties and democracy, see John H. Aldrich, *Why Parties?: A Second Look* (Chicago: University of Chicago Press, 2011); Frances McCall Rosenbluth and Ian Shapiro, *Responsible Parties: Saving Democracy from Itself* (New Haven: Yale University Press, 2018).

4. The early twentieth-century economist Joseph Schumpeter is often credited with first recognizing this analogy, relating parties to firms, voters to customers, votes to currency, and policies to products. See Joseph Schumpeter, *Capitalism, Socialism, and Democracy* (New York, Harper and Brothers, 1942). For good recent summaries, see Ian Shapiro, *The State of Democratic Theory* (Princeton, Princeton University Press, 2003), 50–77; Jeffrey Edward Green, *The Eyes of the People: Democracy in an Age of Spectatorship* (New York; Oxford: Oxford University Press, 2010), 171–177.

5. Katherine M. Gehl and Michael E. Porter, "Why Competition in the Politics Industry Is Failing America: A Strategy for Reinvigorating Our Democracy," Harvard Business School, September 2017, www.hbs.edu/competitiveness/research/Pages/research-details. aspx?rid=84.

6. We're not suggesting bribery. To "pay" is not used literally.

7. Voters whose views are either "consistently conservative" or "consistently liberal" are significantly more likely to vote in primaries than those who are "mostly liberal," "mixed," or "mostly conservative." Primary voters are not only more ideological, but often "very interested in politics." For ideology/partisanship of primary voters as compared to average voters, see, e.g., Pew Research Center, "Political Polarization in the American Public," June 10, 2014, accessed August 2017, http://assets.pewresearch.org/wp-content/uploads/sites/5/2014/06/6-12-2014-Political-Polarization-Release.pdf; Seth J. Hill, "Institution of Nomination and the Policy Ideology of Primary Electorates," *Quarterly Journal of Political Science* 10, no. 4 (2015): 461–487; as well as Gary C. Jacobson, "The Electoral Origins of Polarized Politics: Evidence From the 2010 Cooperative Congressional Election Study," *American Behavioral Scientist* 56, no. 12 (2012): 1612–1630. For engagement with politics, see John Sides, Chris Tausanovitch, Lynn Vavreck, and Christopher Warshaw, "On the Representativeness of Primary Electorates," working paper,

June 2016, http://cwarshaw.scripts.mit.edu/papers/primaries_160617.pdf. We note, however, that Sides et al. find only slight differences between the ideologies of primary and average voters.

8. Author analysis of data from Cook Political Report, "2016 House Election Results by Race Rating," November 8, 2016, http://cookpolitical.com/house/charts/race-ratings/10168; Inside Elections with Nathan L. Gonzales, "House Ratings," November 3, 2016, https://insideelections .com/ratings/house/2016-house-ratings-november-3-2016; and Daily Kos, "Election Outlook: 2016 Race Ratings," http://www.dailykos.com/pages/election-outlook/2016-raceratings#house, accessed March 2017. Estimates for Senate races were not consistent, and the average of the three estimates was used.

9. Data from Michael P. McDonald, "2016 and 2008 Presidential Nomination Contest Turnout Rates," United States Elections Project, accessed March 2017, http://www.electproject.org/2016P and http://www.electproject.org/2008p.

10. Rules governing closed primaries vary greatly between states. They take three basic forms: (1) Closed primaries limit voting only to registered party members, and voters must declare their party affiliation in advance, before arriving at the polling place. (2) Semi-closed primaries vary in how they treat unaffiliated voters. For example, some states allow the party to choose if nonmembers can vote; other states consider voting in a primary as a form of party registration. (3) In a caucus system, the state or political party arranges a meeting where participants vote by openly showing support for a candidate (for example, by raising hands or clustering into groups). Caucuses can be open or closed. According to FairVote, as of May 2016, Republicans held closed or semi-closed presidential primaries or caucuses in twenty-nine states, compared with twenty-six states for Democrats. For congressional races, Republicans and Democrats held twenty-six closed or semi-closed primaries. See "Closed Primary," Annenberg Classroom, accessed March 2017, http://www.annenbergclassroom.org/term/closed-primary; National Conference of State Legislatures, "State Primary Election Types," July 21, 2016, http://www.ncsl.org/research/ elections-andcampaigns/primary-types.aspx; D'Angelo Gore, "Caucus vs. Primary," FactCheck .org, April 8, 2008, http://www.factcheck.org/2008/04/caucus-vs-primary/. For data on primary type by state, see "Presidential Primary or Caucus Type by State," FairVote, accessed March 2017, http://www.fairvote.org/primaries#presidential_primary_or_caucus_type_by_state.

11. Author analysis based on data from "Health," Center for Responsive Politics, accessed March 2017, https://www.opensecrets.org/industries/indus.php?cycle=2016&ind=H.

12. For an overview of rules related to these groups, see "Dark Money Basics," Center for Responsive Politics, accessed August 2017, https://www.opensecrets.org/dark-money/basics.

13. Data from "Revolving Door: Former Members of the 114th Congress," The Center for Responsive Politics, accessed December 7, 2017, https://www.opensecrets.org/revolving/ departing.php?cong=114.

14. Lee Drutman and Alexander Furnas constructed a data set of contract lobbyists (i.e., lobbyists who are not internal to one particular company). In 2012, 44 percent of active contract lobbyists were former government officials. This is up from 17.8 percent in 1998. See Lee Drutman and Alexander Furnas, "How Revolving Door Lobbyists Are Taking Over K Street," *Sunlight Foundation*, January 22, 2014, https://sunlightfoundation.com/2014/01/22/revolving-door-lobbyists-take-over-k-street/. The presence of revolvers, however, may be slightly overstated in these figures. Herschel and LaPira (2017) find that revolvers are much more likely to register than non-revolvers. See Thomas Herschel and Timothy LaPira, "How Many Lobbyists Are in Washington? Shadow Lobbying and the Gray Market for Policy Advocacy," *Interest Groups & Advocacy* 6, no. 3 (2017): 199–214, doi: 10.1057/s41309-017-0024-y. These former government officials have a major impact on the success of lobbying. Baumgartner et al. (2009) finds that hiring "covered officials" (i.e., high-ranking government officials) as lobbyists is the only extra-governmental variable that systematically predicts lobbying success. See Frank Baumgartner et al., *Lobbying and Policy Change: Who Wins, Who Loses, and Why* (Chicago: University of Chicago Press, 2009). Lazarus and McKay (2012) similarly find that universities that hire former government officials as lobbyists are more likely to get earmarks than those that do not: "Having one or more revolvers lobbying on a school's behalf increases the predicted probability of receiving an earmarks by nearly 30 percent in 2002 and almost 35 percent in 2003." See Jeffrey Lazarus and Amy Melissa McKay, "Consequences of the Revolving Door: Evaluating the

Lobbying Success of Former Congressional Members and Staff" (paper presented at the Midwest Political Science Association Annual Meeting, Chicago, April 2012), doi: 10.2139/ssrn.2141416. For this reason, Blanes i Vidal et al. (2012) and Bertrand et al. (2011) find that revolving door lobbyists earn more than other lobbyists. See Jordi Blanes i Vidal, Mirko Draca, and Christian Fons-Rosen, "Revolving Door Lobbyists," *American Economic Review* 102, no. 7 (2012): 3731–3748, doi: 10.1257/ aer.102.7.3731; Marianne Bertrand, Matilde Bombardini, and Francesco Trebbi, "Is It Whom You Know or What You Know? An Empirical Assessment of the Lobbying Process" (NBER working paper 16765, 2011).

15. Martin Gilens and Benjamin I. Page, "Testing Theories of American Politics: Elites, Interest Groups, and Average Citizens," *Perspectives on Politics* 12, no. 3 (September 2014), 564–581.

16. Nickerson and Rogers (2014) explain how campaign data analytics can yield key competitive advantages. They note that "campaign data analysts . . . develop predictive models that produce individual-level scores that predict citizens' likelihoods of performing certain political behaviors, supporting candidates and issues, and responding to targeted interventions. The use of these scores has increased dramatically during the last few election cycles." Further, they found that campaigns "use these [predictive] scores to target nearly every aspect of campaign outreach: door-to-door canvassing; direct mail; phone calls; email; television ad placement; social media outreach (like Facebook and Twitter); and even web page display." The authors' model shows that targeting persuasive communications at voters with a responsiveness score in the top quintile produces three times as many votes as would untargeted efforts. See David W. Nickerson and Todd Rogers, "Political Campaigns and Big Data," *Journal of Economic Perspectives* 28, no. 2 (Spring 2014), 51–74.

17. For example, Comcast notes in its Form 10-K, "Advertising revenue [for its Cable Communications segment] increased 9.6 percent in 2016 primarily due to an increase in political advertising revenue. In 2015, advertising revenue had decreased 3.8 percent over the previous year, primarily due to a decrease in political advertising revenue." See Comcast Corporation, December 31, 2016 Form 10-K (filed February 3, 2017).

18. For a discussion of connections between a polarizing electorate and the increasing influence of partisan news media, see Gary C. Jacobson, "Partisan Media and Electoral Polarization in 2012: Evidence from the American National Election Study," in *American Gridlock: The Sources, Character, and Impact of Political Polarization*, edited by James A. Thurber and Antoine Yoshinaka (New York; Cambridge: Cambridge University Press, 2015), 259–286. For an opposite perspective that argues that the polarization of the media is more of a symptom than a cause of our political problems, see Kevin Arceneaux and Martin Johnson, "More a Symptom Than a Cause: Polarization and Partisan News Media in America," in *American Gridlock*, Cambridge University Press (2015).

19. Thomas Jefferson to Edward Carrington, January 16, 1787, in *The Works of Thomas Jefferson*, vol. 5, *Correspondence 1786-1789*, ed. Paul Leicester Ford (New York and London: G. Putnam's Sons, 1904–1905), http://oll-resources.s3.amazonaws.com/titles/802/ Jefferson_0054-05_EBk_v6.0.pdf.

20. Author Miller, *(London) Observer*, November 26, 1961.

21. See Adam Sheingate, *Building a Business of Politics: The Rise of Political Consulting and the Transformation of American Democracy* (New York; Oxford: Oxford University Press, 2016).

22. David Dodson, a former CEO, experienced the duopoly's power over suppliers firsthand when he challenged Senator John Barroso in the Republican Senate Primary in Wyoming in 2018: "When I tried to hire the law firm to which I'd directed millions of dollars in business while I was a chief executive, it turned me away, explaining that it could work only for Democrats. When I contacted a law firm known to serve Republicans, that firm told me it couldn't work for a candidate running against an incumbent because it would put its entire practice at risk. As I tried to build an organization to run a credible primary challenge, this story repeated itself, whether I was recruiting campaign staff or a marketing firm." See David Dodson, "Why Do We Let Political Parties Act Like Monopolies?" *New York Times*, May 20, 2019, https://www.nytimes .com/2019/05/20/opinion/primary-challengers.html.

23. Jonathon Martin, "Republican Campaign Committee Pushes Back Against Conservative Group," New York Times Blog, *New York Times*, November 1, 2013, https://thecaucus.blogs .nytimes.com/2013/11/01/republican-campaign-committee-pushes-back-against-conservative-group/.

24. Laura Barron-Lopez, Zach Montellaro, Ben White, and David Brown, "New DCCC Chair Bustos Vows to Stay on Offense in 2020," *Politico*, January 6, 2019, https://www.politico.com/ story/2019/01/06/dccc-chair-cheri-bustos-2020-1058174.

25. Number of think tanks from James G. McGann, "2015 Global Go To Think Tank Index Report," February 9, 2016, http://repository.upenn.edu/cgi/viewcontent .cgi?article=1009&context=think_tanks. Budget estimate based on author analysis using the most recent revenue data available for US think tanks identified in table 7 in McGann. Revenue data are available for just sixty-four of the think tanks from McGann's list, totaling more than $2 billion. Revenue data from Guidestar and annual reports.

26. Tevi Troy, "Devaluing the Think Tank," *National Affairs*, Winter 2012, http://www .nationalaffairs.com/publications/detail/devaluing-the-think-tank.

27. For a list of leading US think tanks, see James G. McGann, "2015 Global Go To Think Tank Index Report," February 9, 2016, http://repository.upenn.edu/cgi/viewcontent .cgi?article=1009&context=think_tanks. Political orientation is identified through consultation of multiple sources, including James G. McGann, *Think Tanks and Policy Advice in the United States* (Abingdon, UK: Routledge, 2007); Michael Dolny, "FAIR Study: Think Tank Spectrum 2012," July 1, 2013, http://fair.org/extra/fair%E2%80%88study-think-tank-spectrum-2012/; and InsideGov, "Research Think Tanks," accessed March 2017, http://think-tanks.insidegov.com/.

28. Author analysis, data from Brookings Institution, "Vital Statistics on Congress," https:// www.brookings.edu/multi-chapter-report/vital-statistics-on-congress/.

29. Lee Drutman and Steven Teles, "Why Congress Relies on Lobbyists Instead of Thinking for Itself," *Atlantic*, March 10, 2015, https://www.theatlantic.com/politics/ archive/2015/03/when-congress-cant-think-for-itself-it-turns-to-lobbyists/387295/.

30. "Lobbying Data Summary," Center for Responsive Politics, accessed July 2017, https:// www.opensecrets.org/lobby/.

31. Ezra Klein, "Corporations Now Spend More Lobbying Congress Than Taxpayers Spend Funding Congress," Vox, updated July 15, 2015, https://www.vox.com/2015/4/20/8455235/ congress-lobbying-money-statistic.

32. Direct spending in the political industrial complex does not capture to the full extent the economic influence that politics has on other industries. Researchers have identified several types of "returns" associated with lobbying activity, such as federal tax savings, the enactment of more favorable regulations, delayed fraud detection for corporations, and the allotment of increased federal resources. We group such findings into six broad categories in the list below. While the list is not exhaustive, these studies collectively provide compelling evidence that lobbying is a financially effective mechanism to influence public policy.

1. Lobbying and Tax Savings from the American Jobs Creation Act
   A. Raquel Alexander, Stephen W. Mazza, and Susan Scholz, "Measuring Rates of Return on Lobbying Expenditures: An Empirical Case Study of Tax Breaks for Multinational Corporations," *Journal of Law and Politics* (2009).
   B. Hui Chen, Katherine Gunny, and Karthik Ramanna, "Return on Political Investment in the American Jobs Creation Act of 2004," working paper 15-050, Harvard Business School, December 2014.
2. Lobbying and Trade Policy
   A. Seung-Hyun Lee and Yoon-Suk Baik, "Corporate Lobbying in Antidumping Cases: Looking into the Continued Dumping and Subsidy Offset Act," *Journal of Business Ethics* 96, no. 3 (October 2010).
   B. Patricia Tovar, "Lobbying Costs and Trade Policy," *Journal of International Economics* 83 (2011).

C. Karam Kang, "Policy Influence and Private Returns from Lobbying in the Energy Sector," *Review of Economic Studies* 83 (2016).

3. Lobbying and Legal Leeway (Fraud Detection, SEC Enforcement)

A. Frank Yu and Xiaoyun Yu, "Corporate Lobbying and Fraud Detection," *Journal of Financial and Quantitative Analysis* 46, no. 6 (2011).

B. Maria M. Correia, "Political Connections and SEC Enforcement," *Journal of Accounting and Economics* 57 (2014).

4. Lobbying and Troubled Asset Relief Program Support

A. Benjamin M. Blau, Tyler J. Brough, and Diana W. Thomas, "Corporate Lobbying, Political Connections, and the Bailout of Banks," *Journal of Banking & Finance* 37 (2013).

B. Ran Duchin and Denis Sosyura, "The Politics of Government Investment," *Journal of Financial Economics* 106 (2012).

5. Lobbying and the Public Sector (Education Institutions, Cities)

A. John M. de Figueiredo and Brian S. Silverman, "Academic Earmarks and Returns to Lobbying," *Journal of Law & Economics* 49, no. 2 (2006).

B. Rebecca Goldstein and Hye Young You, "Cities as Lobbyists," *American Journal of Political Science* (April 2017).

6. Lobbying and the Energy Sector

A. Karam Kang, "Policy Influence and Private Returns from Lobbying in the Energy Sector," *Review of Economic Studies* (2016).

33. Total is for 2017–2018 cycle and includes Advisory Opinion 2014-12 (which allows separate contribution limits for national convention committees). Methodology from R. Sam Garrett, "Increased Campaign Contribution Limits in the FY2015 Omnibus Appropriations Law: Frequently Asked Questions," Congressional Research Service, December 19, 2014, http://op.bna .com.s3.amazonaws.com/der.nsf/r%3FOpen%3Dsbay-9s6pa3. Updated contribution limits from "Contribution Limits for 2015–2016 Federal Elections," Federal Election Commission, accessed March 2017, http://www.fec.gov/info/contriblimitschart1516.pdf.

34. The most significant new party since 1860, the Progressive Party (also known as the Bull Moose Party) dates back to the period from 1912 to 1916. It was founded by Teddy Roosevelt so that he could run for president after he lost the 1912 Republican nomination. The party successfully elected thirteen Representatives, but it disintegrated when most of its members rejoined the Republican Party. The Reform Party, the most recent party that achieved any electoral success, grew out of Ross Perot's 1992 presidential candidacy in which he won 19 percent of the popular vote. The Reform Party lasted from 1992 to 2000, with its major success being the election of Jesse Ventura as governor of Minnesota in 1998. Today's most significant third parties, the Libertarians and the Greens, each run numerous candidates every year, but they have yet to win a single congressional or gubernatorial campaign. See "Bull Moose Party," Encyclopædia Britannica, July 12, 2015, https://www.britannica.com/topic/Bull-Moose-Party; "Progressive (Bull Moose) Party (1912)," in *Guide to U.S. Elections*, 6th ed., vol. 1 (Washington: CQ Press, 2010); Reform Party National Committee, "About," accessed March 2017, http://www.reformparty.org/ about/; CQ Voting and Elections Collection, "Third Party Results," CQ Press Electronic Library, accessed March 2017.

35. John Laloggia, "Six Facts About U.S. Political Independents," Pew Research Center, May 5, 2019, https://www.pewresearch.org/fact-tank/2019/05/15/facts-about-us-political-independents/.

36. Federal Election Commission, "Contribution Limits," accessed February 3, 2020, https:// www.fec.gov/help-candidates-and-committees/candidate-taking-receipts/contribution-limits/.

37. See, for example, Office of Commissioner Ann M. Ravel, "Dysfunction and Deadlock: The Enforcement Crisis at the Federal Election Commission Reveals the Unlikelihood of Draining the Swamp," Federal Election Commission, February 2017, https://www.fec.gov/resources/about-fec/commissioners/ravel/statements/ravelreport_feb2017.pdf.

38. Nicholas Confessore and Karen Yourish, "$2 Billion Worth of Free Media for Donald Trump," *New York Times*, March 15, 2016, https://www.nytimes.com/2016/03/16/upshot/ measuring-donald-trumps-mammoth-advantage-in-free-media.html.

39. Dwight D. Eisenhower, "Farewell Address, Delivered January 17, 1961," American Rhetoric, Top 100 Speeches, last updated February 18, 2017, https://americanrhetoric.com/speeches/dwightdeisenhowerfarewell.html.

40. For example, according to the Center for Responsive Politics, the total cost of elections during presidential cycles increased 60 percent from the 1999–2000 cycle to the 2015–2016 cycle, after adjusting for inflation. As noted by the Center for Responsive Politics, 2016 total cost projections include spending by PACs on overhead expenses, which are attributed to Congressional races. The total cost accounts for "all money spent by presidential candidates, Senate and House candidates, political parties, and independent interest groups trying to influence federal elections." "Cost of Election," The Center for Responsive Politics, https://www.opensecrets.org/overview/cost.php, accessed February 2017.

41. For methodology, see Katherine M. Gehl and Michael E. Porter, "Why Competition in the Politics Industry Is Failing America: A Strategy for Reinvigorating Our Democracy" (Boston: Harvard Business School, 2017): Appendix E.

42. These estimates are based on data from various sources. Federal election spending from the Federal Election Commission, https://beta.fec.gov/data/, accessed March 2017, as well as select data from Center for Responsive Politics, http://www.opensecrets.org/outsidespending/fes_summ.php, accessed March 2017. Lobbying data from Center for Responsive Politics, based on data from Senate Office of Public Records, https://www.opensecrets.org/lobby/, accessed March 2017. List of think tanks gathered from James G. McGann, "2015 Global Go To Think Tank Index Report," TTCSP Global Go To Think Tank Index Reports, February 9, 2016, table 7. To gather political orientation of think tanks, we referenced multiple sources: James G. McCann, *Think Tanks and Policy Advice in the United States* (Abingdon, UK: Routledge, 2007); FAIR Think Tank Spectrum Study 2012; and InsideGov.com. Revenue figures of think tanks from Guidestar/organization websites. Advertising revenue to the media from political shows based on author analysis of advertising revenue data provided by Kantar Media. To exclude political advertising from our list of political shows (to avoid double counting), we used data from Political TV Ad Archive, https://politicaladarchive.org/data/, accessed March 2017, and Erika Franklin Fowler, Travis N. Ridout, and Michael M. Franz, "Political Advertising in 2016: The Presidential Election as Outlier?" *Journal of Applied Research in Contemporary Politics*, February 22, 2017.

43. Estimate represents advertising revenue from political coverage on major television shows primarily covering politics. Based on author analysis of advertising revenue data provided by Kantar Media.

44. Total jobs reflects estimated number of registered lobbyists, employees of partisan/partisan-leaning think tanks, individuals earning at least $15,080 (annual earnings for a full-time federal minimum wage worker). "Major" consulting contracts defined as cumulative earnings of at least $50,000 in 2016. Lobbying jobs from Center for Responsive Politics, https://www.opensecrets.org/lobby/, accessed June 2017. Think tank jobs from Guidestar/annual reports. Campaign payrolls and consulting contracts from author analysis of Federal Election Commission data, https://www.fec.gov/data/disbursements, accessed July 2017. Registered lobbyists alone account for 11,170 jobs in 2016. See Center for Responsive Politics, Lobbying Database, https://www.opensecrets.org/lobby/, accessed August 2017.

45. For example, candidates for governor, legislature, and other state offices raised $2.2 billion in campaign contributions in 2018. If we add in all of the other channels of spending—lobbying, advertising, etc.—spending on state elections soars, demonstrating the magnitude of the politics industry. For details on state election spending, see Geoff Mulvihill, "AP: Political Money in State-Level Campaigns Exceeds $2B," AP NEWS, Associated Press, November 1, 2018, https://www.apnews.com/b3ead0614b664bd89fbe1c8c19c42131.

46. See, e.g., Tim LaPira, "How Much Lobbying Is There in Washington? It's Double What You Think," Sunlight Foundation, November 25, 2013, and Emma Baccellieri and Soo Rin Kim, "Boehner Joins the Not-Quite-a-Lobbyist Ranks," Center for Responsive Politics, September 21, 2016.

47. See Leadership Now Project, "Democracy Market Analysis 1.0: Highlights, April 2019," https://app.box.com/s/62p88nxqny80x3efgya079fgt6k92q3j.

48. Industry size determined by value added as a percentage of gross domestic product for "Government" [the combined value added from (a) federal and (b) state and local government] in 2016, versus nonaggregated Bureau of Economic Analysis industries. Data from Bureau of Economic Analysis, GDP-by-Industry data, accessed August 2017; author analysis. Federal outlays data (FY 2016) from Congressional Budget Office, "The Budget and Economic Outlook: 2017 to 2027," Budget Data, January 24, 2017, https://www.cbo.gov/publication/52370.

Chapter 2

1. Samuel F. Toth, *The Political Duopoly: Antitrust Applicability to Political Parties and the Commission on Presidential Debates*, 64 Case W. Res. L. Rev. 239 (2013), https://scholarlycommons .law.case.edu/cgi/viewcontent.cgi?article=1180&context=caselrev.

2. Brennan Center for Justice et al., "Deteriorating Democracy: How the Commission for Presidential Debates Undermines Democracy," August 2004, https://www.opendebates.org/pdfs/REPORT2.pdf.

3. A separate commission at the Harvard University Institute of Politics led by Newton Minow came to a similar conclusion, see the Commission on Presidential Debates, https://www .debates.org/about-cpd/overview/. Minow later became a vice chair for the commission.
See also Robert E. Hunter, *Electing the President: A Program for Reform* (Center for Strategic and International Studies, Georgetown University, 1986), https://www.fordlibrarymuseum.gov/library/document/0375/1682722repro.pdf.

4. Brennan Center for Justice et al., "Deteriorating Democracy."

5. Hunter, *Electing the President*.

6. Phil Gailey, "Democrats and Republicans Form Panel to Hold Presidential Debates," *New York Times*, February 19, 1987, https://www.nytimes.com/1987/02/19/us/democrats-and-republicans-form-panel-to-hold-presidential-debates.html?pagewanted=1.

7. Brennan Center for Justice et al., "Deteriorating Democracy."

8. Toth, *The Political Duopoly*," 249.

9. George Farah, *No Debate: How the Republican and Democratic Parties Secretly Control the Presidential Debate* (New York: Seven Stories Press, 2004).

10. Brennan Center for Justice et al., "Deteriorating Democracy."

11. "Opinion: Fixing the Presidential Debates," *New York Times*, September 18, 1996, https://www.nytimes.com/1996/09/18/opinion/fixing-the-presidential-debates.html.

12. "About the CPD," Commission on Presidential Debates, accessed November 2019, https://www.debates.org/about-cpd/.

13. Data presented as part of Level the Playing Field's lawsuit. "The crux of the petition's factual submissions consists of two reports that purport to show that CPD's 15 percent threshold is designed to result in the exclusion of independent or third-party candidates. The first report, by Dr. Clifford Young, concludes that in order to reach a 15 percent threshold, a candidate must achieve name recognition among 60–80 percent of the population. The second, by Douglas Schoen, estimates that the cost to a third-party or independent candidate of achieving 60 percent name recognition would be over $266 million, including almost $120 million for paid media content production and dissemination, which the report concludes is not a reasonably reachable figure for a non-major-party candidate. Additionally, both the Young and Schoen reports conclude that polling in three-way races is inherently unreliable and not, therefore, an objective measure of the viability of third-party and independent candidates. In reaching their conclusions, both the Young and Schoen reports assert that third-party and independent candidates are disadvantaged by the fact that they do not benefit from a 'party halo effect' by which Democratic and Republican candidates—regardless of name recognition—may garner a minimum vote share in polling merely for being associated with a major party, in addition to benefitting from increased name recognition from media coverage of the major party primary season." See https://www.gpo.gov/fdsys/pkg/FR-2017-03-29/pdf/2017-06150.pdf.

14. "Political Typology Reveals Deep Fissures on the Right and the Left," Pew Research Center, October 24, 2017, https://www.people-press.org/2017/10/24/1-partisanship-and-political-engagement/.

15. This illustrative example is provided by Mickey Edwards in "How to Turn Democrats and Republicans into Americans," in *Politics to the Extreme: American Political Institutions in the Twenty-First Century*, ed. Scott A. Frisch and Sean Q. Kelly (New York: Palgrave Macmillan, 2013) 219–226. See also Will Bunch, "The Backlash," *New York Times*, September 13, 2010, https://www.nytimes.com/2010/09/13/books/excerpt-backlash.html.

16. Jeff Zeleny, "G.O.P. Leaders Say Delaware Upset Damages Senate Hopes," *New York Times*, September 14, 2010, https://www.nytimes.com/2010/09/15/us/politics/15elect.html.

17. Ed Hornick, "Christine O'Donnell: From 'witchcraft' to Tea Party favorite," CNN, October 13, 2010, http://www.cnn.com/2010/POLITICS/10/13/christine.odonnell.profile/index.html.

18. "O'Donnell Winning Tea Party, Losing Delaware," Fairleigh Dickinson University's PublicMind, October 28, 2010, http://publicmind.fdu.edu/winsome/final.pdf.

19. Edwards, "How to Turn Democrats and Republicans into Americans," in *Politics to the Extreme*, 219–226.

20. Mickey H. Edwards, "The Case for Transcending Partisanship," *Daedalus* 142, no. 2 (2013): 84–94, https://www.amacad.org/publication/case-transcending-partisanship.

21. "Sore Loser Laws in the 50 States," Ballotpedia, accessed November 2019, https://ballotpedia.org/Sore_loser_laws_in_the_50_states.

22. This number is down slightly from forty-six after Washington (2004) and California (2011) adopted nonpartisan primaries. For details on the multiple forms of sore-loser laws and when states adopted them, see Barry C. Burden, Bradley M. Jones, and Michael S. Kang, "Sore Loser Laws and Congressional Polarization," *Legislative Studies Quarterly* 39, no. 3 (August 2014): 299–325. Contrary to Burden et al. (2014), we do not categorize a nonpartisan primary as a form of sore-loser law.

23. See Troy K. Schneider, "Can't Win for Losing," *New York Times*, July 16, 2006, http://www.nytimes.com/2006/07/16/opinion/nyregionopinions/16CTschneider.html?mcubz=0.

24. "The Worst Ballot Access Laws in the United States," FairVote, January 13, 2015, https://www.fairvote.org/the-worst-ballot-access-laws-in-the-united-states.

25. Cantor was hardly a compromise-oriented politician. But as one analysis summarizes well: "Over the last few years, it became more apparent to Cantor that if he became Speaker of the House he'd need to work with Democrats to govern, while also presiding over a seemingly ungovernable GOP. He slowly evolved from Speaker John Boehner's top rival into a more conciliatory presence, willing to make deals, for example, on the debt ceiling. He also began devoting more time and energy to articulating conservative policy alternatives than most of his peers in the Republican conference . . . Cantor privately chastised tea partiers in his conference who fomented the 2013 government shutdown, came out in favor of restoring parts of the Voting Rights Act, and helped craft a watered-down DREAM Act that would provide a path to legalization for immigrants who came to the US illegally as children. But he seemed to do so with fairly little regard to how rock-ribbed conservative primary voters back home would react to these pragmatic gestures." See David Wasserman, "What We Can Learn From Eric Cantor's Defeat," FiveThirtyEight, June 20, 2014, https://fivethirtyeight.com/features/what-we-can-learn-from-eric-cantors-defeat/. See also Robert Costa, Laura Vozzella, and David A. Fahrenthold, "Republican House Party Leader Eric Cantor Succumbs to Tea Party Challenge Eric Bratt," *Washington Post*, June 11, 2014, https://www.washingtonpost.com/local/virginia-politics/eric-cantor-faces-tea-party-challenge-tuesday/2014/06/10/17da5d20-f092-11e3-bf76-447a5df6411f_story.html?noredirect=on&utm_term=.f17ee81ef6b7. For more on Cantor's evolution see Ryan Lizza, "The House of Pain," *New Yorker*, February 24, 2013, https://www.newyorker.com/magazine/2013/03/04/the-house-of-pain; Robert Costa, "Eric Cantor Attempts to Remake the House GOP Brand, and His Own," *Washington Post*, March 24, 2014, https://www.washingtonpost.com/politics/eric-cantor-attempts-to-remake-the-house-gop-brand-and-his-own/2014/03/23/

b1a5e430-af9f-11e3-95e8-39bef8e9a48b_story.html?noredirect=on&utm_term=.aae084ba0938; Jason Zengerle, "Eric Cantor's America," *New York*, September 30, 2011, http://nymag.com/news/politics/eric-cantor-2011-10/#print.

26. Cameron Easley, "America's Most and Least Popular Governors: Q1 2018 Rankings," Morning Consult, April 12, 2018, https://morningconsult.com/2018/04/12/americas-most-and-least-popular-governors/.

27. Greg Orman, *A Declaration of Independents: How We Can Break the Two-Party Stranglehold and Restore the American Dream* (Austin, TX: Greenleaf Group Book Press, 2016), 61.

28. Lee Drutman, *Breaking the Two-Party Doom Loop: The Case for Multiparty Democracy in America* (New York; Oxford: Oxford University Press, 2020), 31.

29. Russell Berman, "Cruz: Political 'Tsunami' Needed to Win Fight to Defund Obamacare," The Hill, August 25, 2013, https://thehill.com/video/sunday-shows/318647-cruz-tsunami-needed-to-defund-obamacare.

30. For overview of the shutdown, see Walter J. Oleszek, "The Government Shutdown of 2013: A Perspective," in *Party and Procedure in the United States Congress, 2nd Edition*, ed. Jacob Straus and Matthew Glassman (2017).

31. Leigh Ann Caldwell, "Architect of the Brink: Meet the Man behind the Government Shutdown," CNN, updated October 1, 2013, http://www.cnn.com/2013/09/27/politics/house-tea-party/index.html.

32. For full timeline, see Eric Krupke, "How We Got Here: A Shutdown Timeline," National Public Radio, October 17, 2013, https://www.npr.org/sections/itsallpolitics/2013/10/16/235442199/how-we-got-here-a-shutdown-timeline.

33. Brad Plumer, "Absolutely Everything You Need to Know about How the Government Shutdown Will Work," *Washington Post*, September 30, 2013, https://www.washingtonpost.com/news/wonk/wp/2013/09/30/absolutely-everything-you-need-to-know-about-how-the-government-shutdown-will-work/?noredirect=on&utm_term=.b2871aafe0a4.

34. Oleszek, "The Government Shutdown of 2013: A Perspective," *Party and Procedure in the United States Congress, 2nd Edition*.

35. For an overview of the Hastert Rule, see Sarah A. Binder, "Oh 113th Congress Hastert Rule, We Hardly Knew Ye!" Brookings Institution, January 17, 2013, https://www.brookings.edu/blog/up-front/2013/01/17/oh-113th-congress-hastert-rule-we-hardly-knew-ye/.

36. Shushannah Walshe, "The Costs of the Government Shutdown," ABC News, October 17, 2013, https://abcnews.go.com/blogs/politics/2013/10/the-costs-of-the-government-shutdown/.

37. For overviews of the evolution of the legislative machinery, see Kenneth Shepsle, "The Changing Textbook Congress," in *Can Government Govern?* ed. John Chubb and Paul Peterson (Washington, DC: Brookings Institution Press, 2010); David W. Rohde, *Parties and Leaders in the Postreform House* (Chicago: University of Chicago Press, 1991); Sam Rosenfeld, chapter 1 in *The Polarizers: Postwar Architects of Our Polarized Era* (Chicago: University of Chicago Press, 2017); Jeffrey Jenkins, "The Evolution of Party Leadership," in *The Oxford Handbook of the American Congress* (2011); Barbara Sinclair, *Unorthodox Lawmaking: New Legislative Processes in the U.S. Congress 5th Edition* (Thousand Oaks, CA: Sage CQ Press, 2016), chapter 6; Steven S. Smith, *Party Influence in Congress* (New York; Cambridge: Cambridge University Press, 2007); Steven Smith and Gerald Gamm, "The Dynamics of Party Government In Congress," in *Congress Reconsidered, 10th Edition*, ed. Lawrence Dodd and Bruce Oppenheimer (Thousand Oaks, CA: CQ Press, 2013); Barbara Sinclair, "The Dream Fulfilled? Party Development in Congress, 1950–2000," in *Responsible Partisanship? The Evolution of American Political Parties Since 1950*, ed. John C. Green and Paul S. Hernson (Lawrence, KS: University Press of Kansas, 2002); John Aldrich and David Rohde, "Congressional Committees in a Partisan Era," in *Congress Reconsidered, 8th Edition*, ed. Lawrence Dodd and Bruce Oppenheimer (Thousand Oaks, CA: CQ Press, 2005); Nathan Monroe, Jason Roberts, and David Rhode, *Why Not Parties? Party Effects in the United States Senate* (Chicago: University of Chicago Press, 2008); Sean M. Theriault, *Party Polarization in Congress* (New York; Cambridge: Cambridge University Press, 2008); Barbara Sinclair, *Party Wars* (Norman, OK: University of Oklahoma Press, 2006); Lawrence Dodd and Bruce Oppenheimer, "The House in a

Time of Crisis," in *Congress Reconsidered, 10th Edition*, ed. Dodd and Oppenheimer (2013). Some, however, argue that the party's power in Congress has not changed dramatically over time. This view is associated with the "Cartel Theory" detailed in Gary Cox and Matthew McCubbins, *Legislative Leviathan: Party Government in the House, 2nd Edition* (New York; Cambridge: Cambridge University Press, 2007).

38. The term "Textbook Congress" is accredited to Shepsle, "The Changing Textbook Congress.

39. John H. Aldrich, Brittany N. Perry, and David W. Rhode, "Richard Fenno's Theory of Congressional Committees and the Partisan Polarization of the House," *Congress Reconsidered*, ed. Dodd and Oppenheimer (Washington, DC: CQ Press, 2001).

40. A famous study of Congress summed up the minor role parties played during this period when insisting that "no theoretical treatment of the United States Congress that posits parties as analytical units will go very far. So we are left with individual congressmen, with 535 men and women rather than two parties, as units to be examined." David Mayhew, *The Electoral Connection* (New Haven: Yale University Press, 1974), 27.

41. For the seminal work on congressional committees during this period, see Richard Fenno, *Congressmen in Committees* (1973). For a modern reassessment of Fenno's work in light of recent polarization, see John H. Aldrich, Brittany N. Perry, and David W. Rhode, "Richard Fenno's Theory of Congressional Committees and the Partisan Polarization of the House," in *Congress Reconsidered, 10th Edition*, 193–220. For an opposing account of the role of committees, distributional theories emphasize that the committee system was essentially a system of cross-jurisdictional bargaining and horse trading to pass policies popular with local constituents. See Barry R. Weingast and William J. Marshall, "The Industrial Organizations of Congress; Or Why Legislatures, Like Firms, Are Not Organized as a Market," *Journal of Political Economy* (1988), 132–163; Barry R. Weingast, Kenneth A. Shepsle, and Christopher Johnsen, "The Political Economy of Benefits and Costs: A Neoclassical Approach to Distributive Politics," *Journal of Political Economy* (1981), 642–664; Christopher R. Berry and Anthony Fowler, "Cardinals or Clerics? Congressional Committees and the Distribution of Pork," *American Journal of Political Science* (2015), 692–708. For a recent account of the positive role that the committee system played and the case for why committee power should once again be strengthened, see Kevin R. Kosar and Adam Chan, "A Case for Stronger Congressional Committees," R Street Institute, 2016.

42. See David W. Rohde, *Parties and Leaders in the Post Reform House* (1991); John H. Aldrich, *Why Parties?* (1995); Lawrence Dodd and Bruce Oppenheimer, "The House in a Time of Crisis," *Congress Reconsidered, 10th Edition*.

43. DSG background paper, "The Case for House Democratic Caucus Action against Rep. John Bell Williams and Rep. Albert W Watson" (December 1964). Quoted in Sam Rosenfeld, *The Polarizers* (Chicago: University of Chicago Press, 2018).

44. Shepsle, "The Changing Textbook Congress." The frequency of party caucuses has since soared. See Richard Forgette, "Party Caucuses and Coordination: Assessing Caucus Activity and Party Effects," *Legislative Studies Quarterly* (204), 407–430.

45. Marjorie Hunter, "Seniority System Revised," *New York Times*, January 21, 1971.

46. Kevin R. Kosar and Adam Chan, "A Case for Stronger Congressional Committees," R Street Policy Study No. 66, August 2016, https://www.rstreet.org/wp-content/uploads/2016/08/66.pdf.

47. These messages got through the committee chairs, who changed their behavior in response. See Sara Brandes Cook and John R. Hibbing, "Congressional Reform and Party Discipline: The Effects of Changes in the Seniority System on Party Loyalty in the House of Representatives," *British Journal of Political Science* 15 (1985), 207–226; Fiona M. Wright, "The Caucus Reelection Requirement and the Transformation of Committee Chairs," *Legislative Studies Quarterly* 25 (2000), 469–480.

48. Walter Oleszek, "Speakers Reed, Cannon, and Gingrich: Catalysts of Institutional Change," *The Cannon Centenary Conference: The Changing Nature of the Speakership* (Joint Commission on Printing, 2003).

49. Lawrence Dodd and Bruce Oppenheimer, "The House in a Time of Crisis," 29–31; C. Lawrence Evans and Walter J. Oleszek, *Congress Under Fire: Reform Politics and the*

Republican Majority (Belmont, CA: Wadsworth, 1997); Eric Shickler, Epilogue in *Disjointed Pluralism: Institutional Innovation and the Development of the U.S. Congress* (Princeton, NJ: Princeton University Press, 2001).

50. Paul Glastris and Haley Sweetland Edwards, "The Big Lobotomy: How Republicans Made Congress Stupid," *Washington Monthly*, June/July/August 2014, https://washingtonmonthly.com/magazine/junejulyaug-2014/the-big-lobotomy/.

51. For an overview of the demise of the Office of Technology Assessment, see Grant Tudor and Justin Warner, "The Congressional Futures Offices: A Modern Model for Science & Technology Expertise in Congress," Belfer Center for Science & International Affairs (2019), 28–31.

52. Derek Willis, ProPublica, and Paul Kane, "How Congress Stopped Working," *ProPublica*, November 5, 2018, https://www.propublica.org/article/how-congress-stopped-working.

53. Thomas Spulak and George Crawford, "How to Fix Congress in One Step," *Politico*, September 19, 2018, https://www.politico.com/agenda/story/2018/09/19/house-rules-committee-congress-000699.

54. McKay Coppins, "The Man Who Broke Politics," *Atlantic*, October 17, 2018, https://www.theatlantic.com/magazine/archive/2018/11/newt-gingrich-says-youre-welcome/570832/; Alex Seitz-Wald, "How Newt Gingrich Crippled Congress," *Nation*, January 30, 2012, https://www.thenation.com/article/how-newt-gingrich-crippled-congress/.

55. Ryan Grim and Aida Chávez, "Here's How Much the Democratic Party Charges to Be on Each House Committee," The Intercept, September 3, 2019, https://theintercept.com/2019/09/03/dccc-house-committees-dues/.

56. For example, in 2007 Nancy Pelosi removed John Dingell as chair of the Energy and Commerce Committee after his opposition in the race to become Speaker and disagreements over an energy bill. See David W. Rhode, Edward Stiglitz, and Barry Weingast, "Dynamic Theory of Congressional Organization," Stanford working paper, February 17, 2013, https://web.stanford.edu/group/mcnollgast/cgi-bin/wordpress/wp-content/uploads/2013/10/rsw_dynamics_1302171.pdf. A list of members of Congress facing party discipline can be found in Matthew Green and Briana Bee, "Keeping the Team Together: Explaining Party Discipline and Dissent in the U.S. Congress," in Jacob Straus and Matthew Glassman, *Party and Procedure in the United States Congress, 2nd Edition* (2017), 48–49. Stiglitz and Weingast find that the frequency of partisan punishment appears to be increasingly common, although they acknowledge that this uptick in punishments could simply reflect the fact that recent punishments are better publicized. More often, representatives considered to be "disloyal" to the party are just bypassed altogether. Marge Roukema (R-NJ) was bypassed for the role of chair of the Financial Service Committee due to her willingness to break from the party line. In response, she retired from Congress in "grave disappointment." Sam Theriault, *Party Polarization in Congress* (2008), 132. In *Party Discipline in the U.S. House of Representatives* (2015) Kathryn Pearson finds that the party Steering Committees do consider loyalty when determining which members will receive the limited number of committee transfers to more powerful and prestigious committees and when appointing committee chairs. Further, members who serve on the four most powerful and most sought-after committees—Appropriations, Energy and Commerce, Rules, and Ways and Means—are typically more loyal to their party than members who do not serve on these committees. These results support the findings of Cox and McCubbins: "The statistical evidence is clear: more loyal members [as measured by loyalty in roll call votes] are more likely to transfer (and more likely to get better assignments as freshmen)," *Legislative Leviathan*, 170.

57. Chairs are no longer independent actors but often little more than puppets of the majority party. Dennis Hastert put it bluntly when he said: "The chairs will deliver on the leadership's agenda because they know that if they fail, they won't be chairs anymore." See Cox and McCubbins, *Legislative Leviathan*, 232.

58. Eric Schickler and Kathryn Pearson, "The House Leadership in an Era of Partisan Warfare," in Lawrence Dodd and Bruce Oppenheimer, *Congress Reconsidered, 10th Edition.*

59. J. Lewallen, S. M. Theriault, and B. D. Jones, "Congressional Dysfunction: An Information Processing Perspective," *Regulation & Governance* 10, no. 2 (2016): 179–190.

60. Data on the rise of post committee adjustments can be found in Barbara Sinclair, *Unorthodox Lawmaking: New Legislative Processes in the U.S. Congress, 5th Edition* (Thousand Oaks, CA: Sage CQ Press, 2016): 149. See Mark J. Oleszek, "Post-Committee Adjustment in the Contemporary House: The Use of Rules Committee Prints," Jacob Straus and Matthew Glassman, *Party and Procedure in the United States Congress, 2nd Edition* (Lanham, MD: Rowman & Littlefield Publishers, 2017), 109.

61. "In the late 1980s almost one in five major measures was not considered by a committee in the House. The frequency dropped to an average of about one in ten in the Congresses of the 1990s but then increased again to an average of one in five in the Congress from 2001 to 2006 and further to one in three in the period 2007–2014." See Sinclair, *Unorthodox Lawmaking, 5th Edition,* 18. Data on the increased frequency at which committees are bypassed can be found in Sinclair, *Unorthodox Lawmaking, 5th Edition,* 151.

62. Sinclair, *Unorthodox Lawmaking, 5th Edition,* 20. This followed the example set by the Republicans when they took control of the House in 1995, when Gingrich created task forces to quickly pass the "Contract with America."

63. Bill Pascrell Jr., "Why Is Congress So Dumb," *Washington Post,* January 11, 2019, https://www.washingtonpost.com/news/posteverything/wp/2019/01/11/feature/why-is-congress-so-dumb/?utm_term=.e1927c724b28.

James M. Curry and Frances E. Lee find that bills are increasingly developed outside of the committee process that defines traditional "regular order." Interestingly, they find no connection between whether "regular order" is observed and the partisanship in passage votes. Based on interviews with 24 members of Congress and high-level Congressional staffers, they argue that this is because unorthodox bill development processes are used for reasons other than gaining partisan advantage, such as efficiency, secrecy, and flexibility. See James M. Curry and Frances E. Lee, "What Is Regular Order Worth? Partisan Lawmaking and Congressional Processes," *Journal of Politics* (2018). This finding conflicts with conventional wisdom, as well as other empirical research. For example, see Laurel Harbridge, *Is Bipartisanship Dead? Policy Agreement and Agenda-Setting in the House of Representatives* (New York; Cambridge: Cambridge University Press, 2015). Certainly, more research is required in this critical area.

64. Or, in the famous words of Bruce Oppenheimer, the Rules Committee is now an "arm of the leadership." See Oppenheimer, "The Rules Committee: New Arm of Leadership in a Decentralized House," *Congress Reconsidered.*

The legislative calendar has space for only a small fraction of the thousands of bills and amendments that have been introduced. In the 114th Congress, 5 percent of introduced bills/resolutions got a vote. See https://www.govtrack.us/congress/bills/statistics, accessed February 15, 2018. This gives the majority party leadership leverage over members. Legislators have particular local issues that are highly salient to their constituents. For reelection purposes, legislators also wish to be seen as political entrepreneurs. Their electoral success is therefore contingent on the majority leadership's willingness to bring their bills and amendments to the floor. Pearson (2015) shows how the parties use this leverage point to extract partisan loyalty from their members. Only those who toe the party line receive these coveted legislative opportunities. See Kathryn Pearson, chapter 4 in *Party Discipline in the U.S. House of Representatives* (Ann Arbor, MI: University of Michigan Press, 2015).

65. Technically, members of Congress can bypass the Rules Committee through the use of a Discharge Petition. If 218 members sign a discharge petition, a bill is brought to the floor under the rules specified in the petition. Discharge petitions were created in 1910 as part of the so-called "Cannon Revolt," discussed in chapter 4, and were instrumental in the passage of Civil Rights reform in the 1960s. However, parties do not tolerate members breaking ranks for these types of procedural votes, and successful discharge petitions are incredibly rare. In 1993, the discharge rules were changed to regularly publish the names all signatories of discharge petitions in the *Congressional Record.* See Clifford Krauss, "Public Mood Bolsters Effort to End House's Secrecy Rule," *New York Times,* September 13, 1993, https://www.nytimes.com/1993/09/14/us/public-mood-bolsters-effort-to-end-house-s-secrecy-rule.html. Pearson finds that from then until 2012, just three discharge petitions that were opposed by the majority party

leadership reached the 218-vote threshold. Of note is that the McCain-Feingold campaign finance reform in 2002 was one of these three bills. See Pearson, *Party Discipline in the U.S. House of Representatives*, 58. Of course, the mere threat of a discharge petition can force the majority party leadership's hand, as we have seen recently with bills to reauthorize the Export-Import Bank and to force a vote on immigration reform. See https://www.conginst.org/2015/10/15/the-discharge-petition-bipartisan-effort-might-revive-the-ex-im-bank/; http://time.com/5308755/discharge-petitions-definition-purpose-history/. However, because discharge votes are seen as rebukes of the party leadership, members are reluctant to use this tool. Sara Binder reflects on the resistance to sign discharge petitions when writing "Majority party lawmakers are typically loath to sign discharge petitions that undercut the power of party and committee leaders. We see this more generally in lawmakers' votes on procedural matters, which exhibit much higher levels of partisanship than votes on substance in both the House and Senate." See "Governing from the Monkey Cage: Discharge Rule Edition," *Washington Post*, October 4, 2013, https://www.washingtonpost.com/news/monkey-cage/wp/2013/10/04/governing-from-the-monkey-cage-discharge-rule-edition/?utm_term=.4bf3ad318e5b. Sean Theriault argues that members of Congress have become increasingly less willing to break with their parties on procedural votes since the 1970s, and that this is one of the major causes of the growing partisanship in final roll call votes. See Sean M. Theriault, *Party Polarization in Congress* (2008), 223. For more on discharge petitions, see https://www.brookings.edu/wp-content/uploads/2016/06/Jackman_Discharge-Procedure-Immigration-Reform_v17.pdf. For more on discharge petitions, see Kathryn Pearson and Eric Schickler, "Discharge Petitions, Agenda Control, and the Congressional Committee System, 1929–76," *The Journal of Politics* (Oct, 2009), 1238–1256; Richard Beth, "The Discharge Rule in the House: Recent Use in Historical Context," Congressional Research Service Report for Congress, Report 97–856 (2003).

66. David Hawkings, "Topic for Debate: Time to End Congressional Debates?," *Roll Call*, January 4, 2018, https://www.rollcall.com/news/hawkings/congressional-debates-little-impact.

67. Interestingly, the Senate has experienced a similar level of polarization as the House, but parties in the Senate do not have the same level of control over the legislative machinery. The party's agenda control is curtailed by Senate rules, which, for example, generally require that amendments cannot be restricted (i.e., no closed rules) and need not even be germane (do not have to be relevant to the proposed bill under consideration). See Steven Smith and Gerald Gamm, "The Dynamics of Party Government in Congress" in Lawrence Dodd and Bruce Oppenheimer, *Congress Reconsidered, 10th Edition*. That's not to say that the parties have not taken steps to solidify their power in the Senate over the past fifty years. See Nathan Monroe, Jason Roberts, and David W. Rhode, *Why Not Parties?*; Steven Smith, *The Senate Syndrome: The Evolution of Procedural Warfare in the Modern US Senate* (Norman, OK: University of Oklahoma Press, 2014).

68. Congress.gov, accessed August 2017.

69. Wyden statement on Senate Floor on Republican tax plan Conference, December 6, 2017, https://www.finance.senate.gov/wyden-statement-on-senate-floor-on-republican-tax-plan-conference.

70. Vito J. Racanelli, "Lobbying Index Beats the Market," *Barron's*, April 27, 2018, https://www.barrons.com/articles/lobbying-index-beats-the-market-1524863200.

Chapter 3

1. Ideological preferences are based on roll-call votes. As Frances Lee explains, roll-call votes may not capture true ideological preferences for two major reasons. First, roll-call votes only capture votes on bills that make it to the House floor for a vote. As we will see, as the party leaderships have taken control of the legislative machinery in the past decades, they have systematically screened out bills that would break party unity and gain bipartisan support. This would tend to decrease the number of moderates we would expect to see in Congress, as measured by roll calls. Second, many votes today (like attempts to repeal and replace the ACA) are never going to be enacted. Representatives are not voting on public policy, but are voting on messaging. Nevertheless, the increased levels of party unity on these "show votes" still speaks

to the strength of the parties and the dysfunctional nature of partisan competition today. See Frances E. Lee, "The 115th Congress and Challenges of Measuring Party Unity in a Polarized Era" (paper presented at the Dynamics of American Democracy conference, Brown University, November 14–15, 2018).

2. Many studies of congressional efficiency show a similar decline in laws enacted over time. However, these calculations usually include commemorative legislation. Commemorative laws have little meaningful effect on our daily lives. They often pertain to the naming of a building or the designation of a new holiday, like National Ice Cream Day. Since commemorative laws have little significant impact on the lives of American citizens, we took them out of the data set. We learned to distinguish between commemorative and noncommemorative laws when comparing congressional efficiency from Jonathan Lewallen, "You Better Find Something to Do: Lawmaking and Agenda Setting in a Centralized Congress," (PhD diss., University of Texas Austin, 2017).

Some critics of this measurement of congressional efficiency highlight the increased average length of each bill passed by Congress. They point out that the total number of pages of statutes has actually increased over time. However, this increase can mainly be explained by the rise of omnibus bills, which combine several issues (often completely unrelated) into one large bill. Omnibus bills have been around since our nation's founding, but they have become far more popular in the twenty-first century. These bills are popular, because they're easier to pass. They are a "you scratch my back, and I'll scratch yours" kind of deal. They allow legislators to pass provisions that they support for subject A, while allowing their counterparts to pass provisions that they support for subject B. While this may seem like an efficient form of compromise, it's not that simple. These bills are often incredibly long and are not presented to legislators with enough time to read them. For example, the Consolidated Appropriations Act of 2018 was 2,232 pages. Since legislators needed to pass it in order to avoid a government shutdown, they had to cram it through legislation. Because it was eventually unveiled less than twenty-four hours before legislators voted, the legislators did not read this important bill before voting on it, completely negating the point of our legislative process. Omnibus bills are a Band-Aid to Congress's inability to compromise. For information about the number of laws and number of pages of laws passed over time, see Andrew J. Taylor, *Congress: A Performance Appraisal* (Boulder, CO: Westview Press, 2013), 145. For information on omnibus bills, see Glen S. Krutz, "Tactical Maneuvering on Omnibus Bills in Congress," *American Journal of Political Science* 45, no. 1 (2001): 210–223.

See also Drew Desilver, "A Productivity Scorecard for the 115th Congress: More Laws Than Before, But Not More Substance," Pew Research Center, January 25, 2019, https://www .pewresearch.org/fact-tank/2019/01/25/a-productivity-scorecard-for-115th-congress/.

3. "In Interview, Outgoing House Speaker Ryan Says He Doesn't See Himself Ever Running Again," *Milwaukee Journal Sentinel*, April 11, 2018, https://www.jsonline.com/story/ news/2018/04/11/interview-outgoing-house-speaker-ryan-says-he-doesnt-see-himself-ever-running-again/508830002/.

4. Data from "Public Trust in Government: 1958–2017," Pew Research Center, May 3, 2017, http://www.people-press.org/2015/11/23/public-trust-in-government-1958-2015/.

5. "Congress and the Public," Gallup, November 12, 2019, https://news.gallup.com/ poll/1600/congress-public.aspx.

6. See Lee Drutman, William Galston, and Tod Lindberg, "Spoiler Alert: Why Americans' Desires for a Third Party Are Unlikely to Come True," Voter Study Group, September 2018, https://www.voterstudygroup.org/publication/spoiler-alert.

7. Figures are annual averages calculated from Gallup poll survey on party affiliation. Response to question "In politics, as of today, do you consider yourself a Republican, a Democrat, or an independent?" accessed August 2018, https://news.gallup.com/poll/15370/party-affiliation .aspx.

8. "Gallup Poll Social Series: Governance, Question 20," Gallup, accessed October 2017, http://news.gallup.com/file/poll/219977/170927ThirdParty.pdf. See also Lee Drutman, William Galston, and Tod Lindberg, "Spoiler Alert: Why Americans' Desires for a Third Party Are Unlikely to Come True," Voter Study Group, September 2018, https://www.voterstudygroup.org/ publication/spoiler-alert.

9. A similar point is made in Will Wilkinson, Brink Lindsey, Steven Teles, and Sam Hammond, "The Center Can Hold: Public Policy for an Age of Extremes," Niskanen Center (2018).

10. Robert Stefan Foa and Yascha Mounk, "The Democratic Disconnect," *Journal of Democracy* (2016); see also Yascha Mounk, *The People vs. Democracy: Why Our Freedom Is in Danger and How to Save It* (Cambridge, MA: Harvard University Press, 2018). Mounk argues that the diminishing support for democracy has manifested in populist politicians who attack the idea of liberal democracy. When answering how deconsolidation arose, Mounk points to the deleterious effects of social media and identity politics. Yet he also blames economic stagnation and the fact that the median income in America has remained flat since the 1980s. This poor economic performance has fundamentally changed the way citizens view politics, as the dream of steady progress has dimmed. This focus on the economic, rather than the cultural component, is disputed in Ronald Inglehart and Pippa Norris, "Trump, Brexit, and the Rise of Populism: Economic Have-Nots and Cultural Backlash," working paper RWP16-026, Harvard Kennedy School, Cambridge (2016).

11. "Hart-Cellar Act, which dismantled the national origins quota system, passed in a Democratic-controlled House by a vote of 320 to 70. Of the 262 Democratic representatives who voted, 202, or 77 percent, supported the bill. Of the 127 Republican representatives who voted, just 10, or 8 percent, opposed the bill. In other words, a full 92 percent of Republican representatives joined Democratic representatives in ending the national origins quota system." Tom K. Wong, *The Politics of Immigration* (New York; Oxford: Oxford University Press, 2017).

12. Wong, *The Politics of Immigration*. The Illegal Immigration Reform and Immigrant Responsibility Act of 1996 (IIRIRA) "passed in a Republican-controlled House by a vote of 370 to 37. Of the 226 Republican representatives who voted, 202, or 89 percent, supported the bill. Of the 180 Democratic representatives who voted, just 13, or 7 percent, opposed the bill. This means that a full 93 percent of Democratic representatives joined Republican representatives in passing IIRIRA."

13. See Marc R. Rosenblum, "US Immigration Policy Since 9/11: Understanding the Stalemate over Comprehensive Immigration Reform," Regional Migration Study Group, Woodrow Wilson International Center for Scholars (August 2011), https://www.wilsoncenter.org/publication/us-immigration-policy-911-understanding-the-stalemate-over-comprehensive-immigration.

14. As the former governor of a border state, Bush made immigration a top priority in his 2000 campaign and pursued it aggressively in his first year in office before the attacks of 9/11 shifted focus abroad. Afghanistan and Iraq dominated the national debate for the next several years, but as his second term wound to a close, a door opened for one last immigration push. Immigration was a rare issue that did not cleanly split the parties. Coalitions cut across party lines, with conservative hawks partnering with liberal labor unions to advocate stricter enforcement and lower legal immigration levels, and Republican business leaders aligning with the Democratic base in support of a more open stance. See Rosenblum, "US Immigration Policy Since 9/11."

15. The maverick John McCain and the liberal lion of the Senate Ted Kennedy introduced a bipartisan bill that dealt with all three pillars of comprehensive immigration reform—enhancing border security, creating a pathway to citizenship for undocumented workers, and retooling the visa system to increase skills-based immigration and expand opportunities for temporary workers. Overcoming initial resistance from Democratic leaders Harry Reid and Chuck Schumer, who were reluctant to give President Bush a major policy victory in the run-up to the midterms, the deal passed in the Senate with the backing of almost every Democrat and nearly half of Republicans. See Rosenblum, "US Immigration Policy Since 9/11"; Robert Draper, "The Democrats Have an Immigration Problem," *New York Times*, October 10, 2018, https://www.nytimes.com/2018/10/10/magazine/the-democrats-have-an-immigration-problem.html.

16. Wong, *The Politics of Immigration*.

17. Greg Orman, *A Declaration of Independents: How We Can Break the Two-Party Stranglehold and Restore the American Dream* (Austin, TX: Greenleaf Book Group Press, 2016).

18. Obama proposed that the new merit-based system for green cards be sunset after five years—an idea popular with the Democratic base but toxic to Republicans aiming to increase the number of high-skilled workers. The amendment was rejected, but Obama was not spared

by Kennedy, who reportedly scolded his young colleague: "You can't come in here and undo everything!" See Jake Tapper, "Obama Pushing Immigration Action Today, Said to Have Hurt Effort in the Past," CNN, November 24, 2014, https://www.cnn.com/2014/11/21/politics/obama-immigration-flashback/index.html.

19. The amendment was proposed by North Dakota Senator Bryan Dorgan. Kennedy, knowing that the amendment's passage would tank the bill, again attacked his fellow Democrat: "Who is the senator from North Dakota trying to fool?" See Orman, *Declaration of Independents.*

20. Greg Orman, "Debaters Should Press Biden on Killing Immigration Reform in '07," RealClearPolitics, October 14, 2019, https://www.realclearpolitics.com/articles/2019/10/14/debaters_should_press_biden_on_killing_immigration_reform_in_07_141490.html.

21. On the campaign trail, months after sinking the deal, Obama pledged he would push for immigration reform in his first year. See Orman, *Declaration of Independents.*

22. Republicans had hoped that next president would be Mitt Romney, but the 2012 elections did not go according to plan, in no small part because of Hispanic voters. Eight years earlier, George Bush won over 40 percent of the Hispanic vote. This was a wakeup call for Republicans. In an autopsy after Romney's defeat, the Republican National Committee insisted that to be viable nationally, Republicans must address their Latino deficit by embracing comprehensive immigration reform. With these directives, Senate Republicans partnered with Democrats to form a bipartisan "Gang of Eight," which made one more crack at comprehensive reform in 2013. Their proposal resembled past rounds of failed reform efforts, including a pathway to citizenship, increased border enforcement, and a streamlined legal immigration system. The bill's fate was also recognizable. After passing in the Senate with the backing of every Democrat and fourteen Republicans, it stalled in the House where Speaker Boehner employed the Hastert rule, insisting that "to pass the House it's going to have to be a bill that has the support of the majority of our [i.e., Republican] members." While there was likely a majority in the chamber who would have supported the bill, it never came up for a vote in the House where Republicans were both fearful of primary challenges and skeptical of the RNC autopsy, embracing an alternative route for electoral success that focused not on broadening appeal but driving up support within the base. For more information on Boehner's usage of the Hastert Rule, see Molly Hooper, "Boehner Commits to Hastert Rule on Immigration Reform," *Hill*, June 18, 2013, https://thehill.com/homenews/house/306179-boehner-commits-to-hastert-rule-on-immigration-reform.

23. For example, see Adam Liptak and Michael D. Shear, "Supreme Court Tie Blocks Obama Immigration Plan," *New York Times*, June 23, 2016, https://www.nytimes.com/2016/06/24/us/supreme-court-immigration-obama-dapa.html.

24. Jynnah Radford, "Key Findings about U.S. Immigrants," Pew Research Center, June 17, 2019, http://www.pewresearch.org/fact-tank/2018/11/30/key-findings-about-u-s-immigrants/.

25. Michael E. Porter et al., "A Recovery Squandered: The State of U.S. Competitiveness 2019," Harvard Business School (2019).

26. For more detail and data, please see Michael E. Porter, Jan W. Rivkin, Mihir A. Desai, with Manjari Raman, "Problems Unresolved and a Nation Divided: The State of U.S. Competitiveness 2016," Harvard Business School (2016).

27. Porter, Rivkin, Desai, with Raman, "Problems Unresolved and a Nation Divided."

28. Michael E. Porter, "America Traded One Recession for a Far More Serious One," *Boston Globe*, September 21, 2018, https://www.bostonglobe.com/opinion/2018/09/21/america-traded-one-recession-for-far-more-serious-one/IIl10IwZ7DElJ5YDXJ7BjO/story.html.

29. See the 2019 Social Progress Index scorecard, https://socialprogress.org.

30. Marc F. Plattner, "Illiberal Democracy and the Struggle on the Right," *Journal of Democracy* 30, no. 1 (2019): 5–19 https://www.journalofdemocracy.org/articles/illiberal-democracy-and-the-struggle-on-the-right/.

31. For an overview of the history of social security, see Larry DeWitt, "Social Security Administration," Social Security Administration Research, Statistics, and Policy Analysis, August 1, 2010, https://www.ssa.gov/policy/docs/ssb/v70n3/v70n3p1.html; and "Social Security," Social Security History, https://www.ssa.gov/history/briefhistory3.html.

32. "Social Security," Social Security History, https://www.ssa.gov/history/fdrsignstate
.html.

33. With the exception of Republican Senator Jim Bunning of Kentucky, who did not vote.
United States Senate. "Roll Call Vote 11th Congress – 1st Session," https://www.senate.gov/
legislative/LIS/roll_call_lists/roll_call_vote_cfm.cfm?congress=111&session=1&vote=00396.

34. Tessa Berenson, "Reminder: The House Voted to Repeal Obamacare More Than 50
Times," *Time*, March 24, 2017, http://time.com/4712725/ahca-house-repeal-votes-obamacare/.

35. For a great analysis of show votes, see Frances Lee, *Insecure Majorities: Congress and the
Perpetual Campaign* (Chicago: The University of Chicago Press, 2016).

36. Former Republican Senator Olympia Snowe put it best when she said, "Much of what
occurs in Congress today is what is often called 'political messaging.' Rather than putting forward
a plausible, realistic solution to a problem, members of both sides offer legislation that is designed
to make a political statement. Specifically, the bill or amendment is drafted to make the opposing
side look bad on an issue and is not intended to ever actually pass." See Olympia Snow, "The
Effect of Modern Partisanship on Legislative Effectiveness in the 112th Congress," *Harvard Journal
on Legislation* (2013): 27.

37. The only thing the Republicans were able to do was effectively eliminate the individual
mandate as part of the Tax Cuts and Jobs Act of 2017.

38. The Lead with Jake Tapper, "Republican Health Care Bill Failure," CNN (March 24, 2017),
http://www.cnn.com/TRANSCRIPTS/1703/24/cg.01.html.

39. The discussion of Simpson-Bowles comes from Katherine M. Gehl and Michael E. Porter,
"Why Competition in the Politics Industry Is Failing America: A Strategy for Reinvigorating Our
Democracy," Harvard Business School, September 2017.

40. US Senate, "The National Commission on Fiscal Responsibility and Reform,"
December 2010, https://www.senate.gov/reference/resources/pdf/NationalCommissionon
FiscalResponsibilityandReform_Dec012010.pdf.

41. National Commission on Fiscal Responsibility and Reform, "The Moment of Truth,"
December 2010, https://www.fiscalcommission.gov/sites/fiscalcommission.gov/files/
documents/TheMomentofTruth12_1_2010.pdf, emphasis added.

42. Author analysis of the widely used data set compiled by the Brookings Institution, "Vital
Statistics on Congress," January 9, 2017, tables 2-7 and 2-8, https://www.brookings
.edu/multi-chapter-report/vital-statistics-on-congress/.

Chapter 4

1. "Washington's Farewell Address 1796," The Avalon Project, https://avalon.law.yale
.edu/18th_century/washing.asp.

2. Joseph Stromberg, "The Real Birth of American Democracy," *Smithsonian*, September 20,
2011, https://www.smithsonianmag.com/smithsonian-institution/the-real-birth-of-
american-democracy-83232825/.

3. Quotations on the Jefferson Memorial, *Thomas Jefferson Encyclopedia*, https://www
.monticello.org/site/research-and-collections/quotations-jefferson-memorial.

4. "Waldorf-Astoria—Famous Dinners, Balls, and Guests, Yodelout! New York City
History," https://web.archive.org/web/20181215173537/http://new-york-city.yodelout
.com/waldorf-astoria-famous-dinners-balls-and-guests/.

5. This measure of polarization is based on roll call votes in Congress. While this is the
most common method for measuring polarization, there are important limitations. First, from
studying roll-call votes alone, it is difficult to distinguish between ideological polarization and
partisan teamsmanship. Second, because this data does not capture changes to the legislative
agenda over time, it is difficult to make comparisons across periods. There are, in fact, reasons
to believe that the parties in the Gilded Age were not as ideologically polarized as they are today
and that their divides were more often based on who would capture the spoils of government. See
Hans Noel's *Political Ideologies and Political Parties in America* (New York; Cambridge: Cambridge

University Press, 2013). Noting these limitations and caveats, however, the data still shows important parallels in the breakdown in compromise at the end of the nineteenth century and in the modern era.

6. W. Bernard Carlson writes that, "While one farm worker in 1820 could produce enough food to feed 4.1 people, by 1900 one farm worker could produce food for seven people. How did this remarkable change in food production take place? In the last half of the nineteenth century, Americans increased both the amount of land under cultivation as well as the number of machines used in farming." See W. Bernard Carlson, "Industrialization and the Rise of Big Business," in *The Gilded Age: Perspectives on the Origins of Modern America*, ed. Charles Calhoun (Lanham, MD: Rowman & Littlefield Publishers, Inc., 2007), 31.

7. See Richard White, *Railroaded: The Transcontinentals and the Making of Modern America* (New York: W.W. Norton & Co., 2012); Joshua D. Wolff, *Western Union and the Creation of the American Corporate Order, 1845–1893* (New York; Cambridge: Cambridge University Press, 2013).

8. Alfred Chandler, *The Visible Hand: The Managerial Revolution in American Business* (Cambridge, MA: Harvard University Press, 1977), Ch. 7–11; Glenn Porter, *The Rise of Big Business, 1860–1920* (Wheeling, IL: Harlan Davidson, 1992).

9. Naomi Lamoreaux, *The Great Merger Movement in American Business, 1895–1904* (New York; Cambridge: Cambridge University Press, 1985); Oliver Zunz, *Making America Corporate, 1870–1920* (Chicago: The University of Chicago Press, 1990); William Roy, *Socializing Capital: The Rise of the Large Industrial Corporation in America* (Princeton, NJ: Princeton University Press, 1997).

10. See Robert Wiebe, *The Search for Order, 1877–1920* (New York: Hill and Wang, 1967).

11. Henry Adams wrote that "The American boy of 1854 stood nearer to the year 11 than to the year 1900." See Henry Adams, *The Education of Henry Adams: An Autobiography* (New York; Oxford: Oxford University Press, 1961), 53.

12. "When the Constitution was ratified in 1788 only about 5 percent of the residents of the new nation lives in cities. Today, about 80 percent of the population lives in places defined as urban. Thus, a central theme of US history has been the transition from a rural, agrarian society to one that is highly urbanized. The latter third of the nineteenth century—years when the interrelated processes of urbanization, industrialization, and immigration reached high tide— was a key period in that transition . . . In 1860, on the eve of the Civil War, the nation's urban population defined as those living in places of 2,500 or more stood at 6.2 million, just under one- fifth of the total. By the end of the century 30 million urbanites constituted about two-fifths of the nation's residents. Thus, in just forty years, the number of urban dwellers in the country had almost quintupled, and their proportion of the total population had doubled." See Robert Barrow, "Urbanizing America," in *The Gilded Age*, ed. Calhoun.

Between 1870 and 1900 nearly 12 million people migrated to America. *Historical Statistics of the United States* (1975), 1:106. For overview of the immigrant experience, see Roger Daniels, "The Immigrant Experience in the Gilded Age," chapter 4 in *The Gilded Age*, ed. Calhoun. The percentage of foreign-born citizens has only recently returned to levels reached in the Gilded Age. See https://www.census.gov/newsroom/pdf/cspan_fb_slides.pdf.

13. Calhoun, *The Gilded Age*, 2.

14. See John Higham, chapters 3–4 in *Strangers in the Land: Patterns of American Nativism, 1860- 1925* (Rutgers University Press, 2008); Steven Diner, chapter 3 in *A Very Different Age: Americans of the Progressive Era* (New York: Hill and Wang, 1997).

15. Jean Pfaelzer, *Driven Out: The Forgotten War against Chinese Americans* (New York: Random House, 2007).

16. Eric Arnesen, "American Workers and the Labor Movement in the Late Nineteenth Century," in *The Gilded Age*, ed. Calhoun; Peter Lindert and Jeffrey Williamson, chapter 7 in *Unequal Gains: American Growth and Inequality Since 1700* (Princeton, NJ: Princeton University Press, 2016); Neil Irvin Painter, *Standing at Armageddon: The United States, 1877–1919* (New York: W.W. Norton & Company, 1989), xix-xxviii.

17. Michael McGerr, chapter 1 in *A Fierce Discontent: The Rise and Fall of the Progressive Movement in America, 1870–1920* (New York; Oxford: Oxford University Press, 2003).

18. Estimations differ, but the consensus is that growth was strong throughout the period. See Thomas C. Cochran and William Miller, *The Age of Enterprise: A Social History of Industrial America* (New York: Harper & Row, 1961), 230. N. S. Balke and R. J. Gordon, "The Estimation of Prewar Gross National Product: Methodology and New Evidence," *Journal of Political Economy* 97.1, 38–92; Christina D. Romer, "The Prewar Business Cycle Reconsidered: New Estimates of Gross National Product, 1869–1908," *Journal of Political Economy* 97.1, 1–37.

19. Arnesen, "American Workers and the Labor Movement in the Late Nineteenth Century," *The Gilded Age*, ed. Calhoun, 55–56.

20. Robert Cherny, *American Politics in the Gilded Age: 1868–1900* (Hoboken, NJ: Wiley-Blackwell, 1997), 60.

21. John Lewis and Archie E. Allen, "Black Voter Registration Efforts in the South," *Notre Dame Law Review* 48, no. 1 (October 1972).

22. B. E. H., and J. J. K., Jr. "Federal Protection of Negro Voting Rights," *Virginia Law Review* 51, no. 6 (1965): 1051–213, https://www.jstor.org/stable/1071533?read-now=1&refreqid=excelsior%3A4e762a1fd0ddbe8c6b81dfb52335a8a3&seq=15#page_scan_tab_contents.

23. C. Vann Woodward, *Reunion and Reaction: The Compromise of 1877 and the End of Reconstruction* (New York; Oxford: Oxford University Press, 1991).

24. Cherny insists: "from the 1830s through the 1890s, political parties dominated American political decision making to a greater extent than ever before or since. Parties firmly controlled virtually all access to public office, all aspects of elections, and all aspects of policy-making." See Cherny, *American Politics in the Gilded Age*, 5.

25. Diner writes that "[g]overnment, which according to American ideals should represent the will of the people, appeared a captive of special interests." See Diner, *A Very Different Age*, 5. See also Cherny, *American Politics in the Gilded Age*.

26. The Pendleton Act of 1883 began to wind down the patronage system with the first steps to create a career civil service for federal government.

27. David D. Kirkpatrick, "Does Corporate Money Lead to Political Corruption?" January 23, 2010, https://www.nytimes.com/2010/01/24/weekinreview/24kirkpatrick.html.

28. In 1904, for example, corporations donated 73 percent of Theodore Roosevelt's campaign funds. See Kathleen Dalton, *Theodore Roosevelt: A Strenuous Life* (New York: Vintage Books, 2002), 265.

29. As historian James L. Baughman explained: "Before the Civil War, parties actually subsidized the operations of many newspapers. Sometimes directly, sometimes through government printing contracts. In many cases, the subsidies were indirect and unknown to readers. Editors or their reporters worked part time for state legislators or members of Congress. Some of these relationships continued late in the 19th century." See James L.Baughman, "The Fall and Rise of Partisan Journalism," University of Wisconsin Center for Journalism Ethics, April 20, 2011, https://ethics.journalism.wisc.edu/2011/04/20/the-fall-and-rise-of-partisan-journalism/.

30. Mark Wahlgren Summers, *Party Games: Getting, Keeping, and Using Power in Gilded Age Politics* (Chapel Hill, NC: The University of North Carolina Press, 2004), 75; Cherny, *American Politics in the Gilded Age*, 11; Tim Groeling and Matthew Baum, "Partisan News Before Fox: Newspaper Partisanship and Partisan Polarization, 1881–1972," working paper, Harvard Kennedy School, Cambridge, 2013, https://ethics.journalism.wisc.edu/2011/04/20/the-fall-and-rise-of-partisan-journalism/.

31. Worth Robert Miller, "The Lost World of Gilded Age Politics," in *The Journal of the Gilded Age and Progressive Era* (New York; Cambridge: Cambridge University Press, 2002), 49–67; Calhoun, *The Gilded Age*, 254.

32. In fact, historians often point to the 1896 election as a pivotal point in American history, when politics was nationalized as the businessman and chairman of the Republican National Committee created a strong national organization that strengthened the centralized party apparatus. Sidney Milkis and Anthony Sparacino, "Pivotal Elections," in, *A Companion to the Gilded Age and Progressive Era*, ed. Christopher McKnight Nichols and Nancy Unger (Hoboken, NJ: Wiley Blackwell, 2017).

33. According to Richard McCormick, "As organizations and as objects of loyalty, the major parties enjoyed their golden age during the last three decades of the nineteenth century. Although only loosely coordinated at the national level, the Democrats and Republicans each boasted awesome machines in localities where they were competitive, and on election days they shepherded enthusiastic and committed followers to the polls." See Richard McCormick, *The Party Period and Public Policy: American Politics from the Age of Jackson to the Progressive Era*, 171.

34. Worth Robert Miller, "Farmers and Third-Party Politics," chapter 13 in *The Gilded Age*, ed. Calhoun.

35. Alexander Keyssar, *The Right to Vote: The Contested History of Democracy in the United States* (New York: Basic Books, 2000), 103.

36. Summers, *Party Games*, 131–132.

37. Alan Ware, *The American Direct Primary—Party Institutionalization and Transformation in the United States* (New York; Cambridge: Cambridge University Press, 2002).

38. Thomas Mann and Norman Ornstein, *The Broken Branch: How Congress Is Failing America and How to Get It Back on Track* (New York; Oxford: Oxford University Press, 2002), 31; Steven S. Smith and Gerald Gamm, "The Dynamics of Party Government in Congress," in *Congress Reconsidered, 10th Edition*, ed. Lawrence Dodd and Bruce Oppenheimer (Washington, DC: CQ Press, 2013), 172–182; David W. Brady, *Congressional Voting in a Partisan Era: A Study of the McKinley Houses* (Lawrence, KS: University Press of Kansas, 1973); Eric Shickler, chapter 2 in *Disjointed Pluralism: Institutional Innovation and the Development of the U.S. Congress* (Princeton, NJ: Princeton University Press, 2001).

39. Congressional Record, April 22, 1880, 2661. Quoted in Gary Cox and Matthew McCubbins, "Legislative Leviathan Revisited," University of California working paper, https://law.yale.edu/sites/default/files/documents/pdf/mccubbins.pdf.

40. Summers, *Party Games*, chapter 2.

41. Cherny, *American Politics in the Gilded Age*, chapter 2.

42. Summers writes that "The republic was always at stake. This heightened, apocalyptic sense was one by-product of the political carnival." Summers, *Party Games*, 4.

43. See Mann and Ornstein, *The Broken Branch*, chapter 2.

44. This "spoils system" was central to political competition throughout the Gilded Age, even as it wound down after the Pendleton Act of 1883 that laid the foundation for a career civil service. See Francis Fukuyama, chapter 10 in *Political Order and Political Decay* (New York: Farrar, Straus and Giroux, 2014).

45. Charles Calhoun argues that while legislative action was certainly restricted due to partisan divides, a good amount of real policy solutions were passed during this period. Additionally, Calhoun argues it is improper to apply current standards to a Gilded Age government that was not yet a modern, regulatory state. See *The Gilded Age*, ed. Calhoun. For more on the development of anti-trust law see Wayne Collins, "Trusts and the Origins of Antitrust Legislation," *Fordham Law Review* (New York: Fordham University School of Law, 2013); William Letwin, "Congress and the Sherman Antitrust Law: 1887–1890," *The University of Chicago Law Review* (Chicago: The Law School, The University of Chicago, 1956).

46. Arnesen writes: "Workers living through this period of economic transformation must have felt as if they were riding a roller coaster in slow motion. The economy grew in fits and starts in the late nineteenth century. The United States faced two major economic depressions—from 1873 to 1877 and from 1893 to 1897—and in each crisis, unemployment rose to over 16 percent while substantial numbers of workers faced widespread underemployment and reduced wages. In an era before state-sponsored unemployment insurance or other benefits, losing one's job could mean being deprived of the means to survive." Arnesen, "American Workers and the Labor Movement in the Late Nineteenth Century," in *The Gilded Age*, Calhoun, 56.

47. Worth Robert Miller, "Farmers and Third-Party Politics," in chapter 13, *The Gilded Age*, ed. Calhoun et al.

48. Arnesen writes that "The closing decades of the nineteenth century were marked by a degree of class conflict, much of it violent, as great as any in the industrialized world. During the 1880s,

according the Bureau of Labor Statistics, the United States experienced almost ten thousand strikes and lockouts. In 1886 alone, a year that earned the title the 'great upheaval,' roughly seven hundred thousand workers either went out on strike or were locked out by their employers. Even larger numbers would participate in the titanic clashes of the early 1890s." See Arnesen, "American Workers and the Labor Movement in the Late Nineteenth Century," in *The Gilded Age*, ed. Calhoun.

49. After early progress with the Common School Movement before the Civil War, it wasn't until the Progressive Era that we saw a renewed push for anti-child labor laws and mandatory public education. This would eventually culminate in the High School Movement. See Claudia Goldin and Lawrence Katz, *The Race between Education and Technology* (Cambridge, MA: Harvard University Press, 2008); James Marten, *Children and Youth during the Gilded Age and Progressive Era: Volume Two* (New York: NYU Press, 2014).

50. At the time, these conditions were exposed in the work of Jacob Riis. See Jacob Riis, *How the Other Half Lives* (New York: C. Scribners Sons, 1890). For a more recent assessment, see Sean Dennis Cashman, *America in the Gilded Age, 3rd Edition* (New York: New York University Press, 1993), 146-150. A shocking statistic that highlights the poor social performance is the fact that Pittsburg had among the highest rates of typhoid in the world. See Arthur Link and Richard McCormick, *Progressivism* (Hoboken, NJ: Wiley-Blackwell, 1983), 29.

51. It is fitting that the era began with the takedown of Boss Tweed, who along with his Tammany Hall Allies embezzled millions of dollars from New York City. See "'Boss Tweed,'" *New York Times*, March 27, 2005, https://www.nytimes.com/2005/03/27/books/chapters/boss-tweed.html. But it didn't end there.

52. Henry Adams, *The Education of Henry Adams* (New York: Popular Edition, 1927), 294.

53. This section has benefited from the gracious advice and guidance of David Moss, Nancy Unger, Peter Levine, Robert Johnston, Jack Santucci, Maureen Flanagan, Walter Nugent, and Hahrie Han.

54. In championing the spirit of the Progressive movement, we are not blind to its shortcomings. Aspects of the Progressive movement were stained by prejudices, with reformers suppressing racial and ethnic minorities in the name of "good government." Many within the movement viewed the working class with either indifference or disdain and sought ways to control and limit the voices of average Americans. In promoting the public good and stamping out corruption, the Progressives at times deconstructed systems (like the urban "machines") that facilitated widespread political participation, especially by poor and immigrant communities. And some Progressive reforms, like partisan primaries, have had pernicious unintended consequences, as we have discussed. Yet by focusing narrowly on these deficiencies or limitations, much of the existing literature has overlooked a larger, and vitally important lesson that the Progressives can teach us today: We the people are not powerless. We control our democracy. We can change the rules of the game to deliver different outcomes. That is the Progressive legacy we must inherit.

Flanagan writes that "Progressives did not seek to overturn capitalism. They sought to revitalize a democratic promise of justice and equality and to move the country into a modern Progressive future by eliminating or at least ameliorating capitalism's worst excesses. They wanted to replace an individualistic, competitive society with a more cooperative, democratic one. They sought to bring a measure of social justice for all people, to eliminate political corruption, and to rebalance the relationship among business, labor, and consumers by introducing economic regulation." Maureen A. Flanagan, "Progressives and Progressivism in an Era of Reform," *Oxford Research Encyclopedia on American History* (New York; Oxford: Oxford University Press, 2016). For more on the origins of the movement, see Link and McCormick, *Progressivism*, Part One.

55. After detailing the political machines in several cities, Lincoln Steffens's 1904 book *The Shame of the Cities* (New York: S. S. McClure, 1904) declared that even more to blame than the political bosses were the members of the public who benefitted from the corruption and, more shameful still, those who did not benefit but remained apathetic, complacent, or cynical.

For more, see Frank Norris, *The Octopus: A Story of California* (Leipzig, Germany: Bernhard Tauchnitz, 1901); Ida Tarbell, *The History of the Standard Oil Company* (Mineola, NY: Dover

Publications, 1901); Upton Sinclair, *The Jungle* (New York: Doubleday, 1904); Lincoln Steffens, *The Shame of the Cities* (Bloomingdale, IL: McClure, Philips, and Co, 1904); David Graham Phillips, "The Treason of the Senate,"*Cosmopolitan*, 1906. Link and McCormick write that "Progressivism cannot be understood without seeing how the masses of Americans perceived and responded to such events. Widely circulated magazines gave people everywhere the sordid facts of corruption and carried the clamor for reform into every city, village, and county." Link and McCormick, *Progressivism*, 9.

56. See Link and McCormick, *Progressivism*.

57. Link and McCormick write that "It is not surprising that reformers of the late nineteenth century had little to do with one another. Their protests and programs had in common neither cause nor objective; each addressed a single problem. Few reform movements were based upon and understanding of the fundamental economic and social process of this time." Link and McCormick, *Progressivism*, 16. By contrast, Progressivism was a national movement that spanned social and class groups. Walter Lippmann wrote in 1921 that "An American will endure almost any insult except the charge that he is not progressive." Walter Lippmann, *Public Opinion* (New York: Harcourt, 1922), 71. There is much debate over who the leaders of the Progressive movement were, and what motivated their efforts. See David Kennedy, "Overview: The Progressive Era," *The Historian* 37, no. 3 (1975): 453–468. The traditional "progressive view" is that the reformers were a broad coalition that worked to expand democracy, wrestling control from special interests who exploited government for their own private gain. See Benjamin Parke DeWitt, *The Progressive Movement* (Seattle: University of Washington Press, 1915). In the 1950s a competing view, which rose to prominence with Richard Hofstadter's book *The Age of Reform*, held that the Progressive movement was led by a reactionary upper class who suffered "status anxiety," as their preeminence was challenged by business tycoons and party bosses. Richard Hofstadter, *The Age of Reform: From Bryan to FDR* (New York: Vintage, 1955). Others insist that the Progressive Era was led not by a reactionary old guard, but by the middle class that industrialization produced.

This emergent class sought to build an effective state, equipped with professional and scientific expertise. Samuel P. Hays, *The Response to Industrialism: 1885–1914* (Chicago: University of Chicago Press, 1957); Robert Wiebe, *The Search for Order: 1877–1920* (New York: Hill and Wang, 1967). This diversity in the movement has even led some to question whether Progressivism should be viewed as a unified movement at all. See Daniel T. Rodgers, "In Search of Progressivism," *Reviews in American History* (Baltimore: The Johns Hopkins University Press, 1982), 113–132; Peter G. Filene, "An Obituary for 'The Progressive Movement,'" *American Quarterly* (Baltimore: The Johns Hopkins University Press, 1970), 20-34; John D. Buenker, "The Progressive Era: A Search for Synthesis," in Eileen Tamura, *Americanization, Acculturation, and Ethnic Identity* (Champaign, IL: University of Illinois Press, 1994). However, Peter Levine does identify a common theme in the movement, writing that "The word *progressive*, as used around the turn of the century, was so ambiguous as to be virtually indefinable. However, practically all self-described progressives shared at least one commitment. They believed that there was a 'national interest' or 'public good' superior to special interest and market outcomes." Peter Levine, *The New Progressive Era* (Lanham, MD: Rowman & Littlefield Publishers, 2000), 18.

58. Robert Putnam, chapter 23 in *Bowling Alone: The Collapse and Revival of American Community* (New York: Simon & Schuster, 2001); Gerald Gamm and Robert Putnam, "The Growth of Voluntary Association in America, 1840–1940." *The Journal of Interdisciplinary History* (1999), 551–557; Theda Skocpol, *How Americans Became Civic* (Washington, DC: Brookings Institution Press, 1990); Richard McCormick, "Public Life in Industrial America, 1877, 1917" in Eric Foner, chapter 5 in *The New American History* (Philadelphia: Temple University Press, 1997).

59. Robert Putnam reflects on this transition when writing, "[g]enerally speaking, the wave began in the last third of the nineteenth century with organizations (like fraternal and cultural groups) focused primarily on the private concerns of their members, including leisure and self-help. In the last decade of the nineteenth century and the first decade of the twentieth century these

associations (and new ones spawned in that period gradually turned their attention to community issues and eventually to political reform. The earlier, inward-oriented phase of creating social networks paved the way for the later, outward-oriented phase of political action." Robert Putnam, *Bowling Alone: The Collapse and Revival of American Community* (New York: Simon & Schuster, 2001), 399.

60. Internal divisions have led some to argue it that there were actually many—not one unified—progressive movements, or to do away with the progressive concept entirely. See Peter Filene, "An Obituary for 'The Progressive Movement.'" *American Quarterly*, 20–34; Daniel T. Rodgers, "In Search of Progressivism," *Reviews in American History* (1982), 113–132; Maureen Flanagan, *America Reformed: Progressives and Progressivism: 1890s-1920* (Baltimore: The Johns Hopkins University Press, 2007).

61. This new ballot system was first advocated in 1882 by the Philadelphia Reform Association. Eldon Cobb Evans, *A History of the Australian Ballot System in the United States* (1917), 18. It was then endorsed in 1886 by New York mayoral candidate Henry George and his United Labor Party. Sarah Henry, *Progressivism and Democracy: Electoral Reform in the United States, 1888–1919*, 40. Success came quickly. Spurred by public outrage over vote buying, the first breakthrough was in the city of Louisville in 1888. Greatly impressed with the reform, one Louisville local reported later that year that, "'the election of last Tuesday was the first municipal election I have ever known which was not bought outright. As a matter of fact no attempts at bribery were made.'" David Moss et al., "An Australian Ballot for California?" (Harvard Business School paper, 2017). Ballot reform in Massachusetts was promoted by a diverse group. A Boston elite hoped it would bring order to elections and rein in corrupt party machines. Frank Foster's Boston Central Labor Union viewed it as a way to ensure better representation for workers. Connections within state government were critical to their success. H. H. Sprague, a member of the leading Boston "Dutch Treat" Club reform group, ran for and was elected to the state Senate and became chairman of the committee on election law. Another member of the Club, Richard Henry Danna III, was a central figure in Massachusetts politics and longtime reform champion. Dana crafted the ballot legislation that passed through both chambers with large majorities in May 1888. See Henry, *Progressivism and Democracy*, chapter 6.

62. Ware, *The American Direct Primary*, 31.

63. Ballot reform was not without its flaws. It was supported and exploited by many reformers as a way to restrict voting, serving as a literacy test that disenfranchised many immigrants and poorer voters. The duopoly also crafted ballot access rules to raise the barriers for third parties. While the adoption of the Australian Ballot restrained the party's ability to buy support and restrict vote-splitting (supporting candidates from more than one party), it also led to the disenfranchisement of millions of less-educated Americans, and allowed the parties to create restrictive ballot access rules that suppressed new forms of competition. David Moss writes that "the distinctive ballots that previously had been printed by each political party were replaced with uniform, state-printed 'Australian ballots,' which voters who could not read English often had difficulty using. As a consequence, many Americans who had the right to vote stopped voting or voted less often. In presidential elections, voter participation fell from around 75–80 percent in the 1880s to 1890s to about 60 percent in 1916." See David Moss, "Chapter 13: The Battle over the Initiative and Referendum in Massachusetts (1918)" in *Democracy* (Cambridge, MA: Harvard University Press, 2017); Henry reflects this point when writing "The original proposers quickly became disillusioned with ballot reform as a cure-all, complaining that it was too easily manipulated by machine politicians, who rewrote the provisions of legislation so as to discourage third parties, hampered fusion candidates by prohibiting names appearing in more than one party column, and raised the requirements for having parties appear on the official ballot at all. By the early twentieth century, critics had become outspoken on the adverse effects of such new form on third-party voters, and some had begun to accuse the instigators of the reform of deliberately plotting the disfranchisement of poorer voters, much as historians of a later generation would do." See Henry, *Progressivism and Democracy*, 43. See also Ware, *The American Direct Primary*.

64. The passage of the new ballot in Massachusetts quickly became the model for the rest of the country. Evans (1917) writes that this group was eventually able to infiltrate the legislature

when "one of the members of the 'Dutch Treat', Mr. H. H. Sprague, was elected to the State Senate and was made chairman of a committee on election law. Encouraged by these favorable signs, the club drafted a bill which was presented by Mr. Sprague. Mr. Hayes lent his support to the bill introduced by Mr. Sprague, a large number of petitions for the bill were received, and on May 29, 1888, the law was enacted." Eldon Cobb Evans, *A History of the Australian Ballot System in the United States* (Ann Arbor, MI: University of Michigan Library, 1917), 19. Ware (2002) writes that: "By 1893, thirty-one of the thirty-three non-southern states had adopted some variant of the Australian ballot law, and by 1893 the two remaining states (Iowa and Kansas) had followed suit." Ware, *The American Direct Primary*, 32.

65. The Australian Ballot remains the system we use to cast our ballots today. Many have rightly noted that ballot reform was sometimes exploited during the Progressive movement for partisan gain or to restrict the voting rights of African Americans, immigrants, and the poor. Such practices must be condemned. But despite its misuses, it did clean up elections and prove that reform was possible.

66. Merriam and Overacker write that "The direct primary was established in the United States as a protest against the unrepresentative character of the old-time convention. The abuses of the delegate system had produced widespread dissatisfaction and a general feeling that the nominating conventions did not reasonably reflect the will of the party. It was believed that the conventions were in many cases controlled by political bosses, and further that these bosses were either controlled by greedy and selfish industrial interests." See Charles Edward Merriam and Louise Overacker, *Primary Elections* (Chicago: The University of Chicago Press, 1928).

67. Previously, because the parties themselves printed their own ballots, they were not officially recognized as playing a role in the democratic processes. However, with the Australian Ballot, the government now controlled ballot access, and the parties had to petition to have their nominees included. In exchange for the privilege of having their candidates automatically included on the ballot, the major political parties entered a new relationship with government in which they were not treated like other organizations in civil society. Instead, the government regulated the parties' internal operations. This would become immediately important with the primary reform movement that followed quickly on the heels of ballot reform. The Democratic Mayor of Boston Josiah Quince reflected this second point when writing, " . . . this question of caucus reform has arisen directly and logically out of the adoption of the Australian Ballot . . . I think that today most of us, at least, see that it [the Australian Ballot] logically involves, leads to, and requires, first, the recognition, and second, the regulation of the political party, or of the convention, or of the caucus; it was the right of any citizen, or any number of citizens, to print a ballot and to present any nominations which he or they saw fit at the polls. But under the Australian Ballot system it is different; the State is obliged to recognize the existence of the political party and of political machinery; and the recognition of this inevitably and logically leads up to the regulation of the practices of political parties, of their conventions and of their caucuses." Ware, *The American Direct Primary*, 79. In the decade from 1890–1899, a number of states adopted binding laws, including statutes dictating when conventions should be held, how they should be structured, and what it meant to be a member of a party. These laws were implemented first at the municipal level, in major cities such as Boston, New York, Baltimore, Detroit, Cleveland, Cincinnati, St. Louis, Chicago, and San Francisco. The reforms then ascended to the state level. By the turn of the century, about two-thirds of states had enacted some form of primary law. Merriam and Overacker, chapter 3, in *Primary Elections*.

68. Ware, *The American Direct Primary*, 81.

69. Ware, *The American Direct Primary*, 124. There are two conflicting theories explaining the success of primary reform in the early 1900s. The traditional view, articulated in Merriam and Overacker (1928), is that the rapid spread of direct primaries was a triumph of reformers overcoming party bosses. A revisionist view, posited in Ware (2002), argues that reforms were not achieved in spite of the parties' best efforts, but rather because the parties made the calculation that the convention system, built for an era of local politics, was too unruly for an industrial society. Lawrence et al. (2013) tests these theories by studying the strength of party machines in the states where primary reform was first achieved and finds that anti-party pressure better

explained the data. Many Progressive reforms—including primary reform—were first achieved in Western states, where the party machines were weakest. This is a trend that also holds for the adoption of the initiative and referendum. Eric Lawrence et al., "The Adoption of Direct Primaries in the United States," *Party Politics* 19, no. 1 (2013).

70. J. W. Sullivan, *Direct Legislation by the Citizenship through the Initiative and Referendum* (University of California Libraries, 1893).

71. One leading member of the Direct Legislation League, William Simon U'ren, championed Sullivan's agenda in Oregon with the creation of the Joint Committee on Direct Legislation. The Joint Committee won the backing of farmers and workers and helped elect U'ren to the Oregon state legislature in 1896 as a member of the Populist Party. Yet in office, U'ren was frustrated and unable to pass his agenda.

So he shifted strategy. Rather than bundling structural reform with controversial policies, U'ren split from the Populists. As he separated himself from party politics, he continued to use his government connections to create a broad reform coalition. His new Nonpartisan Direct Legislation League, formed in 1898, framed I&R as a neutral reform. It was neither pro-business nor pro-labor, not pro-Democrat or pro-Republican—just pro-democracy. With this unifying message, I&R gained support from not only Oregon Federation of Labor and the Federated Trade Council, but also local middle managers and business owners, as well as major newspapers. In 1902, U'ren, became a national figure when Oregon adopted I&R, which passed through the legislature and was approved by the electorate in a vote of 62,024 to 5,668. See Moss, "Chapter 13"; Henry, *Progressivism and Democracy*, Part Two.

72. John Matsusaka, State Initiative & Referendum Institute, http://www.iandrinstitute.org/states.cfm. However, it is worth noting that unlike the other reforms, the adoption of the initiative and referendum was almost exclusively a Western phenomenon, with nineteen of the twenty-two states who had adopted I&R prior to 1920 west of the Mississippi. Thomas Goebel, "'A Case of Democratic Contagion': Direct Democracy in the American West, 1890–1920," *Pacific Historical Review* 66, no. 2 (1997). This is likely because Eastern states had much stronger party machines that were able to prevent the spread of I&R. Even in states like Massachusetts that did adopt I&R, it was a long, protracted battle. It was only in 1917, after I&R efforts had been rebuffed for over two decades, that the reform passed through a constitutional convention. Moss, "Chapter 13."

73. David Schmidt, *Citizen Lawmakers: The Ballot Initiative Revolution* (Philadelphia: Temple University Press, 1989), 25.

74. Tolbert finds: "From 1904–1994, voters approved fifty-eight initiatives in the areas of political reform and government organization. Progressive Era political reforms included the Australian (or long) ballot, home rule for local governments and municipalities, secret ballot, manager-council system, nonpartisan local elections, insulation of judges from political pressure, direct primary, direct election of US Senators, women's suffrage . . . The initiative process was first used to establish nomination of candidates through primary elections in Arkansas, Maine, Montana, Oregon and South Dakota." Caroline J. Tolbert, "Direct Democracy as a Catalyst for 21st Century Political Reform"; Schmidt, *Citizen Lawmakers*.

75. No bill was even reported out of committee in the House until 1888. Zachary Clopton and Steven Art, "The Meaning of the Seventeenth Amendment and a Century of State Defiance," *Northwestern University Law Review* 107, no. 3 (2015).

76. University of Chicago Law Professor David Strauss writes that "At most, the (Seventeenth) Amendment served to mop up outliers that were few in number and would probably have fallen into line before long." Strauss links this to a larger point about constitutional amendments. Reviewing the other Constitutional Amendments of the Progressive Era—the Sixteenth which authorized an income tax, the Eighteenth which inaugurated prohibition, and the Nineteenth which extended the franchise to women—Strauss generalizes the point above, writing: "Notwithstanding all the attention that constitutional amendments receive, however, our constitutional order would look little different if a formal amendment process did not exist. At least since the first few decades of the Republic, constitutional amendments have not been an important means by which the Constitution, in practice, has changed. Many changes have come

about without amendments. In some instances, even though amendments were rejected, the law changed in the way the failed amendments sought. Several amendments that were thought to be important in fact had little effect until society changed by other means. Other amendments did little more than ratify changes that had already come about in other ways. If this thesis is correct, it suggests that precedents and other traditions are often as important as the text of the amended Constitution; that political activity, in general, should not focus on proposed constitutional amendments; and that American constitutional law is best seen as the result of a complex, evolutionary process, rather than of discrete, self-consciously political acts by a sovereign People." David Strauss, "The Irrelevance of Constitutional Amendments," *Harvard Law Review* (2001).

77. Moss, *Democracy*, "Chapter 13."

78. In 1901, Oregon held the first "primary" for the Senate in which voters could express their preferences. The parties initially ignored the results, and state legislators picked the candidate of their choosing. Led by William Simon U'ren, however, reformers passed a ballot measure in 1904 that required candidates for the state legislature to pledge whether or not they would respect the results of the Senate primary. A candidate's stance was required to appear next to their name on the ballot. Faced with growing public pressure, almost all candidates agreed to respect the primaries, which became popular elections for the Senate in everything but name. In 1908 Oregon citizens solidified the process by passing another ballot measure making the campaign pledges binding. Henry, *Progressivism and Democracy*, Part Two.

79. Caroline J. Tolbert, "Direct Democracy as a Catalyst for 21st Century Political Reform," *Political Science Quarterly* (September 2003).

80. Jeffrey Jenkins, "The Evolution of Party Leadership," *The Oxford Handbook of the American Congress* (2011); Lawrence Dodd and Bruce Oppenheimer, "The House in a Time of Crisis: Economic Turmoil and Partisan Upheaval," in *Congress Reconsidered, 10th Edition*, ed. Dodd and Oppenheimer, 28.

81. Kenneth Shepsle, "The Changing Textbook Congress," in John Chubb and Paul Peterson, *Can Government Govern?* (Washington, DC: Brookings Institution Press, 1989).

82. Lawrence Dodd and Bruce Oppenheimer, "The House in a Time of Crisis," in *Congress Reconsidered 10th Edition*, ed. Lawrence Dodd and Bruce Oppenheimer.

83. Robert E. Mutch, *Buying the Vote: A History of Campaign Finance Reform* (New York; Oxford: Oxford University Press, 2014), chapters 1–2.

84. Mutch, *Buying the Vote: A History of Campaign Finance Reform*, chapters 3–4.

85. Capturing the magnitude of the change to the industry structure, in 1910 William Allen White wrote that "to have told the campaign managers of '84 or '88 that within a quarter of century the whole nation would be voting by secret ballot, the candidates nominated in two-thirds of the American states by a direct vote of the people, without the intervention of conventions or caucuses, and that further than that every dollar spent by a candidate or by a party committee would have to be publicly accounted for, would have set . . . the managers of those days cackling in derision until they were black in the face." William Allen White, *The Old Order Changeth* (CreateSpace Publishing, 1910), 241.

86. For example, see David Huyssen, *Progressive Inequality* (Cambridge, MA: Harvard University Press, 2014).

87. Attributed to Henry Luce in 1941, the term "American Century" connotes a period of American dominance, in which America led the world politically, economically, and culturally.

88. "World Exports as Percentage of Gross World Product," Global Policy Forum, archived from the original on July 12, 2008, https://web.archive.org/web/20080712023541/http://www .globalpolicy.org/socecon/trade/tables/exports2.htm.

89. United States Census Bureau, *The Foreign-Born Population in the United States*, https://www .census.gov/newsroom/pdf/cspan_fb_slides.pdf.

90. Jynnah Radford, "Key Findings About U.S. Immigrants," Pew Research Center, June 17, 2019, https://www.pewresearch.org/fact-tank/2019/06/17/key-findings-about-u-s-immigrants/.

91. "The Effects of Immigration on the United States Economy," Penn Wharton University of Pennsylvania, June 27, 2016, https://budgetmodel.wharton.upenn.edu/issues/2016/1/27/the-effects-of-immigration-on-the-united-states-economy.

Chapter 5

1. Jason D. Olson and Omar H. Ali, "A Quiet Revolution: The Early Successes of California's Top Two Nonpartisan Primary," Open Primaries, August, 2015, https://d3n8a8pro7vhmx.cloudfront.net/openprimaries/pages/418/attachments/original/1440450728/CaliforniaReportFinal8.24small.pdf?1440450728.

2. Louis Jacobson, "The Six Most Dysfunctional State Governments," *National Journal*, July 13, 2009. http://www.nationaljour-nal.com/njonline/the-six-most-dysfunctional-state-governments-20090713.

3. Charles Munger Jr., "California's Top-Two Primary: A Successful Reform" (paper presented the USC Schwarzenegger Institute for State and Global Policy, February 22, 2019), http://www.schwarzeneggerinstitute.com/institute-in-action/article/californias-top-two-primary-a-successful-reform.

4. The top-two primary yielded eighty same-party general elections in California, for the Assembly, state Senate, and US House of Representatives combined, in the general elections of 2012, 2014, and 2016. Of these same-party district elections, twenty-two saw the reelection of incumbents running against a token opponent of their own party. The remaining fifty-eight were highly competitive: a total of $205 million was spent in those contests; ten incumbents were defeated. In contrast, over the not three but five election cycles from 2002 to 2010, when there were partisan primaries, an incumbent lost to a member of his or her own party in one race for the Assembly, one race for the state Senate, and one race for the US House, for a decade total of three. See http://schwarzeneggerinstitute.com/institute-in-action/article/californias-top-two-primary-a-successful-reform. The Lucy Burns Institute similarly found a jump in the competitiveness of California races after the reform was implemented. See Carl Klarner, "Democracy in Decline: The Collapse of the 'Close Race' in State Legislatures," Lucy Burns Institute, May 6, 2015, http://ballotpedia.org/Competitiveness_in_State_Legislative_Elections:_1972-2014.

5. Taryn Luna, "State Legislature's Approval Rating Hits 50 Percent," *Sacramento Bee*, September 28, 2016, https://www.sacbee.com/news/politics-government/capitol-alert/article104797076.html.

6. Arnold Schwarzenegger and Ro Khanna, "Don't Listen to the Establishment Critics. California's Open Primary Works," *Washington Post*, June 18, 2018, https://www.washingtonpost.com/news/posteverything/wp/2018/06/18/dont-listen-to-the-establishment-critics-californias-open-primary-works/.

7. Nancy Lavin and Rich Robinson, "John McCain Understood How Ranked Choice Voting Strengthens Our Democracy," FairVote, August 27, 2018, https://www.fairvote.org/john_mccain_understood_how_ranked_choice_voting_strengthens_our_democracy.

8. Sarah John and Andrew Douglas, "Candidate Civility and Voter Engagement in Seven Cities with Ranked Choice Voting," *National Civic Review* 106, no. 1 (2017): 25–29.

9. Denise Munro Robb, "The Effects on Democracy of Instant Runoff Voting" (PhD diss., University of California Irvine, 2011).

10. Lee Drutman, *Breaking the Two-Party Doom Loop: The Case for Multiparty Democracy in America* (New York; Oxford: Oxford University Press, 2020).

11. Robert Pear, "If Only Laws Were Like Sausages," *New York Times*, December 4, 2010, https://www.nytimes.com/2010/12/05/weekinreview/05pear.html.

12. Mike Gallagher, "How to Salvage Congress," *Atlantic*, November 13, 2018, https://www.theatlantic.com/ideas/archive/2018/11/gallagher-congress/575689/.

13. See Judy Schneider, Christopher M. Davis, and Betsy Palmer, "Reorganization of the House of Representatives: Modern Reform Efforts," CRS Report for Congress, 2003; Congressional Institute, "Joint Committees on the Organization of Congress: A Short History,"

October 15, 2015; Donald R. Wolfensberger, "A Brief History of Congressional Reform Efforts," February, 2013; Casey Burgat, "Congressional Reorganization Acts," R Street Institute, 2018; Lee Drutman and Kevin R. Kosar, "The Other Biggest Problem in Washington," *New York Times*, September 11, 2018, https://www.nytimes.com/2018/09/11/opinion/congress-senate-house-washington-.html.

14. In April of 1946, one national survey found that only 14 percent of the electorate thought Congress was doing a "good job." See Donald R. Matthews, "American Political Science and Congressional Reform," *The Reorganization of Congress: A Report of the Committee on Congress of the American Political Science Association* (Washington, DC: Public Affairs Press, 1945).

15. Matthews, "American Political Science and Congressional Reform," 92–93.

16. *The Reorganization of Congress: A Report of the Committee on Congress of the American Political Science Association* (Washington, DC: Public Affairs Press, 1945), 10.

17. *The Reorganization of Congress*, 4.

18. *The Reorganization of Congress*.

19. Matthews, "American Political Science and Congressional Reform," 95–98.

20. H. R. 18. 70th Cong., Sec. 2 (February 19, 1945).

21. Roger H. Davidson, "The Advent of the Modern Congress," *Legislative Studies Quarterly* 15, no. 3 (August 1990): 365–370.

22. Davidson, "The Advent of the Modern Congress," 365.

Chapter 6

1. "New State Ice Co. v. Liebmann," 285 U.S. 262, 311 (1932) (Brandeis, J., dissenting).

2. For congressional elections, legislators in Washington, DC, could vote to change the electoral system across the country with a federal law. In the 115th Congress (2017–2018), Representative Donald Breyer of Virginia proposed a bill called the "Fair Representation Act" that would implement ranked-choice voting for all congressional races, and Representative John Delaney of Maryland introduced the "Open Our Democracy Act," which would create top-two primaries in all congressional races. In addition to those top priority political innovations, a dozen bills proposed in this congressional session took on gerrymandering, while many more tackled the issue of money in politics. Some innovative proposals were also offered to restructure the legislative machinery to make it more open to deliberation and compromise, and to retool the FEC to turn it into a real regulator. So far, however, these bills have made little progress in a Congress beholden to the duopoly. But once we begin to see progress in enough states, it is possible that Congress would vote to expand these innovations to the entire nation for congressional elections.

3. See John Matsusaka, "State-by-State List of Initiative and Referendum Provisions," Initiative & Referendum Institute, http://www.iandrinstitute.org/states.cfm.

4. Twenty-one states have both ballot initiatives and referenda. Two states—Maryland and New Mexico—have referenda, but not initiatives. In these two states, citizens cannot totally bypass politicians to pass political innovations. See Initiative & Referendum Institute, "State-by-State List of Initiative and Referendum Provisions," http://www.iandrinstitute. org/states.cfm.

5. "Movement by State," Open Primaries, https://www.openprimaries.org/movement_by _state; "2019 Legislation Advancing Ranked Choice Voting," FairVote, https://www.fairvote .org/2019_legislation_advancing_ranked_choice_voting.

6. In addition to California and Washington, which are covered in this section, Nebraska and Louisiana also have some adopted some version of top-two primaries. Nebraska uses top-two primaries for its nonpartisan state legislature (discussed below). Louisiana, meanwhile, has a runoff election structure that is very similar to top-two. In the "primary," voters can select their favorite candidate, regardless of party. Unlike top-two, if a candidate receives more than 50 percent of the vote in this round, he or she is declared the winner. But if no candidate receives a majority, as with top-two, the two candidates who received the most votes proceed to the "general election" round.

In 2019, Marcia Morey (D-NC), Zack Hawkins (D-NC), and Ray Russell (D-NC) all sponsored a bill for the General Assembly of North Carolina to "establish a process for Top Four Open Primary and three elections and to appropriate funds for that purpose." This bill also includes a provision for the usage of ranked-choice voting in general elections. See https://www.ncleg.gov/Sessions/2019/Bills/House/PDF/H994v0.pdf. Senator Chris Rothfuss proposed a similar bill for Wyoming in January 2019. This bill proposed the use of ranked-choice voting in primary elections to select the top four candidates to move on to the general election. The bill also proposed using ranked-choice voting for the remaining candidates in the general election. See https://wyoleg.gov/Legislation/2019/SF0065.

7. The blanket primary was spurred by support from the Washington State Grange, which sponsored a successful initiative in 1935. "History of Washington State Primary Systems," https://www.sos.wa.gov/_assets/elections/historyofwashingtonstateprimarysystems.pdf; "Initiative 872," *Spokesman-Review*, July 1, 2009, http://www.spokesman.com/stories/2004/oct/26/initiative-872/.

8. A federal district court initially ruled that Washington's blanket primary was constitutional in 2002. The parties then appealed this decision to the Ninth Circuit, which found that the blanket primary was unconstitutional because it violated the rights of free association. The State of Washington and the Grange then appealed this decision to the Supreme Court, but in February 2004 the Supreme Court refused to hear the case, which meant that the Ninth Circuit decision declaring the blanket primary unconstitutional stood. "History of Washington State Primary Systems," accessed November 2019, https://www.sos.wa.gov/_assets/elections/historyofwashingtonstateprimarysystems.pdf.

9. Secretary of State Sam Reed first introduced the idea of the top-two to the legislature in the 2001 session and, with the help of the Grange's lobbying efforts, he was able to create a coalition of Democratic and Republican legislators to support the bill. While the bill survived the Senate, the Speaker of the House ultimately refused to call a vote on the measure. Sam Reed, telephone conversation with author, April, 2019.

10. Reed, telephone conversation with author.

11. Following the gubernatorial veto, the ballot initiative campaign entered into full force. Secretary Reed held a press conference with key legislators from both parties and the Grange, where they announced the top-two initiative. Reed, telephone conversation with author. That same week, the Grange launched its first wave of statewide radio advertising campaign condemning the governor and encouraging voters to sign Initiative 872 petitions. In June 2004, Initiative 872 qualified for the November ballot with 308,402 valid signatures. See http://blanketprimary.org/pressroom/release-2004-04-05.php. On November 2, 2004, voters approve Initiative 872 and Washington becomes the first state to adopt a top-two primary system for congressional and state-level elections, https://ballotpedia.org/Top-two_primary.

12. Susan Gilmore, "Supreme Court Rules in Favor of Washington State Top-Two Primary," *Seattle Times*, March 18, 2008, https://www.seattletimes.com/seattle-news/supreme-court-rules-in-favor-of-washington-state-top-two-primary/.

13. Eric McGhee, "Political Reform and Moderation in California's Legislature," Public Policy Institute of California, May 2018, https://www.ppic.org/wp-content/uploads/r-0517emr.pdf.

14. Phillip Reese, "California Legislators Rarely Break from Party Line in Floor Votes," *Sacramento Bee*, October 11, 2012.

15. Arnold Schwarzenegger and Ro Khanna, "Don't Listen to the Establishment Critics. California's Open Primary Works," *Washington Post*, June 18, 2018, https://www.washingtonpost.com/news/posteverything/wp/2018/06/18/dont-listen-to-the-establishment-critics-californias-open-primary-works/?noredirect=on&utm_term=.42066db02666.

16. "Grading the States 2005: A Look Inside," Government Performance Project, Pew Charitable Trust, 2004–2006, http://www.pewtrusts.org/~/media/legacy/uploadedfiles/pcs_assets/2004-2006/GPPReport2005pdf.pdf.

17. "Californians and Their Government," Public Policy Institute of California, March 2010.

18. Schwarzenegger and Khanna, "Don't Listen to the Establishment Critics."

19. Jason D. Olson and Omar H. Ali, "A Quiet Revolution: The Early Successes of California's Top Two Nonpartisan Primary," OpenPrimaries, August 2015, https://www.openprimaries.org/research_california.

20. Olson and Ali, "A Quiet Revolution."

21. "California Proposition 62, 'Modified Blanket' Primaries Act (2004)," https://ballotpedia .org/California_Proposition_62,_%22Modified_Blanket%22_Primaries_Act_(2004).

22. Christopher Caen, "The Consequences of California's Top-Two Primary," *Atlantic*, December 29, 2015, https://www.theatlantic.com/politics/archive/2015/12/california-top-two-open-primary/421557/.

23. "The Unforgivable State," *Economist*, February 19, 2009, https://www.economist.com/united-states/2009/02/19/the-ungovernable-state.

24. Jesse McKinley, "Calif. Voting Change Could Signal Big Political Shift," *New York Times*, June 9, 2010, https://www.nytimes.com/2010/06/10/us/politics/10prop.html.

25. "USC Dornsife/Los Angeles Times California Poll," USC Dornsife/Los Angeles Times, May 25, 2018, https://drive.google.com/file/d/1g5uibGxcEuknURkZZvT4Ah4Q9-IvalVz/view.

26. See http://schwarzeneggerinstitute.com/institute-in-action/article/californias-top-two-primary-a-successful-reform. The Lucy Burns Institute similarly found a jump in the competitiveness of California races after the reform was implemented. See Carl Klarner, "Democracy in Decline: The Collapse of the 'Close Race' in State Legislatures," Lucy Burns Institute, May 6, 2015, http://ballotpedia.org/Competitiveness_in_State_Legislative_Elections:_1972-2014.

27. In 34 percent of competitive same-party general elections, the winning candidate in the top-two primary would not have a partisan primary in the old primary system, http://schwarzeneggerinstitute.com/institute-in-action/article/californias-top-two-primary-a-successful-reform.

28. Olson and Ali, "A Quiet Revolution."

29. Christian Grose, "Political Reforms in California Are Associated with Less Ideological Extreme State Legislators." The Public Policy Institute of California (PPIC) finds that while "both Democrats and Republicans in other states have been polarizing . . . The fact that California's representatives have not moved closer to the poles or have moved slightly in a more moderate direction stands out." See https://www.ppic.org/wp-content/uploads/r-0517emr.pdf. Eric McGhee and Boris Shor similarly find a small increase in moderation in the California state legislature in recent years. See Eric McGhee and Boris Shor, "Has the Top Two Primary Elected More Moderates?" *Perspectives on Politics* 15, no. 4 (2017): 1053–1066.

30. Schwarzenegger and Khanna, "Don't Listen to the Establishment Critics"; Li Zhou, "Washington Has a Top-Two Primary. Here's How It Works," Vox, August 7, 2018, https://www.vox.com/2018/8/7/17649564/washington-primary-results.

31. Zhou, "Washington Has a Top-Two Primary."

32. Adam Nagourney, "California Sees Gridlock Ease in Governing," *New York Times*, October 18, 2013, https://www.nytimes.com/2013/10/19/us/california-upends-its-image-of-legislative-dysfunction.html?%20r=1&amp.

33. "California Top-Four Primary Initiative (2018)," Ballotpedia, https://ballotpedia.org/California_Top-Four_Primary_Initiative_(2018); "FairVote California," FairVote, https://www .fairvoteca.org/.

34. Marina Villeneuve, "AP EXPLAINS: Maine Tries Ranked-Choice Voting," *U.S. News*, June 11, 2018, https://www.usnews.com/news/best-states/maine/articles/2018-06-11/ap-explains-maine-tries-ranked-choice-voting.

35. Jessie Scanlon, "Could Maine's New Ranked-Choice Voting Change American Elections?" *Boston Globe Magazine*, October 17, 2018, https://www.bostonglobe.com/magazine/2018/10/17/could-maine-new-ranked-choice-voting-change-american-elections/6VqNC73bQzMrPd0RSepA8L/story.html.

36. Editorial Board, "Ranked-Choice Voting Unlikely to Gain Traction in Maine," *Sun Journal*, November 11, 2010, https://www.sunjournal.com/2010/11/11/ranked-choice-voting-unlikely -gain-traction-maine/.

37. "Spotlight: Maine," FairVote, https://www.fairvote.org/spotlight_maine#portland.

38. Howard Dean, "Howard Dean: How to Move Beyond the Two-Party System," *New York Times*, October 7, 2016, https://www.nytimes.com/2016/10/08/opinion/howard-dean-how-to-move-beyond-the-two-party-system.html.

39. "Portland: Ranked Choice Voting in Portland, Maine," FairVote, https://www.fairvote.org/portland; Matt Dunlap radio interview, 100.5 WLOB News Talk Maine, September 15, 2017, https://wlobradio.com/index.php/2017/09/15/09-15-17-matt-dunlap/.

40. "Spotlight: Maine," FairVote, https://www.fairvote.org/spotlight_maine#portland.

41. Colin Woodard, "Maine's Radical Democratic Experiment," *Politico Magazine*, March 27, 2018, https://www.politico.com/magazine/story/2018/03/27/paul-lepage-maine-governor-ranked-choice-voting-217715.

42. "Timeline of Ranked Choice Voting in Maine," FairVote, https://www.fairvote.org/maine_ballot_initiative.

43. Larry Diamond, "How to Reverse the Degradation of Our Politics," *American Interest*, November 10, 2017, https://www.the-american-interest.com/2017/11/10/reverse-degradation-politics/.

44. Larry Diamond, "A Victory for Democratic Reform," *American Interest*, June 15, 2018, https://www.the-american-interest.com/2018/06/15/a-victory-for-democratic-reform/.

45. Cara McCormick, interview by author, May 2019.

46. Diamond, "A Victory for Democratic Reform."

47. Edward D. Murphy and Peter McGuire, "As Mainers Vote in First Ranked-Choice Election, LePage Says He 'Probably' Won't Certify Referendum Results," *Press Herald*, June 12, 2018, https://www.pressherald.com/2018/06/12/voters-turn-out-for-historic-election-day/.

48. "Enough's Enough," *Ellsworth American*, May 9, 2018, https://www.ellsworthamerican.com/opinions/editorials/enoughs-enough/.

49. Dennis Hoey, "Oscar Winner Jennifer Lawrence Lends Support to Ranked-Choice Voting," *Press Herald*, June 7, 2018, https://www.pressherald.com/2018/06/07/oscar-winner-jennifer-lawrence-lends-support-to-ranked-choice-voting/.

50. "Maine Question 1, Ranked-Choice Voting Delayed Enactment and Automatic Repeal Referendum (June 2018)," Ballotpedia, https://ballotpedia.org/Maine_Question_1,_Ranked-Choice_Voting_Delayed_Enactment_and_Automatic_Repeal_Referendum_(June_2018).

51. Larry Diamond, "A New Age of Reform," *American Interest*, November 16, 2018, https://www.the-american-interest.com/2018/11/16/a-new-age-of-reform/.

52. "Maine Gov. Signs Off on Congressional Race Results, But Calls the Election 'Stolen,'" CBS News, December 28, 2018, https://www.cbsnews.com/news/maine-congressional-race-governor-paul-lepage-signs-off-on-jared-golden-winner/.

53. Diamond, "How to Reverse the Degradation of Our Politics."

54. As of 2019, seven states—Maine, California, Colorado, Maryland, Massachusetts, Minnesota, and New Mexico—contain cities that have already implemented ranked-choice voting for municipal elections. On top of this, another four states—Florida, Michigan, Oregon, and Tennessee—contain cities that have adopted but not yet implemented ranked-choice voting for municipal elections. In 2018, Utah passed a pilot program that allows municipalities to use ranked-choice voting for 2019 elections (participating cities: Cottonwood Heights, Lehi City, Payson City, Vineyard City, and West Jordan City). See, "Ranked Choice Voting," Ballotpedia, accessed April 2019, https://ballotpedia.org/Ranked-choice_voting_(RCV)#Ranked_choice_voting_in_the_United_States.

55. Iowa and Nevada plan to allow early voters to use it, while Hawaii, Alaska, Kansas, and Wyoming plan to allow all voters to use it. "Where Ranked Choice Voting Is Used," FairVote, https://www.fairvote.org/where_is_ranked_choice_voting_used.

56. See USC Price, "Terminate Gerrymandering: Engineering Victories in Michigan, Colorado, Utah, Missouri and Ohio," YouTube, January 15, 2019, https://www.youtube.com/watch?v=vWUXpMO3-88&t=102s.

57. David Brooks, "The Localist Revolution," *New York Times*, July 19, 2018, www.nytimes.com/2018/07/19/opinion/national-politics-localism-populism.html.

58. Roger Davidson, "The Advent of the Modern Congress: The Legislative Reorganization Act of 1946," *Legislative Studies Quarterly* 15, no. 3 (1990): 360.

59. Paul Kane, "Against the Odds, Select Committee Aims to Push Congress into the 21st Century," *The Washington Post*, May 25, 2019, https://www.washingtonpost.com/powerpost/against-the-odds-select-committee-aims-to-push-congress-into-the-21st-century/2019/05/24/3dff17f6-7d97-11e9-8bb7-0fc796cf2ec0_story.html.

60. John F. Kennedy, chapter 8, in *Profiles in Courage* (1956). In his autobiography (1945), George Norris recounts his dismay for the "autocratic power that the rules of the House gave to the Speaker." In Norris's first meeting on the House Committee on Public Grounds and Buildings, he learned—and could not understand why—the Speaker had the power to decide whether or not the committee could draft an omnibus public building bill: "Then, right then, I believe the light dawned upon me and I began to see for the first time that the Republican party was subject to influences similar to those that I believed controlled the Democratic party; and soon I learned there was no difference between the parties in this respect. Both of them were machine-controlled, and the Democratic and Republican machines often worked in perfect harmony and brotherly love." See George Norris, *Fighting Liberal: The Autobiography of George W. Norris* (New York: Macmillan, 1945), 96.

61. Momentum toward Nebraska's one-branch legislature stemmed in large part from progressive ideals that required "adapting the machinery of state government to social and economic change." See John P. Senning, *The One-House Legislature* (New York: McGraw-Hill Book Company, 1937), 42.

62. In 1915, a Nebraskan joint legislative committee led by Rep. John N. Norton—which had investigated how to align political reform with progressive ideals—advanced a recommendation for a unicameral legislature, but no action was taken. Legislative proposals for a unicameral legislature, advanced by Norton and others, further failed in 1917, at Nebraska's 1919–1920 constitutional convention, and in 1923, 1925, and 1933. However, the public appetite for structural change grew after the 1933 session "fumbled badly on tax legislation, liquor regulations, and reapportionment" and failed to an appropriations bill. See James R. Rogers, "Judicial Review Standards in Unicameral Legislative Systems: A Positive Theoretic and Historical Analysis," *Creighton Law Review* 33 (1999) 69–70; Nebraska Legislature, "Inside Our Nation's Only Unicameral," (2018) 13; Charlyne Berens, *One House: The Unicameral's Progressive Vision for Nebraska* (Lincoln: University of Nebraska Press, 2005).

63. Seth Masket and Boris Shor, "Polarization without Parties: Term Limits and Legislative Partisanship in Nebraska's Unicameral Legislature," *State Politics & Policy Quarterly* (2014).

64. Berens, *One House*, 36; Senning, *The One-House Legislature*.

65. Berens, *One House*; Senning, *The One-House Legislature*. A poll taken in fall of 1934 by the American Legislators' Association found that the majority (i.e., over 50 percent) of the following groups were against one-house legislatures: Nebraska Representatives, United States Representatives, State Senators, United States Senators, American Bankers Associations, State Representatives, American Bar Association members, Nebraska Senators, newspaper editors, and business executives. In majority support of one-house legislatures were: American Association of University Women, American Foundation of Labor, League of Women Voters, Government Research Association, American Political Science Association. See "Two Houses—or One?" *State Government*, 207–208, as cited in *Unicameralism in Practice: The Nebraska Legislative System*, compiled by Harrison Boyd Summers, vol. 11, no. 5 (1937).

66. Minnesota had a nonpartisan legislature from 1913 until 1973. Unlike Nebraska, Minnesota's adoption of the nonpartisan ballot was not the result of a grassroots movement. Rather, it was the initiative of the state legislators. Interestingly, the adoption of this system in Minnesota was somewhat of an accident. In 1913, there was a legislative proposal to require nonpartisan elections in municipal and judicial elections, a common proposal throughout the Progressive states in the early twentieth century. A. J. Rockne, leading a group of conservative Republicans, attempted to kill the bill by attaching a poison-pill amendment mandating nonpartisanship in state legislative elections, as well. Much to their surprise, it passed. Despite the nonpartisan intentions behind the bill, two dominant ideological factions—the Liberals and Conservatives—had formed in the state legislature by the late 1930s. Seth Masket argues

that organized interests outside of the chamber served to maintain the legislative caucuses. Consequently, Minnesota's nonpartisan legislative machinery did not last long, and the shift back to party balloting in 1973 was merely a "formality." See Seth E. Masket, *The Inevitable Party: Why Attempts to Kill the Party System Fail and How They Weaken Democracy* (New York; Oxford: Oxford University Press, 2016), 84–104. It is likely that the different outcomes in Nebraska and Minnesota can be attributed to the different ways in which their nonpartisan legislatures were established. In Nebraska, it was a multiyear, public campaign. In Minnesota, it was rapid and largely contained within the confines of the state legislature. The lesson might be that such a monumental reform requires time, transparency, and public support.

67. Despite nonpartisan election processes, elected officials still have a Democrat or Republican affiliation, which voters can ascertain through other means. Seth Masket of University of Denver and Boris Shor of Georgetown University, for example, note: Newspaper and online coverage of campaigns often refers explicitly to the party affiliations of the candidates, and researchers and political activists can readily learn this information from the media, from state legislative voter records, and from a roster published by the state government. See Masket and Shor, "Polarization without Parties," 4.

68. As noted by Masket: "There is no official majority or minority caucus in the legislature (known popularly as the Unicam), nor are there whips or party leaders. The Speaker is elected by his colleagues through a secret ballot, as are the chairs of all the standing committees." See Masket and Shor, "Polarization without Parties," 4.

69. Michael Dulaney, "Committee Structure of the Nebraska Legislature," Nebraska Council of School Administrators, accessed February 10, 2018, http://legislative.ncsa .org/nebraska-unicameral/committee-structure-nebraska-legislature.

70. Kim Robak, the 35th Lieutenant Governor of Nebraska, said that "the Speaker does not owe the political party loyalty; rather, the Speaker owes allegiance to the members as a whole." See Kim Robak, "The Nebraska Unicameral and Its Lasting Benefits," *Nebraska Law Review* 76 (1997).

71. *Lincoln Star*, January 5, 1937, as cited in Berens, *One House*, 45.

72. Studies examining roll call voting in Nebraska consistently fail to find partisan underpinnings. Welch and Carlson identify a "randomness" in voting behavior by Nebraska legislators in a study of Nebraska's roll call vote, with a notable decline in the relationship between party and roll call voting after 1947, relative to 1927 (when the legislature was partisan) and 1937 (when most members had previously served in the partisan legislature). Data from Eric H. Carlson and Susan Welch, "The Impact of Party on Voting Behavior in the Nebraska Legislature," in *Nonpartisanship in the Legislative Process*, John C. Comer and James B. Johnson (Washington, DC: University Press of America, 1978), as cited in John C. Comer, "The Nebraska Nonpartisan Legislature: An Evaluation," *State & Local Government Review* 12, no. 3 (1980), 101. In their examination of at least mildly contentious roll calls in 1999–2000, Wright and Schaffner reaffirm that "Nebraska legislators vote with each other across issues almost at random." See Gerald C. Wright and Brian F. Schaffner, "The Influence of Party: Evidence from the State Legislatures," *American Political Science Review* 96, no. 2 (2002), 374. Again, using mildly contentious roll calls in 1999–2000, Schaffner found that "members of Nebraska's parties are dispersed throughout the ideological space, with the distributions of both parties almost entirely overlapping." See Brian F. Schaffner, "Political Parties and the Representativeness of Legislative Committees," *Legislative Studies Quarterly XXXII*, no. 3 (August 2007), 489. However, Shor and McCarty captured state legislative roll call votes from 1993 through 2013 and found that the Nebraska legislature is not uniquely ideologically un-polarized, though it was in the mid-1990s. See Masket and Shor, "Polarization without Parties," 5. This is likely related to the imposition of term limits starting in 2000. The law resulted in the forced retirement of a large cohort of incumbents in 2006, when the law first became effective. The parties exploited the cohort of forced retired legislators in 2006 to recruit, train, and fund candidates that will likely adhere to the party agenda.

73. Masket and Shor, "Polarization without Parties," 6–10.

74. These outcomes have recently deteriorated due to the misguided implementation of term limits. Masket and Shor found that a Nebraska initiative that limited state legislators to two consecutive four-year terms, which passed in 2000, has had a major impact on polarization in the Unicameral. The law resulted in the forced retirement of a large cohort of incumbents in 2006, when the law first became effective. The parties exploited the cohort of forced retired legislators in 2006 to recruit, train, and fund candidates that will likely adhere to the party agenda. As a result, while the Nebraska state legislature was one of the least polarized in the country in the mid-1990s, it has now moved toward the middle of the pack (although it is still below average). See Masket and Shor, "Polarization without Parties."

75. "Unicameral Update," accessed February 25, 2018, http://update.legislature. ne.gov/?p=15429.

76. Mark Berman, "Nebraska Lawmakers Abolish the Death Penalty, Narrowly Overriding Governor's Veto," *Washington Post*, May 27, 2015, https://www.washingtonpost.com/ news/post-nation/wp/2015/05/27/nebraska-lawmakers-officially-abolish-the-death-penalty/.

77. "Nebraska Lawmakers Override Veto to Allow Undocumented to State License," Fox News, April 12, 2016, http://www.foxnews.com/politics/2016/04/21/nebraska-lawmakers-override-veto-to-allow-undocumented-to-obtain-state-licenses.html.

78. Press Release, Nebraska State Legislature, accessed February 2018, https://bloximages .chicago2.vip.townnews.com/journalstar.com/content/tncms/assets/v3/editorial /7/59/7593b6c2-5e4a-5718-9024-6e0329d85f8f/574db362c5137.pdf.pdf.

79. We already see a great deal of energy around the idea of reengineering the legislative machinery in Washington. In addition to the Problem Solvers, there is now a bipartisan Select Committee on the Modernization of Congress, which was spurred by Issue One and the Harvard Negotiation Project's multiyear Rebuild Congress Initiative. The Bipartisan Policy Center's "Congress That Works" project has devised a set of recommendations for how Congress can revamp its rules to become more efficient and effective. Other groups, including the R Street Institute and the Congressional Institute, are also actively working to promote structural innovation in Congress.

80. Nancy C. Unger, "Passive Citizenship Is Not Enough," *Origins*, March 29, 2007, http:// origins.osu.edu/history-news/passive-citizenship-not-enough.

81. "Liberty Medal Ceremony," CNN, October 16, 2017, https://www.cnn.com/2017/10/16/ politics/mccain-full-speech-liberty-medal/index.html.

Conclusion

1. State spending excludes federal transfers. State spending (FY 2017) from National Association of State Budget Officers, State Expenditure Report (Washington: National Association of State Budget Officers, 2018), "Archive of State Expenditure Report," National Association of State Budget Officers, accessed June 2019, https://www.nasbo.org/reports-data/state-expenditure-report/state-expenditure-archives; author analysis (excludes spending of federal funds by states). Federal outlays data (FY 2017) from Congressional Budget Office, "The Budget and Economic Outlook: 2017 to 2027," January 24, 2017, "The Budget and Economic Outlook: 2017 to 2027," Congressional Budget Office, January 24, 2017, https://www.cbo.gov/publication/52370; author analysis.

2. Melinda Gates, "The Best Investment America Can Make," CNN, April 20, 2017, https:// www.cnn.com/2017/04/20/opinions/melinda-gates-the-best-investment-america-can-make/ index.html.

3. Seema Chowdhry, "Bill and Melinda Gates: The World Needs to Adapt to What's Happening and What We Know Is Coming," livemint, February 14, 2018, https://www.livemint .com/Companies/6XSuKEMMkD81F1Be6WJ04K/Bill-and-Melinda-Gates-The-world-needs-to-adapt-to-whats-h.html.

4. David G. Crane, "Tithe to Democracy—Donate to Well-Meaning Candidates," SFGATE, May 17, 2014, http://www.sfgate.com/opinion/article/Tithe-to-democracy-donate-to-well-meaning-5484784.php.

5. Crane, "Tithe to Democracy."

6. "Benjamin Franklin: Founding Father Quote," Founding Father Quotes, http://www.foundingfatherquotes.com/quote/913.

7. Suzy Platt, ed., "Respectfully Quoted: A Dictionary of Quotations Requested from the Congressional Research Service," in *Washington: Library of Congress, 1989, no. 1593*, via Bartleby.com, accessed March 2017, http://www.bartleby.com/73/1593.html.

Index

Acknowledgments

We find it a joy and a privilege to reflect on all those who helped us along this journey.

A number of distinguished thought leaders have really impacted us. The work of author and former US Representative Mickey Edwards as well as Greg Orman and Charlie Wheelan, pathbreaking political innovators and talented writers, thinkers, and doers, shaped much of Katherine's early thinking on these issues. We are grateful to Alan Murray and Clifton Leaf at *Fortune* for their early and influential buy-in. We thank Howard Shultz for his engagement with our work and for bringing vitally important visibility to the high barriers to entry for new competitors.

We owe an enormous debt of gratitude to our two lead writing and research partners. The talented researcher and writer Liam Gennari helped us master the literature, and his enormous effort got us through the first draft. The phenomenal Solomon Lieberman joined us not a moment too soon to get us over the finish line. His talent as a writer, his insight as a researcher and strategist, his dedication to excellence, and his passion for the work contributed immeasurably.

Our politics work and outreach has been led by two remarkable women, Sara Eskrich and Alexandra Houghtalin. We can't ever thank you enough.

We are grateful to a number of other deeply talented researchers from both our teams who have also made important contributions. Harvard Business School's senior researcher Grant Tudor and research associate Andrew Speen provided invaluable research support. HBS research associates Brad Desanctis, Jacob Clemente, Don Maruyama, and Emily Tedards each contributed along the way.

We could not have done any of this without the essential help of our highly capable support teams, past and present: Katie Boyce, Erin Collins, Kendra Hartman, Jill Hogue, Laura Hennigan, Darlene Ahlstedt, Lauren Dombkoski, Jacob Ringer, Charlotte Cunningham, Stuart Gardner, Angie Koput, Katie Warjas, Julie Costello, and Lori Wernicke.

We are deeply indebted to Harvard Business School for its extensive support and encouragement, in particular to Dean Nitin Nohria for his continued encouragement and leadership. We also draw heavily on Harvard Business School's U.S. Competitiveness Project. Special thanks to cochair Jan Rivkin for his insights, for hosting an early presentation on politics involving HBS colleagues that provided important feedback, and for his welcoming expansion of the project to include this work. We also thank program director Manjari Raman for her insights and support. With its incredible alumni and reach, Harvard Business School has also provided many enormously valuable opportunities to present this work, and the resulting dialogues have contributed immensely to its improvement. A grateful thank-you as well to the fabulous event and technical staff at the world-class Klarman Hall venue.

We are also indebted to the team at the Social Progress Imperative, especially Scott Stern and Michael Green, who were instrumental in working with Michael to develop data on the social performance of countries that has been essential to our work.

A number of generous academics and thought leaders have provided critical data, ideas, and insights for the book: Lee Drutman, David Moss, Mihir Desai, Jeffrey Green, Kenneth Shepsle, Nancy Unger, Peter Levine, Robert Johnston, Jack Santucci, Maureen Flanagan, Walter Nugent, Laura Philips Sawyer, Hahrie Han, Sara Binder, Robert Boatright, Julian Zelizer, Nolan McCarty, David E. Lee,

Maya Sen, Brian D. Feinstein, Jon Jacoby, Sarah Bonk, and David Gilmour. The team at the Leadership Now Project also provided highly useful data and input.

We are very appreciative of reviews and feedback from Scott Page, Austin Ramirez, Daniella Ballou-Aares, Erik Kesting, Margo Weinstein, Greg Orman, Bill Eggers, Adam Corndorf, Brent Gottlieb, Robert Secter, David Epstein, Gabrielle Lieberman, and one anonymous reviewer (you know who you are).

Many others contributed by providing valuable support, input, platforms, and settings that allowed us to speak about and promote this movement. They include the *Boston Globe*'s Linda Henry, Chrissy Houlahan, the Skoll Foundation and Sally Osberg, Kitty Boone and the Aspen Institute, Bill Ackman, Sarah Longwell, Seth and Beth Klarman, Wendy Dodson, Alan Schwartz, Bill George, Charlie Frankel, Edward Chapman, Theresa Mintle, Anke Faber, Dan Tierney, Steve Schaumberger, Michael Sanchez, Anne Wedner, Jamie Clare Flaherty, Sam Elghanayan, Jason Childress, Ray Carey, and the Detroit Regional Chamber's Sandy Baruah.

We thank Ike Williams, our literary agent, John Butman, who helped create the book proposal, and Jeff Kehoe, our editor at Harvard Business Review Press. Thanks to each of you for believing in this book and for your patience with the journey, and together with our speakers' agent Danny Stern, for helping us to spread our urgent message.

. . .

There are also many who helped us beyond direct contributions to the ideas, research, writing, and outreach for the book. We both received tremendous individual and personal support, for which we will be eternally grateful.

I (Katherine) never dreamed of writing a book, and yet here we are. Wow. I definitely didn't get here on my own—far from it.

My deepest appreciation goes to two people: Mickey Edwards and Michael Porter. Mickey turned the proverbial light on for me with his brilliant insight: "Washington isn't broken—it's delivering exactly what it's designed to deliver." Without Mickey there would be no Politics Industry Theory. And without Michael's generous contributions to our Gehl Foods strategy project and his later agreement to join me in this work, there would be no book. Thank you both.

The women of WIPI-WTAFN and the patriotic folk of P&P teach, inspire, and motivate me on an ongoing basis.

My friends Kathryn Flores, Kendra Hartman, Lane Jabaay, D'Ann Adams, and Margo Weinstein keep me sane and happy (through much more than the book). Emily Broadfoot, Jean Gales, Katie Galvan, Fadia Elzingi, Hannah Horwatich, and Scotty Wagner supported me in so many ways that made this effort possible. My father, John Gehl, gave me the opportunity to lead Gehl Foods, without which this work would simply not be happening. My sister, JoJo Neumann, helped me immensely in the early years of my CEO tenure, as did Mike Betzhold, Kendra Hartman, Sherry Majewski, Mike Sowieja, John Shaughnessy, Tim Preuninger, Jeff Chaley, and John Slawny throughout. I am indebted also to Mike Stewart, Rachel Corn Kluge, Steve Barth, and Spencer Moats.

Thank you to Eleanor Estes, Mary Nelson, Chad Boeding, Ben Hamer, Fabienne Tronel, Chris Jackson, Lauri Badar, Donna Wilkerson, Henry Woodruff, Rebecca Gallagher, Kathy Creighton, Deb Leinart, Keith Vallely, Mary Nelson, Dale Bredesen, Julie Kochenek, Jen Brea, Gary Shunk, Julia Stasch, Beth Hamilton, Cheri Knerr, Heidi Pietenpol, Joel Dudley, Cassandra Jackson, Michael Krauss, Tony Komaroff, and Elizabeth Littlefield for all the impact they've made. Special appreciation to S.A.C. I will always be grateful to all of you.

To the delights of my life, my children—Alexandra, who gives me all my best laugh lines, makes me laugh more than anyone, and is always supportive of my work, even when it takes my time away.

As a mutual friend of ours once said, "It's the job that's never started as takes longest to finish." And Teddy, whose birth postponed our original Harvard Business School report and who slept on my lap for much of the first three months of his life while I typed it to completion. I love, love, love you both. And Michael thanks you, too!

Finally, to Jeff Wilmore, who changed my life also—even though he doesn't know it.

I (Michael) owe my deepest gratitude to my two daughters, Lana Porter and Sonia Smyth, as well as my son-in-law, Peter Smyth, and Boston Book Festival's Debbie Porter, for their encouragement and moral support throughout this project.

. . .

Lastly, while the lens we bring is unique, we are just one part of a broader community of political innovators and reformers. We are deeply indebted to them for what they've taught us and for the work they do every day. Many fantastic political reform and innovation organizations are noted on our website, www.political-innovation .org, but here we want to call out some wonderful individuals whose passion inspires us and from whose work we all benefit. Progressive Era reformer, Robert "Fighting Bob" La Follette, said it best:

> *America is not made but is in the making. There is an unending struggle to make and keep government representative. Mere passive citizenship is not enough. Men must be aggressive for what is right if government is to be saved from those who are aggressive for what is wrong.*

We are the makers. And every day, these makers are getting the work done: Cara McCormick, Daniella Ballou-Aares, Jeanne Massey, Ruth Greenwood, Nick Troiano, Chad Peace, Peter Ackerman, Kent Thiry, David Crane, Anne-Marie Slaughter, Maya MacGuineas, Kyle Bailey,

Larry Lessig, Andrew Shue, Mike Murphy, Betsy Wright Hawkings, David Schoenbrod, Steve Peace, Dan Howle, John Opdycke, Katie Fahey, Marc Merrill, Jason Bertolocci, John Pudner, Sam Reed, Sam Mar, Mark Schmitt, Nancy Jacobson, Adam Friedman, Mac D'Alessandro, JB Lyon, Jim Jonas, Bill Walker, Kaia Los Huertos, Evan McMullin, Matthew Dowd, Stefani Mills, Lenny Mendonca, Mindy Finn, Meredith McGehee, Steven Olikara, Brian Mistrot, Lisa Rice, Drisana Hughes, Kathryn Murdoch, Brooke Russell, Mort Kondracke, Dave Dodson, Emily Cherniack, Jim Pederson, Perry Waag, Josh Silver, Ralph Becker, Alexandra Shapiro, Seth London, Andrew Crutchfield, Phil Keisling, Conyers Davis, Shawn Griffiths, Christian Gross, Joshua Graham Lynn, Cynthia Ritchie Terrell, Gerry Herbert, Nicholas Stephanopoulos, Rob Ritchie, Rye Barcott, Debilyn Molineaux, David Nevins, Neal Simon, and the many others.

The leaders of Democracy Found, and their investment in Wisconsin, gives us real hope that change will happen. They are Austin Ramirez and Heather Ramirez, Lynde Uihlein, Andy Nunemaker, Sarah and Steve Zimmerman, Kathryn Quadracci Flores and Raja Flores, Madeleine and David Lubar, Linda and Greg Marcus, Mary Jo and Don Layden, Sue and Bud Selig, Gus and Becky Ramirez, and Sara Eskrich. We appreciate all of you. The courageous leadership of Mike Gallagher, Dale Kooyenga, and Danny Riemer is so important. Thank you.

While all those we've acknowledged deserve our great appreciation, this does not mean to imply that they agree with us. We alone bear full responsibility for our analysis, conclusions, and recommendations. Finally, to anyone we have inadvertently omitted, please accept both our apology and our appreciation. So many have done so much. We feel blessed.

—*Katherine and Michael*

About the Authors

KATHERINE M. GEHL is a business leader, entrepreneur, author, and speaker. She is the CEO of Venn Innovations, a new organization focused on powerful and achievable change around a short list of consequential issues requiring breakthrough thinking. The first focus for Venn Innovations is American politics.

Corresponding with the release of this book, Gehl is founding the Institute for Political Innovation (IPI), a not-for-profit organization with the mission of guiding theory and practice around nonpartisan political innovation in America.

Gehl is the former president and CEO of Gehl Foods, a $250 million high-tech food manufacturing company in Wisconsin, where she led an aggressive and transformational turnaround, receiving multiple awards, before selling the company in 2015—in part to dedicate more time to political innovation. In 2013 Gehl applied the traditional tools of business analysis for the first time to politics in order to uncover the root cause of its dysfunction—the unhealthy competition in what she called the politics industry. In 2016 she invited Michael Porter to join her in her work, and they coauthored the 2017 Harvard Business School publication "Why Competition in the Politics Industry Is Failing America: A Strategy for Reinvigorating Our Democracy." Its enthusiastic reception led to this book.

Gehl serves on the boards of Unite America, Business for America, and New America. She is the honorary cochair of the National Association of Nonpartisan Reformers (NANR). In 2018 Gehl cofounded Democracy Found, an initiative dedicated to establishing Final-Five Voting in Wisconsin for congressional elections.

Gehl received a BA from the University of Notre Dame, an MA from the Catholic University of America, and an MBA from Northwestern University's Kellogg School of Management.

MICHAEL E. PORTER is an economist, researcher, author, adviser, and teacher. Throughout his career at Harvard Business School, he has brought economic theory and strategy concepts to bear on many of the most challenging problems facing corporations, economies, and societies, including market competition and company strategy, economic development, the environment, and health care. Porter's work has shaped the modern strategy field, and his ideas are taught in virtually every business school in the world. While Porter is, at his core, a scholar, his work has also achieved remarkable acceptance by practitioners in governments, corporations, and NGOs globally. He advises *Fortune* 100 and *Fortune* 500 companies and heads of state from around the world, and he is the most cited scholar today in economics and business.

Porter has received numerous honors, including the Adam Smith Award of the National Association for Business Economics, the John Kenneth Galbraith Medal, and—seven times—the McKinsey Award for best *Harvard Business Review* article of the year. He has been awarded twenty-six honorary doctorates from universities around the world, as well as the first-ever Lifetime Achievement award from the US Department of Commerce for his contribution to economic development.

In 2000 Harvard Business School and Harvard University jointly established the Institute for Strategy & Competitiveness to provide a base for Porter's research. He was named a University Professor by Harvard University, the highest recognition that can be awarded to a Harvard faculty member.

Porter received a BSE in aerospace and mechanical engineering from Princeton University, an MBA from Harvard Business School, and a PhD in business economics from Harvard University.

To take action go to:

political-innovation.org

All proceeds from this book benefit

The Institute for Political Innovation